THE CONSTITUTION FOR E

There is much confusion over the 'Constitution', and this book provides an in-depth legal analysis of the key aspects of the Constitutional
Treaty which, if ratified by the 25 EU Member States, would govern the
European Union. Piris argues that, despite its ratification being rejected
by the French and the Netherlands referenda in 2005, the Treaty should
not be discarded, as it will inevitably be the point of departure for the
future of European integration. He places this analysis in an historical
and political context and explains the origin, meanings and legal and
political effects of all proposed changes to the present treaties.

JEAN-CLAUDE PIRIS is Director-General of the Legal Service of the
Council of the European Union. He is a Member of the French Conseil
d'Etat, Paris, a former French diplomat to the United Nations in
New York, and former Director of the Legal Service of the OECD,
Paris. He was the Legal Adviser and Head of Secretariat of the Intergovernmental Conference (IGC) which adopted the Constitution, as
well as the Legal Adviser of the preceding IGCs which negotiated and
adopted successively the treaties of Maastricht, Amsterdam and Nice.

CAMBRIDGE STUDIES IN EUROPEAN LAW AND POLICY

This series aims to produce original works which contain a critical analysis of the state of the law in particular areas of European Law and set out different perspectives and suggestions for its future development. It also aims to encourage a range of work on law, legal institutions and legal phenomena in Europe, including 'law in context' approaches. The titles in the series will be of interest to academics; policymakers; policy formers who are interested in European legal, commercial, and political affairs; practising lawyers including the judiciary; and advanced law students and researchers.

Joint Editors

Professor Dr Laurence Gormley
Rijksuniversiteit Groningen, The Netherlands

Professor Jo Shaw
University of Edinburgh

Editorial advisory board

Professor Richard Bellamy, University of Reading; Ms Catherine Barnard, University of Cambridge; Professor Marise Cremona, Queen Mary College, University of London; Professor Alan Dashwood, University of Cambridge; Professor Dr Jacqueline Dutheil de la Rochère, Université de Paris II, Director of the Centre de Droit Européen, France; Dr Andrew Drzemczewski, Council of Europe, Strasbourg, France; Sir David Edward KCMG, QC, former Judge, Court of Justice of the European Communities, Luxembourg; Professor Dr Walter Baron van Gerven, Emeritus Professor, Leuven & Maastricht and former Advocate General, Court of Justice of the European Communities; Professor Daniel Halberstam, University of Michigan, USA; Professor Dr Ingolf Pernice, Director of the Walter Hallstein Institut, Humboldt Universität, Berlin; Michel Petite, Director General of the Legal Service, Commission of the European Communities, Bruxelles; Professor Dr Sinisa Rodin, University of Zagreb; Professor Neil Walker, University of Aberdeen and EUI, Fiesole.

Books in the series

THE CONSTITUTION FOR EUROPE

A Legal Analysis

JEAN-CLAUDE PIRIS

CAMBRIDGE
UNIVERSITY PRESS

CAMBRIDGE UNIVERSITY PRESS
Cambridge, New York, Melbourne, Madrid, Cape Town, Singapore, São Paulo

Cambridge University Press
The Edinburgh Building, Cambridge CB2 2RU, UK

Published in the United States of America by Cambridge University Press, New York

www.cambridge.org
Information on this title: www.cambridge.org/9780521682183

First published 2006

Printed in the United Kingdom at the University Press, Cambridge

A catalogue record for this publication is available from the British Library

ISBN-13 978-0-521-86353-7 hardback
ISBN-10 0-521-86353-8 hardback
ISBN-13 978-0-521-68218-3 paperback
ISBN-10 0-521-68218-5 paperback

TABLE OF CONTENTS

TABLE OF CONTENTS

FIGURES

TABLES

BOXES

SERIES EDITORS' PREFACE

The adoption of the Constitution for Europe, on 29 October 2004 in Rome, in a return to the venue where the old EEC Treaty was signed, was hoped to be a great leap forward for European integration. Its ratification, however, proved to be a bridge too far for the populations of France and the Netherlands. Significantly, given that many voters simply used the referenda in those countries to express a general dissatisfaction with the political class, Jean-Claude Piris begins this major study of the central and most characteristic aspects of the Constitution for Europe with the question whether the Constitution is now dead and buried. While he rightly concludes that it is too early for the requiem, he gives a careful analysis of the scenarios resulting from these referenda results.

This work makes a seminal contribution to the understanding of the core aspects of the Constitution, with the advantage of the author's unique insights into the processes by which it came about. Whatever the result of the further political deliberations, the Constitution stands as a reference point for the future development of integration, and it may be anticipated that this work will become the focus of much attention by scholars, politicians and others interested in the development of the European Union. Piris points out the innovations and improvements which the Constitution would introduce, building on the unfinished work of Maastricht, Amsterdam, and Nice. He highlights the improvements which it would make in the democratic structure of the Union and in streamlining decision-making, with notable improvements in the protection of fundamental rights within the ambit of the Union's activities and clarification of the Union's competences. In the mists of the political half-truths, deliberate misrepresentation and intentional inaccuracies which have characterised much of the discussion about the Constitution, this work forms a beacon of light to show the way forward. It is elegantly yet accessibly written and is a singularly well-informed and articulate contribution to writings in the field.

Accordingly, it is with great pleasure that we welcome this, the third book in the series Cambridge Studies in European Law and Policy, as a combination of law and policy analysis which will be essential reading in the disciplines which it covers.

Laurence Gormley
Jo Shaw
10 October 2005

ACKNOWLEDGMENTS

The author thanks Ms Thérèse Blanchet, adviser in the Legal Service of the EU Council, for her invaluable assistance in the writing of this book.

TABLE OF CASES

Court of Justice of the European Communities

Other Courts

European Court of Human Rights (ECHR) and European Human Rights Commission

National Constitutional and Other Courts

ANNEXES

Introduction

In the time-scale of history, sixty years is very short. For centuries, ever since the Greeks and the Romans, since the Normans and the Germans, not to mention the British and the French, the peoples of Europe have constantly waged war on each other. During the last century alone, from 1914 until 1918 and from 1939 until 1945, merciless wars inflamed the European continent causing hatred and massive destruction, leaving its peoples bled white and prey to starvation.

What is the situation of Europe today, only sixty years on?

Europe is at peace. Europe is democratic. Europe is prosperous. War has become unthinkable among the peoples which have united within the European Union. The dense web of commercial, economic, political and legal links they have built between them are such that it is difficult to realise nowadays that the blitz on London, the flattening of Dresden and the occupation of Paris by the German army only took place around sixty years ago.

In simple terms, the present situation might be described as follows: the European Union (EU) has its own law-making institutions, including a Council composed of Ministers who are members of national governments of the Member States, and a directly elected European Parliament. The Council and the European Parliament share the power of co-deciding legislative, administrative and budgetary acts, which are proposed by the Commission. The Commission, which exercises the powers conferred on it by the Council for the implementation of Community law, also ensures that this law is applied and may take a Member State to court if it fails to fulfil its obligations. The European Parliament shares with the Council the power to approve the appointment of the President of the Commission and of the Commission as a whole; the Parliament also has the power to remove the Commission from office. The 'laws' (regulations and directives) adopted by these institutions within the fields of power of the European Community (EC) are superior to the laws of the Member States and may have direct effect on the citizens. The Union has a single market and manages a single currency and monetary union for a number of its Member States. There are a number of fields for which the Member States have lost power to adopt legislation or to negotiate international agreements. There are other fields where laws or treaties can be imposed on the Member States and which they are obliged to implement, or else be faced with having to make lump sum or penalty payments, as well as paying compensation to adversely affected people. The European Court of Justice has the power to rule on disputes between the institutions, between institutions and Member States about the extent of their respective powers, and on the rights and obligations of Member States and citizens under European law.

How did that happen in such a short period of time? and
how did this fabulous adventure begin?

Immediately after World War II, the old dreams of a reconciled, if not united, Europe began to take a concrete shape in the economic and political fields. On the economic side, financial help from the United States, symbolised by the speech of General Marshall on 5 June 1947, was followed by the establishment of the Organisation for European Economic Cooperation (OEEC, which became OECD[1] in 1961) at the Hague Congress in 1948. This was quickly followed, on the political side, by the establishment of the Council of Europe and the signature of the European Convention on Human Rights respectively in 1949 and 1950. On the military side, the Western European Union (WEU) and the North Atlantic Treaty Organisation (NATO) were established respectively in 1948 and 1949.[2]

At the same time, following the speech of the French Foreign Minister Robert Schuman on 9 May 1950, efforts began to build a smaller but more integrated Europe, around France and Germany. This attempt relied on powerful institutions and using the so-called 'Monnet method' of progressive building up 'through practical achievements which will first of all create real solidarity, and through the establishment of common bases for economic development'.[3] The European Coal and

---

[1] OECD : Organisation for Economic Cooperation and Development.
[2] A Treaty establishing the European Community of Defence was signed in May 1952, but it was rejected by the French Parliament in 1954.
[3] Quoted from the third paragraph of the Preamble to the Coal and Steel Treaty.

The founding Member States and the successive enlargements

1952
Belgium
France
Germany
Italy
Luxembourg
Netherlands

1981
Greece

1995
Austria
Finland
Sweden

1973	1986	2004
Denmark	Portugal	Cyprus
Ireland	Spain	Czech Republic
UK		Estonia
		Hungary
		Latvia
		Lithuania
		Malta
		Poland
		Slovakia
		Slovenia

Figure 0.1. The founding Member States and the successive enlargements.

Steel Community was launched by its six founding States in 1951 and entered into force in July 1952 (it lapsed on 23 July 2002). Then followed the Conference of Messina in June 1955 after which the Treaty establishing the European Economic Community was signed in Rome on 25 March 1957 and entered into force on 14 January 1958.[4]

That was the real start of the historic adventure which led to the establishment of the European Union. Since then, the original Treaty of Rome has been modified several times and the six founding States have admitted among them, in successive 'enlargements', 19 other European countries (see figure 0.1). The enlargement process reached its culmination on 1 May 2004, with the accession of ten new countries, including eight former communist countries from the other side of the Iron Curtain, which had divided the European continent since the end of World War II.

The different treaties establishing the European Community and the Union (see box 0.1) were the first ones in European history where the issues at stake were not about delimiting borders between States or to establish the power of one State over another. Their aim was to multiply

[4] Together with the Treaty establishing the European Atomic Energy Community, known as 'Euratom'.

and strengthen the links between European countries in order to prevent war and to help them to entrench democracy, to respect human rights and to ensure prosperity and security for their peoples.

Box 0.1   The main amending Treaties

The Single European Act (signed on 17 Feb. and 28 Feb. 1986)

This Treaty, which entered into force on 1 July 1987, gave a decisive impulse for the completion of the Internal Market with a deadline (1992) and the means to achieve it through the possibility for the Council to adopt by qualified majority the legal texts establishing the internal market.

The Treaty establishing the European Union (EU) (signed on 7 Feb. 1992)

Also known as the 'Maastricht Treaty', it added two 'pillars' to the Community pillar, i.e. the pillar on the Common Foreign and Security Policy and the pillar on Justice and Home Affairs. It also created a single currency, the euro, and provided for a timetable for its establishment. Following a narrow 'Yes' vote in France and a 'No' vote in Denmark, later on reversed by a 'Yes' vote, the EU Treaty entered into force on 1 November 1993.

The Amsterdam Treaty (signed on 2 Oct. 1997)

This Treaty entered into force on 1 May 1999. It 'communitarised', i.e. submitted to ordinary Community rules, parts of the Justice and Home Affairs chapter of the Treaty on European Union (the chapter on visas, asylum, immigration and civil judicial cooperation) and integrated into the EC Treaty the so-called 'Schengen *acquis*', on the removal of controls of persons at internal borders, which had been developed by certain Member States outside the Treaties. It created the office of High Representative for the Common Foreign and Security Policy.

The Nice Treaty (signed on 26 Feb. 2001)

The main purpose of this Treaty was to adapt the institutions to the enlargement to ten new Member States by adapting the size of the Commission and the weighting of votes in the Council. This Treaty entered into force on 1 February 2003, following hurdles in the ratification process in Ireland.

I

Is the Constitution for Europe 'dead and buried'?

In 2004, on the basis of the numerous Treaties which had built the EU over the years, the Heads of State or Government of the 25 States members of the European Union decided to take yet another step, through adopting a 'Constitution for Europe'. On 29 October 2004, in Rome, in the very room where the original 1957 Rome Treaty was signed, 25 European Heads of State or Government solemnly signed the 'Treaty establishing a Constitution for Europe' on which they had reached a political agreement on 18 June 2004.[1]

This Treaty, they declared, '*completes* the process which began when the Treaty of Rome established the basic framework for European integration' and 'like the Treaty of Rome, it will serve for many years as the foundation of a Union at the service of its citizens'.[2]

This ambiguous formula contains, in a nutshell, two different interpretations which could be given of this new Treaty.

According to the first interpretation, this formula means that the Constitution would finally mark the end of European integration: it declares it completed, so that it will not go any further. This explains the reason for the deletion of the famous first paragraph of the preamble to the original Rome Treaty about laying 'the foundations of an ever closer union among the peoples of Europe', which was repeated by the Maastricht Treaty in Article 1 of the EU Treaty.

According to the second interpretation, this formula shows that the Constitution would be yet another step in the ever deeper European

---

[1] The Constitution text, as signed on 29 October 2004, has been published in the Official Journal of the European Union, OJ 2004 No. C310, 16 December 2004 (accessible from the internet site 'europa', http://europa.eu.int/constitution/index_eu.htm).

[2] See the Conclusions of the Presidency of the European Council, Brussels, 17 and 18 June 2004, doc. 10679/04 ADD 1. All Presidency Conclusions since 1998 may be found on the internet site of the Council: http://ue.eu.int, under 'documents' and 'European Council'. The verb 'completes' is emphasised by the author.

integration, sowing the seeds for further integration. This latter interpretation is supported by the express mentioning in the Constitution of symbols usually associated with a State, such as a flag, an anthem, a motto and a 'Europe day', the names 'Union Minister for Foreign Affairs' and 'European law' and, above all, the name 'Constitution for Europe' which would be given to the new Treaty on European Union (see box 1.1).

Box 1.1   Article I-8 of the Constitution reads:

'The symbols of the Union

The flag of the Union shall be a circle of twelve golden stars on a blue background.

The anthem of the Union shall be based on the "Ode to Joy" from the Ninth Symphony by Ludwig van Beethoven.

The motto of the Union shall be: "United in diversity".

The currency of the Union shall be the euro.

Europe day shall be celebrated on 9 May throughout the Union.'

Would these symbols allow for a sort of 'creative utopia' and prepare the minds of the peoples for something more integrated to come later? Or would they remain a sort of 'compensation gift' conceded to the Euro-enthusiasts for not having made in the Constitution the great leap forward the latter would have liked, or even a kind of apology for the 'stop' to further integration which might be contained in this Constitution?

On the one hand, some Euro-enthusiasts claim to be disappointed that the new Treaty does not deliver on its promises because the actual content of the so-called 'Constitution' does not correspond to the grandeur of its name. On the other hand, the Euro-sceptics denounce the symbols which have been retained as an alleged proof of yet another undemocratic plot towards the creeping transformation of the EU into a State.

From the outset, some people feared that the choice ('the fatal choice' according to the journalist Christine Ockrent) of such a heavily loaded symbol as the name 'Constitution'[3] for this new European basic Treaty would run the double risk of triggering hopes and illusions on the part of the Euro-enthusiasts, followed by disillusion and disappointment, while

---

[3] On the issue of the name 'Constitution' and its use for an EU Treaty, see my article 'Does the European Union have a Constitution? Does it need one?' (1999) 6 *European Law Review* 557–585.

at the same time provoking concern and criticism on the part of the Euro-sceptics. Added to each other, it was considered by some that these negative reactions could imperil the very ratification of the Treaty, particularly in the Member States which had decided to submit the authorisation to ratify it to a popular referendum.

Therefore, one might think that instead of clarifying the debate on Europe for the citizens,[4] the choice of the name 'Constitution for Europe' has confused the elements of the choice given to the voters in the referenda: did they have to vote for a strengthening of the EU as it is or for an EU radically transformed into a new project? Strong efforts of explanation had to be made on the part of national governments and political parties to clarify the debate. Obviously, these efforts have not been sufficient. Both in France and in the Netherlands, the referenda gave a clear result against the ratification of the Constitution. For a lot of commentators, the story finishes here: the Constitution is 'dead and buried'.

Section 1: The ratification process of the Constitution

Article IV-447 of the Constitution sets out the legal requirements for the Constitution's entry into force:

> This Treaty shall be ratified by the High Contracting Parties in accordance with their respective constitutional requirements . . . [it] shall enter into force on 1 November 2006, provided that all the instruments of ratification have been deposited, or, failing that, on the first day of the second month following the deposit of the instrument of ratification by the last signatory State to take this step.

This is, as it ought to be, in accordance with Article 48 of the EU Treaty: a modification (and, thus, a repeal) of the EU Treaty may only enter into force if approved by all the Member States' Governments and ratified by all Member States according to their constitutional requirements.

---

[4] See the European Parliament's Resolution on the Constitution: 'Welcomes the fact that the Constitution provides citizens with more clarity as to the Union's nature and objectives and as to the relations between the Union and the member States, notably because: . . . (i) it provides guarantees that the Union will never be a centralised all-powerful "superstate" . . . (j) the inclusion of the symbols of the Union in the Constitution will improve the awareness of the Union's institutions and their action.' (doc. A6-9999/2004, 9 December 2004).

Therefore, legally, the rule is quite straightforward: if a State fails to ratify the Constitution, it will not enter into force.[5]

Of the Governments of the 25 Member States which signed on 29 October 2004, in Rome, the draft Treaty establishing a Constitution for Europe, about 15 have decided to request the authorisation to ratify the Treaty from their national Parliaments. At the time of writing (September 2005), 11 of them had obtained this authorisation: Lithuania (11 November 2004), Hungary (20 December 2004), Slovenia (1 February 2005), Italy (6 April 2005), Greece (20 April 2005), Slovakia[6] (11 May 2005), Austria (25 May 2005), Germany (27 May 2005), Latvia (2 June 2005), Cyprus (30 June 2005) and Malta (6 July 2005). In Belgium, the two Chambers of the Federal Parliament approved the Treaty in April and May 2005, as well as most of the regional and community Parliaments, but the process still had to be completed in one of the regional Parliaments. Estonia is due to submit the Treaty to its Parliament in the autumn of 2005. Finland and Sweden have announced that they would postpone their parliamentary ratification.

About ten Governments decided instead, for constitutional or for political reasons, to organise a national referendum in order to allow their people to decide directly on the ratification of the Treaty. That was the case in Denmark, Ireland, Luxembourg, France, the Netherlands, Spain, Poland, Portugal and the UK, the Czech Republic not yet having decided whether it would proceed through a referendum or through parliament. At the time of writing (September 2005), four Member States have proceeded with a popular vote; two said 'Yes' and two said 'No':

---

[5] Right after the end of the negotiations on the Constitution, speculation quickly started on what would happen in case of non-ratification by one or several Member States. See, among others: B. de Witte 'The Process of Ratification and the Crisis Options: A Legal Perspective' in *The EU Constitution: The Best Way Forward?*, Asser Institute Colloquium on European Law, The Hague, 13–16 October 2004; L. S. Rossi 'What If the Constitutional Treaty Is Not Ratified?' (30 June 2004) *EPC Commentary*; L. S. Rossi, 'En cas de non-ratification . . . Le destin périlleux de ce Traité-Constitution' (2004) 4 *Revue trimestrielle de droit européen* 621–637; C. Grant, *What Happens if Britain Votes No? Ten Ways Out of a European Constitutional Crisis* (Centre for European Reform, March 2005); J. Shaw 'Failure to Ratify the Constitutional Treaty: What Next?' in Ingolf Pernice/Jiří Zemánek (eds.), *A Constitution for Europe: The IGC, the Ratification Process and Beyond* (Nomos Verlag, Baden-Baden, 2005, European Constitutional Law Network-Series, Bd. 5).

[6] In July 2005, the Supreme Court of Slovakia suspended the process, pending judgement of an application claiming that it is legally necessary for the ratification to be through a referendum.

- the first referendum took place in Spain on 20 February 2005, where the Treaty was approved by a very high majority of 76.7%, with a relatively low turnout of 42.3%;
- the second referendum took place in France on 29 May 2005, where the French people rejected the ratification of the Treaty by a clear majority of 54.87%, with a high turnout of 69.3%;
- the third referendum took place three days later in the Netherlands, on 1 June 2005, and the Treaty was again rejected by an even clearer majority of 61.6%, with a high turnout of 62.8%;
- the fourth referendum took place in Luxembourg on 10 July 2005 where the Treaty was approved by a clear majority of 56.52% and a very high turnout of 86.8% (voting is compulsory in Luxembourg).

The referendum was legally binding in France. In the Netherlands, where it was the first ever nationwide referendum in modern times, it was consultative, but the major political parties had agreed that a turnout rate above 30% would be considered as producing a result that the Parliament would agree to follow. The results of the French and Dutch referenda were considered as a political earthquake in Europe.

Section 2: Analysis of the negative referenda in France and in the Netherlands

Following those two 'No' votes, taking into account the legal rule according to which a single failure to ratify is enough to prevent the Constitutional Treaty from entering into force, many observers concluded that the Treaty would never enter into force.

The British press declared the Treaty 'dead and buried' (*Guardian*, 4 June 2005).[7] The British Government decided immediately to postpone the ratification procedure which had to begin in the British Parliament before the referendum.

---

[7] The difference between the quasi-unanimous jubilation of the British press and the quasi-unanimous sadness of the French press was striking: Martin Wolf wrote: 'The French and the Dutch have demolished the road to "ever closer Union". . . Perfidious Albion wins again . . . The French (and Dutch) have answered the UK's European question : vive la France', *Financial Times*, 3 June 2005. Less serious British newspapers went as far as celebrating the end of European integration.

By contrast, the French press was on a very sad note: Serge July wrote: '. . . un désastre général et une épidémie de populisme qui emportait tout sur leur passage, la construction européenne, l'élargissement, les élites, la régulation du libéralisme, le réformisme, l'internationalisme, même la générosité' (a general disaster and an epidemic

Is that final? Should we indeed consider the Constitutional Treaty as being dead and forget about it? On the face of it, in principle, yes: for the time being, it is, at least, frozen. However, both French and Dutch political authorities, after the referenda, have called on the other Member States to continue the ratification process. Moreover, this was unanimously confirmed by the 25 Heads of State or Government at their meeting in Brussels on 16 and 17 June 2005: despite media pressure to issue the Constitution with a death certificate, and despite the difficulties some of them face in the ratification process, they have decided, in their wisdom, that this process should effectively continue, albeit with an adjusted timeframe. This means that all Member States remain committed, at the highest level, to the ratification process in the terms of the conclusions of 17 June 2005.

Therefore, things are not as simple as they might appear at first sight. If the ratification process is still going on, how could one affirm that the Constitutional Treaty must be forgotten?[8]

In order to try and determine what could be the political consequences of the two failed referenda for the fate of the Constitutional Treaty and for the future of European integration, two questions deserve to be raised:

1. Were these results a political surprise, representing a brutal reversal of the opinions of the Dutch and French people as regards European integration, as might appear at first glance?
2. Should these results be interpreted as a refusal, by two founding Member States, of the continuation of European integration?

In order to try and answer the first question, one may take into account several elements, among which the evolution of the turnout in

of populism which wiped out everything in its path, European integration, enlargement, elites, the regulation of liberalism, reformism, internationalism, even generosity), *Libération*, 30 May 2005; the cover page of *L'Express* read: 'Chirac défait, la gauche éclatée, la France isolée, l'Europe en crise' (Chirac defeated, the left blown up, France isolated, Europe in crisis) (no. 2813, 30 May to 5 June 2005); the cover page of *Le Nouvel observateur* read: 'Etat de choc, le pouvoir rejeté, les élites désavouées, l'Europe sanctionnée' (state of shock, the governing power rejected, the elites disavowed, Europe punished) (no. 2117, 2 to 8 June 2005) and the title of the editorial of *Le Point* read: 'L'Europe en berne et la France au piquet' (Europe at half-mast and France in the corner) (no. 1707, 2 June 2005).

[8] One might think about Mark Twain: when an obituary of him was published while he was still alive, he is reported to have cabled the press to say that reports of his death had been greatly exaggerated.

successive elections to the European Parliament, might serve as a benchmark. For the whole of the European Union, since 1979, when the Members of the European Parliament were for the first time elected by a direct vote, the evolution shows a steady decrease in the turnout (from 63% to 45.7%) (see figure 1.1).

As for France and the Netherlands more specifically, the figures show a similar trend, the turnout in both countries being lower than the average EU turnout (see figure 1.2).

In the June 2004 elections to the European Parliament, there were 41.5 million voters in France, and only 17.7 million of them took part in the vote. There were 12.1 million voters in the Netherlands, and only 4.7 million of them took part in the vote.

These figures were obviously very alarming, as they demonstrated:

- either a lack of interest for European issues (which the very high turnout in the 2005 referenda tends to deny);
- or a lack of trust in the fact that the election of the Members of the European Parliament could have an influence on the direction, rhythm, or purpose of European integration.

Another element which one may take into account in order to judge the political significance of the French 'No' in 2005 is a comparison with the previous referendum in that country on a Treaty on a European issue: it took place in 1992 and concerned the Maastricht Treaty. In a nutshell, this was the Treaty which formally established the European Union (on top of the existing European Communities). It contained the agreement to create an EU single currency and paved the way for the EU to develop both a foreign policy ('CFSP', the Common Foreign and Security Policy) and a policy concerning internal security ('JHA', Justice and Home Affairs). Therefore, the project put to the approval of the French citizens in 1992 was rather clear: it was even possible to sum up its content in a few sentences. That is not the case for the 'Constitution for Europe', as this book will show. However, in spite of this relative clarity of the issue at stake, the results of the 1992 Maastricht referendum in France were very close: 49.2% of the voters voted against and 50.8% in favour (with a high turnout of 70%).

With regard to France, what has happened on the EU scene since this referendum of 1992? How could the development of the EU have been perceived from a French point of view? In other words, during the period which elapsed from 1992 to 2005, what were the events which could have

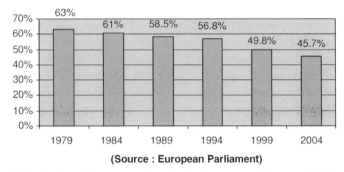

Figure 1.1. Evolution of the turnout for the elections to the European Parliament for the whole European Union *(Figure 1.1)*.

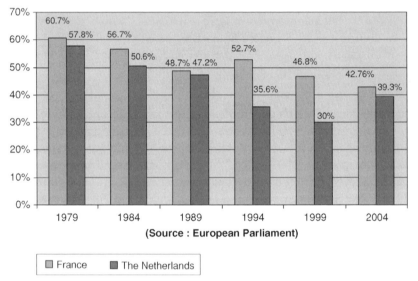

Figure 1.2. Evolution of the turnout for the elections to the European Parliament for France and the Netherlands *(Figure 1.2)*.

attracted the French voters either to a 'Yes' vote or to a 'No' vote with regard to the 'European Project'?

The following elements might be taken into account in this regard:

- The number of EU Member States grew first from 12 to 15, and then, in 2004, just one year before the date of the French referendum, from 15 to 25. Bulgaria and Romania signed their accession Treaty in April 2005 and are scheduled to become EU members on 1 January 2007.

Croatia and Turkey are official candidates and their accession negotiations are foreseen to begin during the year 2005. The former Yugoslav Republic of Macedonia and the other Western Balkan States are seen as possible candidates in the medium term.

- The resignation of all the members of the Santer Commission in 1999 attracted a lot of criticism and, as a consequence, a bad image of the EU institutions has been given by the media. This has sometimes been encouraged by a 'Brussels-bashing' tendency on the part of some Ministers about the Brussels bureaucracy and its supposed powers.

- The war in Iraq demonstrated a deep political division among the EU Member States: this made the EU appear as having largely failed in its efforts to forge a common foreign policy, despite the formidable work done by Javier Solana, the EU High Representative for the CFSP.

- On the economic front, the rate of unemployment in France has stubbornly remained stuck at around 10% of the active population for about 20 years. This is partly perceived by the French people as the result of globalisation, mixed up in the minds of many of them with the EU and its enlargement. In the year 2000, the EU itself had claimed *urbi et orbi* that, with the so-called 'Lisbon Process', Europe will become, in 10 years time, 'the most competitive economy in the world'. Through this solemn statement, the EU looked as if it had assumed all responsibilities for this into its hands. Since the expected results did not follow, the EU appeared as having also failed in the economic field, notwithstanding the fact that the main responsibilities in that field do not fall within its competences, but within those of the Member States.

- The first round of the elections for the French President in 2002 (21 April) gave the following results:

  - Jacques Chirac   19.88%
  - Jean-Marie Le Pen   16.86%
  - Lionel Jospin   16.18%
  - together the 13 other candidates received 47.08% of the votes.

These results show that a majority of the French voters had decided to vote in the first round in favour of candidates who did not have any chance of being elected in the second round.[9] These elections were seen

---

[9] That was obviously also the case of Jean-Marie Le Pen: in the second round of the elections which opposed Jacques Chirac to Jean-Marie Le Pen, Jacques Chirac got a massive 82.22% of the votes.

as a political earthquake in France: it was apparent that voters did not trust the major political parties any more and that the gap between the voters and the political elite was growing dangerously.

As for the situation in the Netherlands, the love-story with European integration, which used to characterise the three Benelux States, had already become less obvious over the years. Things appeared to go too fast and too far, citizens having the feeling that they had lost control over the way Europe was going. The fact that the turnout for the European Parliament elections did not reach 40% three times in a row, in 1994, 1999 and 2004, was quite revealing. In addition, it was widely advertised that the Dutch tax-payers were paying more per capita to the EU budget (without stressing the modesty of the sums involved, i.e. 333 euros per year per capita for the Netherlands in 2004 or less than one euro per day per capita)[10] than tax-payers from any other Member State. Political parties from the extreme right and from the extreme left had made substantial progress in the elections. Moreover, the political turmoil which followed the assassination of Pim Fortuyn in May 2002 and of Theo Van Gogh in November 2004 was accompanied by a psychological drama, as a people who were tolerant and open to immigration suddenly discovered that there was, in their country, a real and deep problem with the failed integration of immigrants.

In both France and the Netherlands, as well as in several other European countries, political analysts did draw, over these past ten years, attention to the problem of the growing distance between citizens and the political elites and to the risks of 'populism' which that entails.[11]

Actually, a great number of surveys, opinion polls and electoral studies have shown that, for at least a decade,[12] the trust of citizens has gone down, both as regards the EU institutions and as regards their own national government and political authorities.[13] Rates of abstention in

---

[10] Source: European Commission, Eurostat, Dutch Finance Ministry (reported in *International Herald Tribune*, 17 June 2005).

[11] See Y. Meny and Y. Surel, *Par le peuple, pour le peuple: le populisme et les démocraties* (Paris, éd. Fayard, 2000).

[12] See the successive 'Eurobarometers' on the 'europa' internet site: http://europa.eu.int/comm/public_opinion/index_en.htm.

[13] See D. Reynié and B. Cautrès, *L'opinion européenne* (Paris, IEP, 2001); P. Bréchon, 'Des valeurs politiques entre pérennité et changement' (2002) 277 *Futuribles* 92–128.

elections have increased, not only in European elections, but also in national ones.[14] In national elections in Europe, both the extreme right (exploiting the impact of immigration) and the extreme left (exploiting unemployment and the weaknesses of the welfare State confronted with the effects of globalisation) have made progress and weakened the major political parties. That was the case not only in France, with the impressive total of votes of candidates of both extreme left and right in the 2002 Presidential elections, but also in Austria, in Denmark, in Belgium, in Italy, in the Netherlands, etc. The legislative elections in Germany on 18 September 2005 confirm this trend. Both major parties lost a significant share of the vote from the last elections in 2002, the SPD falling from 38.5% to 34.3% of the votes and the CDU-CSU from 38.8% to 35.2%. Each of them lost around 2 million voters, whereas the newly created Linkspartei allied with the neo-communist PDS got over 2 million more votes as compared with 2002 (from 4% to 8.7% of the votes).

Both phenomena, at the EU level *and* at the national level, must be considered together.

It is obvious that part of the democratic control of the EU institutions is not exercised at the European level (role of the European Parliament), but at the national level (through democratic control of the national political authorities). Actually, it may be argued that the most effective democratic representation of the citizens and the best political control exercised over the EU for them takes place indirectly, through their nationally elected representatives in the Council and in the European Council, while their direct representation through the European Parliament is in fact weaker, as it fails to reflect a collective will. This might be explained by the lack of a true European political space, the lack of an EU political debate, the lack of EU-wide media and the lack of an EU public opinion.[15] As a result, the European Parliament elections are being transformed into what specialists call elections of a 'second-order'

---

[14] H. D. Klingemann, 'Mapping Political Support in the 1990's: A Global Analysis' in Pippa Norris (ed.), *Critical Citizens: Global Support for Democratic Governance* (Oxford University Press, 1999); S. Pharr and R. Putnam, *Disaffected Democracies* (Princeton University Press, 2000).

[15] J. Habermas, *Between Facts and Norms: Contributions to a Discourse Theory* (Cambridge, Polity Press, 1996); D. Grimm, 'Does Europe Need a Constitution?' (1995) 1–3 *European Law Journal* 282–303; J. H. H. Weiler, *The Constitution of Europe* (Cambridge University Press, 1999).

nature,[16] allowing citizens to punish the political parties which are in power. This was the case in 2004 in more than two-thirds of the 25 Member States. Another explanation, given by Mark Leonard, is the fact that the Union has no competence to legislate on issues which matter most for the voters in Europe, as such competences belong to Member States:[17]

> The reason that people do not turn out in their droves to vote for the European Parliament is not because it has no powers. It is because none of the issues in which the EU specializes – trade liberalization, monetary policy, the removal of non-tariff barriers, technical regulation in the environmental and other areas, foreign aid, and general foreign policy co-ordination – appears anywhere on the list of issues that voters care about. In fact, none of the policies in the five most important issues for voters in Europe – health care provision, education, law and order, pension and social security policy, and taxation – are set by the European Union.

Elections to the European Parliament are not used in order to answer political questions at an EU level. European citizens identify themselves much more with their country of origin than with Europe. The image of Europe which is given to them by their national leaders differs according to their country of origin.[18] If one adds to this the lack of a common language and the lack of a European political leadership, the situation is not favourable either to a political election campaign at EU level or to strong EU institutions elected directly by the people(s). Therefore, as Vivien A. Schmidt remarks:[19] 'The "will of the peoples" can still be expressed, and is, indirectly and strongly through the national executives sitting in the Council of Ministers, directly but much more weakly through the elected members of the European Parliament.'

This might change in the future, but not in the short term. In any case, the situation would not change dramatically with the entry into force of

---

[16] K. Reif and H. Schmitt, 'Nine Second-Order National Elections' (1980) 8 *European Journal of Political Research* 3–44; C. van der Eijk and M. N. Frank, *Choosing Europe* (University of Michigan Press, 1996).

[17] M. Leonard, *Why Europe Will Run the 21st Century* (London, Fourth Estate, Harper Collins Publishers, 2005).

[18] T. Risse 'Who Are We? A Europeanization of National Identities?' in M. G. Cowles, J. A. Caporaso and T. Risse (eds.), *Transforming Europe* (Ithaca, Cornell University Press, 2001).

[19] V. A. Schmidt, *The EU: Democratic Legitimacy in a Regional State* (Centre for European Studies, Working Paper no. 112, 2004), http://www.ces.fas.harvard.edu/publications/VSchmidt.pdf.

the Constitution, even if it would arguably be significantly improved. Actually, the conceivable measures which could deliver a real 'solution' would be much more drastic and politically unacceptable for the Member States, at least for the time being. It would consist in a system of a direct election, either of the President of the Commission or of the President of the European Council. This would establish a powerful – because fully legitimate – institution and would be a radical step on the way towards establishing a Federation. That is the reason why such a measure is not contemplated by the Member States, which desire neither the establishment of too powerful a European institution, nor the establishment of a Federal State. From there it flows that, when people have the feeling that mistakes have been made at the European level, they do not have a 'scapegoat' which they could punish directly. This situation is not likely to disappear soon.

Therefore, in the future, political control over the EU institutions will largely continue to be exercised through national institutions, in addition to the control exercised through the European Parliament. It flows from that that one should stop trying to look for solutions to the so-called 'European democratic deficit' through institutional means modelled on nation-states' institutions.

The political discourse in Europe comes essentially through national politicians talking to national public opinions through national mass media. As national leaders project their own image of the EU, they are held responsible for the supposed faults of the EU. The extreme right makes the major political parties responsible for immigration, whether legal or illegal, whether coming from the new EU Member States or from African or Asian countries. The extreme left makes them responsible for unemployment, and the consequences of globalisation (such as deloca-lisations),[20] as well as for the pressures of European Monetary Union (the Stability and Growth Pact, the European Central Bank's policy on interest rates) on the welfare state ('Europe is not social enough'). The powers of national governments appear increasingly eroded by the internationalisation of economic transactions. In the minds of most people, this globalisation has come at the same time as the integration

---

[20] Which, in reality, still mainly benefit the 15 'old' EU Member States, in particular the UK and France: in 2004, out of 2885 new foreign investments in Europe (including from other EU States), 567 went to the UK and 490 to France as compared with 148 to Poland and 42 to Turkey (OECD and Ernst and Young, reported in *Le Monde*, 30 June 2005).

of the EU and both are seen together. As a result, rather than a protection, the EU is seen as a threat to national identities and to the national sovereignty of the old nation-states of Europe.

The phenomenon is therefore at both levels: citizens may feel that the well-known 'democratic deficit' at the EU level is increasingly accompanied by a 'democratic deficit' at the national level as well. As Larry Siedentop puts it: '. . . democratic political cultures are being weakened in the Member States, without being replaced' (*The Wall Street Journal*, 17 June 2005). If this were to be true, at least in some European countries,[21] this would require changes and remedies at the national level as well, and should not be looked for at the EU level or, at any rate, not only at the EU level.

Therefore, one could expect that, in this context and at this juncture, asking the people, both in France and in the Netherlands, to vote by a referendum on 'the European Project' would not be an 'easy-to-win' bet. One has to add to those elements the fact that the message offered by the Constitutional Treaty is not that clear.

Firstly, the concept of 'Constitution' is often linked to the concept of 'State', whereas the purpose of the Constitutional Treaty is not at all to establish a federal State.

Secondly, the content of the Constitutional Treaty is not easy to summarise in a few sentences: is it about more powers for the EU, or more democratic control over the EU institutions, or more means given to the EU to enable it to speak with one voice in the world? Or is it about adapting the EU to its increased membership? Or is it about codifying and simplifying the too many and too complicated Treaties and rules governing the EU? Or all of that together? It is not easy to get an answer by 'Yes' or 'No' when the question is so complex.

Therefore, the negative results were perhaps less surprising than seen at first sight.

But should these results be interpreted as a vote 'against' Europe ? It appears from the opinion polls conducted right after the referenda that neither the French, nor the Dutch people, are against their country continuing to participate actively in the development of European

---

[21] However, on this point, some may argue that there is not so much a problem of democratic deficit at the national level (see the last national elections in Greece, Spain or Portugal) but a problem of elites in some European countries.

integration. This was shown by a large-scale survey which was conducted immediately after the two referenda,[22] the purpose of which was to better understand the factors which determined the results and the motivations of the voters. The outcome was very interesting.

Factors which determined the results of the referenda and motivations of the voters

The Netherlands

More than half (51%) of the 37.2% of people who abstained in the referendum said it was because they believed that they were not sufficiently informed about the Constitution. Most people (whether having voted or not) said that the debates about the Constitution started too late in the Netherlands (67%). 26% of those who abstained thought that the text of the Constitution was too complicated for them. Only 16% of them presented their abstention as an opposition to European integration.

The three primary motivations of the 'Yes' voters in the Netherlands were:

- the belief that the Constitution was essential in order to pursue European integration (24%);
- the belief that the Constitution would strengthen European identity (13%);
- the belief that the Constitution was essential for ensuring the smooth functioning of the European institutions (12%).

The reasons for the 'No' vote in the Netherlands were very diverse; the four most important ones being:

- the lack of information, which was by far the main reason, since 32% of the 'No' voters indicated that as the reason for their negative vote;

[22] This survey was conducted on 30 and 31 May 2005 in France (2015 interviews) and from 2 to 4 June 2005 in the Netherlands (2000 interviews). Flash Eurobarometer no. 171 and 172, TNS SOFRES c/o EOS Gallup Europe.
On internet: http://europa.eu.int/comm/public_opinion/flash/fl171_en.pdf and
http://europa.eu.int/comm/public_opinion/flash/fl172_en.pdf.
For a report analysing the referendum, made by the Dutch Cultureel Planbureau, which is a government advisory body, see at the following address: http://www.cpb.nl/eng/pub/ bijzonder/58/ bijz58.pdf.

- the supposed loss of national sovereignty (19.5%);
- opposition to the government or to some political parties (14%);[23]
- the 'cost' of Europe (13%).

Most Dutch citizens did not have a good image of the European institutions: 61% negative opinion, only 31% positive opinion.

A vast majority of the Dutch (2/3) thought that the rejection of the Constitution would allow for a renegotiation of the Constitution in order to achieve 'a more social text'. A similar majority believed that a new renegotiated Constitution would allow for the interests of their country to be better defended within the EU.

A slight majority of the Dutch people did not consider that the Constitution was essential in order to pursue European integration (50%); whereas 41% of the Dutch thought that the Constitution was essential in that regard.

One of the major elements of the survey is that a vast majority of Dutch citizens, i.e. 82% of them, support the Netherlands' membership of the EU as being 'a good thing' (see figure 1.3). This was the opinion of 98% of those having voted 'Yes' and of 78% of those having voted 'No'.

France

The campaign preceding the referendum in France raised passions in the whole country. The turnout was very high: nearly 70% of the voters participated, so approximately the same rate as for the 1992 referendum on the Maastricht Treaty.

Despite the fact that two-thirds of the people said they had enough information to vote, 37% thought that the debates in France began too late. Among the people who abstained, 60% said that the reason for their abstention was the excessive complexity of the text, and 49% said that they were not sufficiently informed about the Constitution to vote on it

---

[23] A 1995 study of the four referenda which took place on the Treaty of Maastricht in Denmark, France and Ireland in 1992 and in Denmark in 1993 'demonstrates clearly that [these] referenda . . . turned out to a great extent to reflect the popularity of the government . . . Among those unhappy with the performance of the government, a majority voted "No", with remarkable similarity between the percentages in each of the three countries . . . These findings raise the concern that, by giving too much credence to referenda about the future of Europe, politicians and commentators could in the wrong circumstances wreck the whole European project' (see M. N. Franklin, C. van der Eijk and M. Marsh, 'Referendum Outcomes and Trust in Government: Public Support for Europe in the Wake of Maastricht' (1995) 18–3 *West European Politics* 101–117).

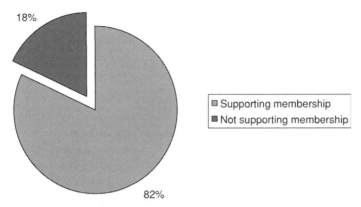

Figure 1.3. Percentage of the Dutch people supporting the membership of their country in the European Union.

(that was the case of 75% of the 18–24 age-group). Only 14% of the abstainers presented their abstention as an opposition to the EU or to European integration.

The two main reasons for the 'Yes' vote were :

• the belief that the Constitution was necessary in order to pursue European integration (39%);
• the positive opinion of the voters towards European integration in general (16%).

The reasons for the 'No' vote were more diversified; the six most important ones were that:

• the Constitution would have negative effects on employment in France (31%);
• the economic situation of France was too bad (26%);
• the Constitution was economically too 'liberal' (19%);
• it was an expression of opposition to the President of the Republic or to the Government (18%);
• there was not enough 'social Europe' (16%);
• the Constitution was too complicated (12%).

In other words, the majority of the 'Yes' voters voted on European matters (in general) whereas the vast majority of the 'No' voters voted more on the economic and social situation in France and the fear that the European Constitution might worsen rather than improve that situation.[24]

Actually, their opinion on the actual text of the European Constitution was the reason behind only 20% of the 'No' voters and 16% of the 'Yes' voters!

One of the major elements to come out of the survey is that 88% of the French citizens believe that France's membership of the EU 'is a good thing' (only 10% disagree) (see figure 1.4). This was the case for 99% of those having voted 'Yes' and for 83% of those having voted 'No' (only 15% disagree).

A large majority of the French people considered that the European Constitution was necessary in order to pursue European integration: 75% of the total (only 21% disagreed), i.e. 90% of the 'Yes' voters (8% disagreed) and even 66% of the 'No' voters (30% disagreed). Among those who participated in the vote ('Yes' and 'No' together), a majority of 90% recognized the necessity to have a European Constitution. As for the image of the European institutions, it is better in France than in the Netherlands: 53% of the French have 'a good image' of them, whereas 43% have a negative impression.

A majority of French citizens (52%) believed that the success of the 'No' vote would make any future enlargement of the EU more difficult, probably linking this to the case of Turkey.

As in the Netherlands, 62% of the French thought that the success of the 'No' vote would allow for a renegotiation of the Constitution in order to obtain a 'more social' text, although this opinion, which was shared by most of those having voted 'No' (83%), was not supported by the 'Yes' voters (only 30%). And, as in the Netherlands, about 60% of the citizens believed that the text of the Constitution would be renegotiated in order to better defend the interests of their country within the EU.

---

[24] This shows how difficult it is to explain to people what European integration is and where are its limits. Economic and social policies are mostly in the hands of Member States' authorities. The EU institutions have few and weak powers in these domains. Moreover, there would be no consensus among the 25 governments to agree on common policies in this respect. However, during the referendum's campaign in France, the 'social issue' was at the centre of the debate and a lot of voters held the Union responsible for unemployment and the bad economic situation.

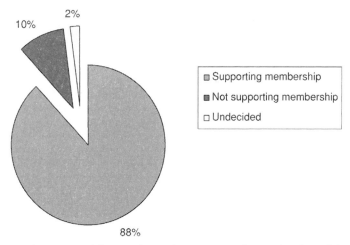

Figure 1.4. Percentage of the French people supporting the membership of their country in the European Union.

Conclusion of the analysis

On the basis of the above analysis, one may conclude that:

- a better economic and social situation;
- and/or a greater popularity of the Government in power;
- and/or better information about economic and social factors, on the rules governing a common economic market, on the real costs and benefits of the EU, on the exact content of the Constitution, in particular on economic and social matters, as well as on the future shape of the European project (federal State or not) and on its final geographical borders (Turkey or not),

would have led to a different result, given the basic wish of both the Dutch and the French people for their country to continue to participate in European integration.

In any case, one of the factors which explains the results of both referenda is the lack of any negative consequence for the country concerned in case of a 'no' result. That country remains a full member of the EU and its situation will not be concretely altered. Therefore, the choice is between, on the one hand, the status quo, i.e. a situation which is well-known, and, on the other hand, the adoption of a text which, being long and complex, necessarily contains here or there some elements which one may dislike or which might be seen as having unknown consequences. The choice would of course have been much clearer or if it had been between either remaining a member of a new EU ruled by the Constitution, or leaving the EU altogether.

Actually, whatever the depth of the analysis, whatever the real motivations of the voters (if it were possible to determine them), the fact remains that, politically and historically, the two 'No' votes are perceived and will remain perceived as being 'Nos' to the European Project.

From here, what might happen next?

It might be useful to have a look back to what happened in the past when one of the Member States failed to ratify a draft Treaty amending the existing European Treaties. This has happened twice, in Denmark and in Ireland.

Section 3: The experience of the two previous instances of negative referenda in Denmark and in Ireland

In 1992, the Danish people rejected the ratification of the Maastricht Treaty. In 2001, the Irish people rejected the ratification of the Nice Treaty. In both cases, their respective governments decided to ask the question a second time to their people on the same Treaty, although accompanied with some clarifications. In both cases, the second referendum gave a clear positive result (respectively 56.7% 'Yes' in Denmark and 62.9% 'Yes' in Ireland).

The case of Denmark

The first referendum on the Maastricht Treaty took place in Denmark on 2 June 1992 and the results were close: 50.7% 'No' and 49.3% 'Yes' (1.65 million votes v. 1.6 million),[25] with a turnout of 83%. The reaction of both the Danish Government and of the Governments of the 11 other European Community Member States was unanimous and immediate

---

[25] See M. N. Franklin, C. van der Eijk and M. Marsh, 'Referendum Outcomes and Trust in Government: Public Support for Europe in the Wake of Maastricht' (1995) 18–3 *West European Politics* 101–117. For an analysis of the referendum campaign and the reasons of the 'No' vote in Denmark, see O. V. Ryborg, *Det utaenkelige nej . . . ! Historien om 6 måneder, 0 dage og 17 timer, der rystede Europa* (Copenhagen, Schultz ed. 1998).

(Ministers of Foreign Affairs held a meeting in Oslo on 4 June 1992, in the margins of a NATO meeting): the ratification process would continue in other countries, and 'the door would remain open for Denmark'.

The difficulty for the Danish Government was how to interpret the reasons for its country's 'No' vote. In order to do that, meetings were organised where all the main political parties actively participated. Finally, this led to the adoption of a Memorandum, listing a number of issues which were considered to reflect the concerns of the Danish people. Among the main issues highlighted were the insufficient transparency of the European institutions, concerns about the future single currency, concerns about the European foreign policy which could lead to a common defence policy, and concerns about the possible development of a European policy on justice and home affairs.

On that basis, the Danish authorities worked during the second semester of 1992, with the help of the General Secretariat of the Council and with the UK presidency, in order to try and find a solution. This had to be done while keeping in mind the absolute necessity of not changing a single word of the Maastricht Treaty, so as not to oblige Member States which had already ratified it to do so again.

Finally, the Danish Government decided to put the Maastricht Treaty, unchanged, to a second referendum, accompanied by declarations and other texts which, without modifying in any way the Treaty itself, sought to provide answers to the concerns of the Danish citizens. These texts were approved by the 12 Governments during the European Council which took place in December 1992 in Edinburgh.

On 18 May 1993, the second referendum on the Maastricht Treaty took place in Denmark and gave a clear positive result: 56.7% 'Yes' (1.93 million votes) and 43.3% 'No' (1.47 million votes), with a turnout of 86.5%.[26]

---

[26] Later on, the Danish Government asked the other EU Member States to transform the texts agreed in Edinburgh into legally binding 'opt-outs' for Denmark, as far as the euro, the EU defence policy and some parts of the justice and home affairs area were concerned. These opt-outs were incorporated into the Treaties by the Amsterdam IGC and could now only be abandoned through a change in the Treaties.

The case of Ireland

The first referendum on the Nice Treaty took place in Ireland on 7 June 2001 and the result was clearly negative: 54% 'No' (0.53 million voters) and 46% 'Yes' (0.45 million votes), with a very low turnout of only 33.7%. These results were even more surprising than the 1992 referendum in Denmark, where, as in other Nordic countries, the feelings towards European integration are traditionally rather lukewarm. Ireland is probably the EU country which has benefited the most from the Union, both in terms of improving its governance and in terms of obtaining 'cohesion funds', resulting, with a clever tax and economic policy by the Irish Government, in a very positive influx of investments and a rapidly growing economy. From being one of the four poorest countries of the Union (with Greece, Portugal and Spain), Ireland has become one of the richest.

It was therefore very difficult to interpret the reasons for the 'No' vote. One of the reasons for the referendum failure might have been over-confidence, on the part of the Government, in a positive result of the referendum; this resulted in the Irish political authorities not campaigning rigorously enough, whereas the 'No' campaign was quite effective, with catchy slogans like 'If you don't know, vote No'. Others hold the view that it was not an Irish problem but a European one (namely that citizens do not identify sufficiently with what happens in Brussels) which had an Irish manifestation only because a referendum was held in Ireland.

After the negative referendum, the Irish Government almost immediately decided that the Nice Treaty, which symbolised the next enlargement of the Union to 10 new Member States, would be put again to the voters. Following thorough consultation of the main political parties, the accent was put on preserving Ireland's policy of neutrality. At the European Council meeting in Seville on 21 and 22 June 2002, Ireland made a 'National Declaration' reaffirming that the provisions of the EU Treaty relating to the CFSP did not undermine its traditional policy of military neutrality and that this would continue to be the case after its ratification of the Treaty of Nice. The European Council adopted a Declaration whereby it confirmed that this traditional Irish policy was not called into question by the Nice Treaty.

The Government then organised a very effective campaign of information, and the second referendum, which took place on 19 October 2002, was very clearly won, by a majority of 62.89% 'Yes' (0.9 million votes) against only 37.11% 'No' (0.53 million votes), and with a higher turnout of 48.45%.

Comparison with the referenda in France and in the Netherlands

Obviously, both the cases of Denmark and of Ireland were very different from what happened in 2005 in France and the Netherlands. Both the former cases involved relatively small States, which had not been among the founding States of the EEC and which were not 'central' to the history of European integration. Still, in both cases, all their major political parties were determined that the future of their country remained with its continued participation in the Union and they were clever enough to consult each other in order to try and find ways and means to obtain this result. In 2005, however, there were *two* negative referenda, not just one, and they were both held in two founding Member States, where people have the feeling that it would be inconceivable that their country could be pushed out of the EU.

With regard, however, to the reasons for the 'No' votes, some similarities might be noted. The reasons for the French and Dutch 'No' were probably even less 'European driven' than in the Danish and Irish cases, as they were much more linked to the state of the economy and/or to the lack of popularity of the governments in power. As far as European issues were concerned, the reasons were probably less linked to the precise text of the Treaty to be ratified than to other, larger questions, such as Europe's supposed responsibility for the general state of the economy, globalisation, immigration, unemployment, social policy and reforms, etc. In 2005, as was the case both in 1992 and in 2001, the voters said they were not sufficiently informed.

Globally, the situation is not very different from what it was both in 1992 and in 2001: the reasons for the Danish and Irish 'No' voters were no better known than those of the French and the Dutch 'No' voters today. In both previous cases, the Governments concerned decided to consult political parties and managed to come to common conclusions. That could also theoretically be the case today as far as France and the Netherlands are concerned; but it is true that the current internal political situation in both countries might not allow for that.

One also has to take into account an additional problem which is that, contrary to what happened in 1992 and in 2001, where the other Member States did not have any concern about their own ratification process, in 2005 the situation is different in this regard. A number of EU

Member States' Governments fear that, in the present circumstances, the referendum which they had called in their country, due either to a constitutional obligation (Denmark and Ireland) or to their own political choice (e.g. Poland or the UK), would not be easy to win. One must note that the double French and Dutch 'No' was very quickly followed by a British statement according to which, in these circumstances, there was no point in pursuing the ratification process of a Treaty which might never come into force.

Section 4: The continuation of the ratification process

The June 2005 Declaration on the ratification of the Constitution

The question of what to do with the on-going ratification process of the Constitution was discussed during the European Council in June 2005, where the 25 Heads of State or Government unanimously adopted the following Declaration (see box 1.2).

Box 1.2   Declaration on the ratification of the Treaty establishing a Constitution for Europe
(European Council, 15 and 16 June 2005)

We have held a wide-ranging review of the process of ratification of the Treaty establishing a Constitution for Europe. This Treaty is the fruit of a collective process, designed to provide the appropriate response to ensure that an enlarged European Union functions more democratically, more transparently and more effectively.

Our European ambition, which has served us so well for over 50 years and which has allowed Europe to unite around the same vision, remains more relevant than ever. It has enabled us to ensure the well-being of citizens, the defence of our values and our interests, and to assume our responsibilities as a leading international player. In order to fight unemployment and social exclusion more effectively, to promote sustainable economic growth, to respond to the challenges of globalisation, to safeguard internal and external security, and to protect the environment, we need Europe, a more united Europe presenting greater solidarity.

To date, ten Member States have successfully concluded ratification procedures, thereby expressing their commitment to the Constitutional Treaty. We have noted the outcome of the referendums in

France and the Netherlands. We consider that these results do not call into question citizens' attachment to the construction of Europe. Citizens have nevertheless expressed concerns and worries which need to be taken into account. Hence the need for us to reflect together on this situation.

This period of reflection will be used to enable a broad debate to take place in each of our countries, involving citizens, civil society, social partners, national parliaments and political parties. This debate, designed to generate interest, which is already under way in many Member States, must be intensified and broadened. The European institutions will also have to make their contribution, with the Commission playing a special role in this regard.

The recent developments do not call into question the validity of continuing with the ratification processes. We are agreed that the timetable for the ratification in different Member States will be altered if necessary in response to these developments and according to the circumstances in these Member States.

We have agreed to come back to this matter in the first half of 2006 to make an overall assessment of the national debates and agree on how to proceed.[1]

Note: [1] Emphasis by the author.

Following this Declaration, Cyprus and Malta decided to proceed with ratifying through their Parliaments (30 June and 6 July 2005 respectively), and so did Belgium and Estonia.

Among the States which have planned to ratify through a referendum, only Luxembourg has so far decided to go ahead as scheduled and it held a successful referendum on 10 July 2005: 56.52% 'Yes' against 43.48% 'No'.

One has to recall that, according to Declaration no. 30 annexed to the final Act of the IGC: 'The Conference notes that if, two years after the signature of the Treaty establishing a Constitution for Europe, four fifths of the Member States have ratified it and one or more Member States have encountered difficulties in proceeding with ratification, the matter will be referred to the European Council.'

This Declaration was suggested to the IGC by the Convention. This was seen as a 'compensation' given to those who wanted the Constitution to expressly provide that it would enter into force even after a non-unanimous ratification, i.e. as soon as a given qualified majority – both of States and of population – had been reached. This suggestion was rejected both as legally incorrect and as politically unacceptable, and the Declaration was adopted instead. Actually, it only states the obvious: when a serious problem happens in the EU, the European Council discusses it. However, the way the Declaration is formulated seems to imply that, if it so happens that a large majority of Member States ratify the Constitution, the few States which have failed to do so could be invited to leave the Union. One has to stress that, as is the case with the other Declarations annexed to the Final Act of the IGC, this text is a political statement which has no legal value. Moreover, its authors did not have in mind France and the Netherlands as the most probable countries not being able to ratify the Constitution quickly. Nevertheless, it does stress the importance given to the Constitution by the Heads of State or Government, as it is the first time that an IGC having revised the founding Treaties has adopted a statement of this kind.

When the Heads of State or Government meet to examine the situation, in June 2006, under the Presidency of Chancellor Wolfgang Schüssel, they might either take a decision on the substance, or decide to wait for one more year before doing so, given the fact that the French or the Dutch Governments might be unable to give a precise answer already in 2006. They might also take a procedural decision in order to prepare some options to be examined later. Actually, it will take time to re-build a favourable climate towards European integration in the public opinions of several European countries. To re-open a debate too soon on the reform of institutions and on the European Constitution might prove to be counter-productive. It would probably be wiser to concentrate on concrete projects and to show that Europe is working on economic realities, rather than to re-open a constitutional debate prematurely.

What next?

On the basis of this analysis, one might think that it is too early today to pronounce the Constitution, or at least its context, 'dead and buried'.

The final answer to that question remains to be given.

The day will come anyway, probably at the latest in 2007, when both the French and the Dutch Governments will have to tell the others whether they consider it realistic to put the text of the Constitutional

Treaty[27] back to a second referendum. So long as they have not decided to do so, some other Governments, such as most likely the British and the Danish ones, will not be in a position to organise a referendum in their own countries.

If the French and/or the Dutch Governments announce that they will not organise a second referendum, it would still remain to be seen what could be done in the future in order to improve the content of the existing EU Treaties which are presently in force. Since European integration will go on, it will be necessary to try and simplify them, as well as to make the Union more democratic and more efficient. In particular, there seems to be a wide agreement on the fact that the EU institutions should be reformed in order to adapt them to the present and future number of members of the EU.

In that case, the idea of using the substance of the Constitution as a basis for a future work, in order to negotiate a new, simplified, reduced future Treaty, which might incorporate some, but not all, of the elements of the Constitution,[28] looks attractive and will have to be examined. However, one should not ignore the fact that this will be politically difficult to implement. Each part of the Constitution (in itself) was a compromise between the 25 Member States, but some parts were accepted by some States only in exchange for obtaining other parts, which were not wished by others. Reaching another compromise of this magnitude would be difficult. For instance, some countries, such as Poland or Spain, would resist the adoption of institutional changes without any change of substance. Therefore, one may wonder if there would be any enthusiasm in launching a negotiation for another Treaty based on a content similar to the Constitution, given the probable

---

[27] In order to avoid new ratification procedures in the Member States which have already ratified this Treaty, it would have to be 'unchanged'. However, 'unchanged' does not necessarily mean 'without any addition'. It is conceivable that 'something' might be added to the text of the Treaty itself. It might be either in a non-legal form, which does not need to be ratified (e.g. a 'Solemn Declaration'), or in a legal form which would not necessitate a new ratification of the Constitutional Treaty itself in the Member States which have already done so, but which might be ratified separately through a lighter procedure, in accordance with their national constitutional requirements.

[28] See for instance the idea of the Bertelsmann Foundation, developed in June 2005, together with its academic partner, the Centre for Applied Policy Research (CAP) in Munich, which would consist in retaining only some of the innovations of the Constitution, see http://www.cap.lmu.de/download/2005/2005_Treaty.pdf, namely some of the reforms of the EU institutions; the development of the decision-making and voting procedures; the reform and enhancement of the instruments of differentiated integration; and some structural provisions.

difficulty of negotiating such a text for no substantial gain. Another idea would be to cut the Constitution into pieces, and to adopt bits of its provisions, one at a time. That is not excluded, but it would not be politically easy either.

It might perhaps appear easier not to cut the content of the Constitution into pieces, but, if the political climate is favourable, to take it (or at least its new or essential context, i.e., Part I, Part II and the related provisions, in Part III) as a whole and add something to it, be it one or several Declarations, or one or several Protocols. This would allow those Member States which have already ratified the Constitution not to begin a new ratification procedure (in the case of one or several Declarations) or to proceed with a light procedure (in the case of one or several Protocols). The new texts could touch upon concrete policies and actions of the EU in fields which matter most to its citizens.

Whatever happens, one may wonder if France would be able to avoid another referendum on the subject of European integration during the next few years. While it is difficult to conceive any kind of European integration without France, it looks very difficult to conceive any kind of further European integration possible so long as France continues to appear as having said 'No' to Europe by the 2005 referendum.

Therefore, one may argue that France will probably have, sooner rather than later, to organise another referendum. It is impossible today to foresee what could be the date on which such a referendum might take place (sometime between 2007 and 2010?) and what its subject might be: the same Constitutional Treaty with the addition of a Solemn Declaration or of a Protocol? a simplified Treaty based on some of the content of the failed Constitution? another kind of Treaty with fewer participants than in the present EU?

If this political analysis were to be correct, one might however wonder whether it would be possible to hold such a referendum, which would amount to asking the French people whether they favour greater European integration, without having first clarified more precisely for them what 'the European Project' is about.

The unavoidable questions on the shape of the 'European project'

Over the past decades, European Governments have carefully managed not to answer this question collectively. That was either because they did not know the answer, or (most probably) because not all of them agreed on the possible answer.

The time might come in the next few years, when the voters will demand to have clearer information – if not exhaustive – about the shape of this 'European project' which they have constantly been asked to support. They might, in particular, ask three simple questions, all of which could help to give the EU 'frontiers, in minds as well as in space':[29]

1. Will the final form of this project be:

   - a mere customs union with some common policies? or
   - a partially federal Union with significant competences but mostly preserving the sovereignty of its constituent Member States? or
   - a fully-fledged Federal State?

It is worth stressing that the Constitution gives the second answer to this question, clearly rejecting the other two.

2. Will the final geographical borders of this project include:

   - the Western Balkan countries?
   - Turkey?
   - Ukraine?
   - other countries?

On this question, the Constitution does not give any answer.

3. What will be the limits of the competences conferred on the EU, will they include in particular:

   - culture? education?
   - health? social security?
   - tax harmonisation?
   - social harmonisation?

On this question, the Constitution does give the beginning of an answer.

It would obviously be very difficult to reach a common answer of the 25 EU Member States to these three questions, but the French authorities (as well as the national authorities of the other Member States) might be obliged to give their own position to their own citizens.

---

[29] L. Siedentop, 'Giving the EU Frontiers, in Minds as well as in Space remains a Priority', *Wall Street Journal*, 17 June 2005. On this issue, and the 'European Neighbourhood Policy', see T. Blanchet 'Le succès silencieux de dix ans d'Espace économique européen: un modèle pour l'avenir avec d'autres voisins?', *Liber Amicorum in Honour of Sven Norberg* (Brussels, Bruylantéd, to be published in 2006).

For their part, the EU institutions might also be called upon to give some clarifications to EU citizens, for instance by not creating misunderstandings and ambiguities about the respective powers of the EU and its Member States in economic and social matters. In particular, regarding the 'Lisbon process' and the so-called 'open method of coordination',[30] the question: 'who is responsible for what?' should always get clear answers when measures are being adopted 'in Brussels'.

At the same time, a lot of effort should be made in trying to put an end to the lack of knowledge on the part of the citizens about the EU's institutions and functioning.[31] EU citizens should also be aware that, through their votes, both in the national and in the EU elections,

---

[30] In the Brussels jargon, when the European Council tries to influence Member States in a domain where only the latter have the power to decide, the 'recommendations' or 'guidelines' which are adopted are called an 'open method of coordination'.

[31] On 22 November 2004, i.e. before the referendum, Jean-Pierre Raffarin, then Prime Minister of France, requested a report to be drawn up on the lack of information of French people about Europe. This report, 270 pages long, was written by M. Herbillon, MP, and published in June 2004 under the title: *La Fracture européenne : Après le Référendum du 29 mai, 40 propositions concrètes pour mieux informer les Français sur l'Europe* (Paris, La documentation française, June 2004).

On 20 July 2005, the European Commission adopted an 'Action Plan' in order to 'better explain how the policies of the EU have an influence on the everyday life of the citizens and what their added value is'. This plan provides for the implementation of some 50 concrete actions aiming to make better use of resources already in existence and to improve the capacities for communication and information within the Commission. The action plan makes the following provisions, amongst others:

– better coordination of the various communication activities within the Commission, in order to get the most out of efforts made and make the best possible use of existing communication tools;

– to make better use of the communication tools which the public prefers in the languages it understands, particularly the Internet and audiovisual services;

– to professionalise communication by providing specific training for European civil servants and by recruiting communications specialists using specific recruitment competitions;

– creating summaries to accompany the main proposals of the Commission, describing, in comprehensible language, the tangible benefits of these proposals for the citizens;

– to reinforce the representative presence of the Commission in the Member States to keep the citizens informed of policies and initiatives which may be of interest and/or concern to them, in the language they understand.

In a second phase of the action plan, the Commission plans to present a White Paper in the autumn of 2005, in which it is to propose a more global political vision of communication and initiatives to be carried out in the medium and long terms, together with other institutions and players. This White Paper will also address the role that the governments of the Member States will have to play in keeping the citizens informed. (See *Agence Europe*, 21 July 2005.)

they are the real masters of the game.[32] In order to contribute to this aim, the EU should develop a proactive communication strategy, with long-term goals.[33]

These goals should not be for the EU institutions to present a positive image and a self-congratulating message. They should be to explain why some issues are discussed at EU level, what are the draft pieces of legislation being discussed, what are the arguments in favour and against, and who are the actors in the decision-making process. It is not enough to tell the people that a decision has been or will be taken on a given issue: they must know what the background is, the context, what are the different positions, and the results to be expected. The aim should not be self-congratulation on each and every EU initiative, but to obtain increased media attention, so as to stimulate a public debate and a political discussion. European issues will most likely hit the news, especially on television, if they are presented as a matter for true political debate or even conflict, which they actually are in most if not all cases.

This implies that, rather than hiding disputes and difficulties, the EU decision-making process should make them more apparent, in order to better attract the attention of the media. One should not forget either that, in our countries, political communication is mostly national. Therefore, the EU institutions should be seen from a national viewpoint in order to try and attract the attention of national media: one might think about more frequent presence of the Members of the European Parliament and European Commissioners in their countries of origin, as well as a greater involvement of the members of national Parliaments in European issues and of enhanced efforts of information on the part of the Governments of the Member States.

This will inevitably lead to some criticisms, but it should be positive in the longer term. In any case, it is better to attract both negative and positive news coverage for the EU than no news coverage at all.

One of the aims would be to demonstrate that, contrary to what people think, the EU political system does allow for control of its decision-making process by the citizens, no less than for their own

---

[32] See *European Democracy: A Manifesto* (T. Arbuthnott and M. Leonard eds, the Foreign Policy Centre, British Council, Nov. 2003) [http://fpc.org.uk/fsblob/219.pdf].

[33] See C. de Vreese, 'Communicating Europe' in the above-mentioned *European Democracy: A Manifesto*. The 'Eurobarometer' (opinion polls) constantly shows that a majority of EU citizens feel that their voice does not count in the EU (52% in autumn 2004, 53% in spring 2005) – see Eurobarometer 63, conducted in May–June 2005, published in July 2005: http://europa.eu.int./comm/public_opinion/index_.

national governments. It is a fact that the increase in the powers of the European Parliament has not produced the results expected by some. The turnout in European Parliament elections fell lower and lower in the very same period when its powers were increased.

One must find the means to reverse this trend. Citizens must feel that, by voting in the European Parliament elections, they can 'really' influence the EU decision-making process.[34] This is one more reason why public debates should be conducted on the issues debated at the European level. In order to do that, another way might be to increase the use of information and communication technologies.[35] The European Commission has already launched electronic consultations on the internet for important new legislative proposals. This should be generalised. The results should be published. The Commission should show how they have been utilised in order to modify its initial proposals. The websites of the different EU institutions should be improved and made more user-friendly: access to documents is good for lobbies and interested parties, but it is far from being the best means to inform the citizens better ('no political system can be legitimate which its citizens do not understand' wrote Larry Siedentop).

After the failure of the referenda in France and in the Netherlands, neither the French nor the Dutch Government asked (yet) for the ratification process to be stopped. On the contrary, the French President Chirac, after the failed French referendum, wrote to his 24 colleagues : '[cette situation] ne remet nullement en cause l'engagement historique et profond de la France dans la construction européenne . . . Alors que neuf pays l'ont déjà approuvé, il appartient maintenant à tous les autres Etats membres de s'exprimer à leur tour sur ce Traité.' ([this situation] does not in any way put into question the historic and profound commitment of France to European integration . . . While nine countries have already approved this Treaty, it is now up to all the other Member States to express themselves on it.)

This continuation of the ratification process was unanimously approved by the 25 Heads of State or Government on 17 June 2005.

---

[34] See proposals by G. Durand for *A European Parliament really closer to the people* (European Policy Centre, Ideas Factory Europe no. 5, December 2004) [http://www.theepc.be/].

[35] See M. Engström, *Rebooting Europe: Digital Deliberation and European Democracy* (The Foreign Policy Centre, Nov. 2002).

The only logical explanation for this decision cannot be anything else than that the common belief of the 25 European leaders was that they have not excluded, for the time being, that there might be a chance (slim as it appears to be for now) of holding a second referendum on the context of the Constitution, perhaps improved with some additions, both in France and in the Netherlands. Responsible political authorities would not play around with going through heavy national procedures just because they would like to know how many Member States could agree on the content of the Constitution, in order to make a decision on how to continue at a later stage. Therefore, if the functioning of the Union were to be made more effective, democratic and transparent, now or in the foreseeable future, the substantive new provisions of the Constitutional Treaty would probably be the or a basis for any further work.

That is the reason why it is worth having an in-depth legal analysis of these provisions. This is the purpose of this book. It endeavours to explain the legal content of the Constitution and its political meaning, while trying to answer the following questions:

- Would this new Treaty constitute a great leap forward, a legal-political revolution that would transform the nature of the relationship of the Union with the Member States, by transforming it into a sort of 'pre-federal State'?
- Or would it rather be an additional step, albeit significant, but still a mere evolutionary step on the road towards further European integration?
- In other words, would this Treaty be the last one for 40 or 50 years as President Valéry Giscard d'Estaing said, or would the so-called Monnet method, the step-by-step confidence-building between the Member States which creates inextricable links and mutual trust, continue to be applied in the future, through other Treaties?

II

The process that led to the Constitution

The Treaty establishing a Constitution for Europe is the result of a long process.

Section 1: A short history of the idea of establishing a European Union

The idea of transforming the European Economic Community into a 'European Union', a single entity which would integrate all aspects of European integration, officially emerged for the first time at the 1972 Summit of the Heads of State or Government in Paris. It was then stated that 'Member States of the Community, the driving wheels of European integration, declared their intention of converting their entire relationship into a European Union before the end of this decade'.[1] However, the idea got lost in the turmoil of the economic crisis of the seventies, despite the recommendations made in the 'Report on European Union', known as the 'Tindemans Report', which was submitted, at their request, by the Belgian Prime Minister to the Heads of State or Government in December 1975.[2]

Ten years later, the 'Solemn Declaration on European Union', signed (which is very unusual for a Declaration) at the European Council in Stuttgart in June 1983, re-launched the idea by reaffirming the 'will to transform the whole complex of relations between their States into a European Union'.[3] For its part, in 1981, the European Parliament had mandated Altiero Spinelli, one of its members and a former Commissioner,

---

[1] See para. 7 of the Communiqué of the Conference of the Heads of State or Government, Paris, 19 and 21 October 1972 (Bull. EC 10–1972, p. 16). For a good collection of historic documents in an electronic form, see the internet site Archive of European Integration (AEI) of the University of Pittsburgh (http://aei.pitt.edu).

[2] Bull. EC Supplement 1/76. Available on the above-mentioned internet site (http://aei.pitt.edu).

[3] Bull. EC 6–1983, pp. 24–29. Available on the above-mentioned internet site (http://aei.pitt.edu). Denmark had reservations about some of the paragraphs of this Declaration.

together with an institutional committee, to propose amendments to the existing treaties. This work resulted in a 'draft Treaty instituting the European Union', known as the 'Spinelli Treaty'[4] which was voted on and accepted by the European Parliament on 14 February 1984 (by a majority of 237 votes against 31). However, the Member States did not follow up on this draft which proposed a very coherent and very bold text, going quite far in the direction of more European integration.

On this issue, the Single European Act of 1986 limited itself to recalling, in its Preamble, the will of the High Contracting Parties 'to transform relations as a whole among their States into a European Union'.

It was the fall of the Berlin Wall in 1989, the end of the Cold War and the ensuing reshaping of the geo-political landscape in Europe which, in 1993, more than 20 years after the Paris Summit of 1972, finally triggered the formal establishment of the 'European Union' by the Maastricht Treaty.[5] Although placed, together with the European Communities, under the same umbrella of a 'single institutional framework' (Article 3 EU Treaty), the European Union was established in a separate Treaty, while the European Community, the Coal and Steel Community and Euratom remained separated legal entities, each of them governed by its own founding Treaty.

It was only ten years later, in the 'Convention on the Future of Europe', that the drafters of the Constitution would propose to merge the Union and the Communities into a single entity,[6] to repeal their

---

[4] Bull. EC 2–1984, pp. 7–28.

[5] For an assessment of the Maastricht Treaty, see J.-C. Piris, 'After Maastricht, Are the Community Institutions More Efficacious, More Democratic and More Transparent?' (1994) 19–5 *European Law Review* 449–487.

[6] The technical feasibility of such an operation had already been checked. During the negotiations of the Amsterdam Treaty, the IGC had asked a Group of Legal Experts representing the then 15 Member States, which had worked on the simplification of the Treaties agreed in Amsterdam, to make a full codification of the existing Treaties. This Group made, 'for information purposes' only, two codifications: the first one (merged the EC and EU Treaties into a single Treaty) (CONF/4160/97 of 19 November 1997) and the second one merged the four Treaties existing at the time, i.e. the EC, EU, Euratom and Coal and Steel Treaties (CONF 4161/97 of 19 November 1997). These two consolidations were made public on 14 July 2000, in accordance with Declaration no. 42 to the Final Act of the Amsterdam IGC (SN 1845/00 of 14 July 2000).

Pending such a fully fledged merger, a first step towards a more readable Treaty was made by the Amsterdam IGC when it agreed on a simplification of the Treaties which repealed obsolete provisions and renumbered the Treaties (see Part Two, Arts. 6 to 8 of the Amsterdam Treaty). This is explained in an Explanatory Report made under the

founding Treaties and to replace them by a single Treaty text which they proposed to name 'Constitution'.

Section 2: The political background which led to the constitution

It was essentially the pressure of the coming enlargements, which would more than double the membership of the Union, and the necessity to adapt the EU institutions to this new reality, which convinced the 12, and then 15, Member States to start thinking seriously about reviewing the basic institutional structure of the EU, which had remained essentially the same since the Community of Six was established in 1957.

The political reality was that in June 1993, while at the same time negotiating the accession of Austria, Finland, Norway and Sweden to the EU, the European Council meeting in Copenhagen had 'agreed that the associated countries in Central and Eastern Europe that so desire shall become members of the European Union'.[7] In June 1995, it further agreed that the accession negotiations with Malta and Cyprus would start six months after the end of the Amsterdam Intergovernmental Conference (IGC) of 1996.[8] In December 1997, it decided to start accession negotiations in the spring of 1998 with six countries, i.e. Cyprus, Hungary, Poland, Estonia, the Czech Republic and Slovenia.[9] In December 1999, meeting in Helsinki, the European Council decided to start accession negotiations in February 2000 with six other countries, i.e. Romania, Slovakia, Latvia, Lithuania, Bulgaria and Malta; at the same meeting, the European Council decided to grant Turkey the status of 'candidate destined to join the Union'.[10] It is worth noting that this

responsibility of the Council Secretariat in OJ No. C340, 10 November 1997; see also J.-P. Jacqué, 'La simplification et la consolidation des traités' (1997) 33(4) in *Le traité d'Amsterdam*, (1998 no. 4–1997) *Revue trimestrielle de droit européen* 195–205.

The internet sites of the 1996 Intergovernmental Conference which led to the Amsterdam Treaty and of the 2000 Intergovernmental Conference which led to the Nice Treaty may be found on the internet site of the Council [http://ue.eu.int], under 'documents' and 'IGC'.

[7] See Presidency Conclusions, Copenhagen, 21 and 22 June 1993, page 13. These Conclusions set out the famous 'Copenhagen criteria' for the future enlargements of the EU. With regard to Norway, it is recalled that, following the negative referendum on accession to the EU in 1994, it did not become a member of the EU. A first accession attempt had already failed in 1972.

[8] See Presidency Conclusions, Cannes, 26 and 27 June 1995, second para. under II 'External Relations'.

[9] See Presidency Conclusions, Luxembourg, 12 and 13 December 1997, para. 27.

[10] See Presidency Conclusions, Helsinki, 10 and 11 December 1999, paras. 10 and 12.

massive enlargement of the EU membership, which would obviously completely transform its very nature, was not put to a popular referendum in any of the pre-existing Member States and has not been properly explained to the people of those States.

However, in spite of this pressure from the enlargement calendar, the Amsterdam IGC, which took place from March 1996 to June 1997, did not solve the most contentious institutional issues. At the end of the IGC, a number of Member States felt that the level of ambition for reform had been far too low.[11] The IGC therefore registered its disagreement in a Protocol, which would become known as the 'Amsterdam leftovers', and agreed that before the next enlargement, another IGC would be convened to address the unresolved institutional issues (see box 2.1).

Box 2.1 Protocol on the institutions with the prospect of enlargement of the European Union (1997)

'Article 1

At the date of entry into force of the first enlargement of the Union . . . the Commission shall comprise one national of each of the Member States, provided that, by that date, the weighting of the votes in the Council has been modified, whether by reweighting of the votes or by dual majority, in a manner acceptable to all Member States, taking into account all relevant elements, notably compensating those Member States which give up the possibility of nominating a second member of the Commission.

Article 2

At least one year before the membership of the European Union exceeds twenty, [an IGC] shall be convened in order to carry out a comprehensive review of the provisions of the Treaties on the composition and functioning of the institutions.'

Moreover, two Declarations were made on this Protocol. The first one, adopted by the IGC, said that, by the date of the first enlargement, 'a solution for the special case of Spain will be found'. The second one was

---

[11] For a good account of the Amsterdam IGC, see B. McDonagh, *Original Sin in a Brave New World, An Account of the Negotiation of the Treaty of Amsterdam* (Dublin, Institute of European Affairs, 1998).

made by Belgium, France[12] and Italy, in which they considered 'that a significant extension of recourse to qualified majority voting forms part of the relevant factors which should be taken into account'.

The main reason for this disagreement in Amsterdam, which was to be also one of the most difficult issues in the two following IGCs (the one which approved the Treaty of Nice and the one which approved the Constitution) was the composition of the Commission, and how to 'compensate' the large Member States, through an increase in their respective weighted votes in the Council, for both the planned loss of 'their' second Commissioner and for the erosion of their voting power in the Council at each successive enlargement.

Since 1957, the large Member States (i.e. at the time of the Amsterdam IGC: France, Germany, Italy, Spain and the UK) had two Commissioners each and the other Member States had one. In the hypothesis of an EU of 28 which would have included seven large Member States (with Poland and Turkey added to the then five large States), the Commission would have numbered 35 members, which was felt, at least by some, to be unmanageable, hence the whole debate about reducing the number of Commissioners and the related issue of 'compensation' for the large Member States.

On the basis of the 'Amsterdam leftovers' Protocol, it was decided to convene the IGC which was to approve the Treaty of Nice. The five topics to be discussed in the Nice IGC were the size of the Commission, the weighting of votes in the Council, the possible extension of qualified majority voting in the Council, the Court of Justice and enhanced cooperation.[13]

The Nice IGC did its best to give at least minimal answers to these issues. However, the horse-trading way in which it finished its work, after

---

[12] In the law authorising the ratification of the Amsterdam Treaty, the French Parliament inserted a provision whereby the French Republic expressed its determination to see, beyond Amsterdam, substantial progress being made in institutional reform in order to make the Union function more efficiently and more democratically, before the conclusion of the first enlargement negotiations (see Law no. 99–229 of 23 March 1999, French Republic OJ of 25 March 1999, p. 4463).

[13] For an assessment of the Treaty of Nice, see the article I wrote: 'The Treaty of Nice: an Imperfect Treaty but a Decisive Step Towards Enlargement' (2000) 3 *The Cambridge Yearbook of European Legal Studies* 15–36, based on a lecture I gave on 8 March 2001 in the Mackenzie-Stuart Lecture in the Centre for European Legal Studies, Faculty of Law, University of Cambridge. See also D. Galloway, *The Treaty of Nice and Beyond, Realities and Illusions of Power in the EU* (Sheffield Academic Press, 2000).

several days and nights of tough bargaining, did not leave a good atmosphere.

Moreover, again, some Member States were quite unhappy about what they considered to be the unsatisfactory results of the negotiations. Therefore, they convinced the IGC to adopt, in December 2000, a 'Declaration on the Future of the Union' (no. 23), known as the 'Nice Declaration' (hereafter '2000 Nice Declaration'), in which the IGC called 'for a deeper and wider debate about the future of the European Union' which should address, *inter alia*, four questions (see box 2.2).

Box 2.2   The four questions put by the 2000 Nice Declaration on the Future of the Union

(1) How to establish and monitor a more precise delimitation of competences between the European Union and its Member States, reflecting the principle of subsidiarity;
(2) the status to be given to the Charter of Fundamental Rights of the Union;
(3) a simplification of the Treaties with a view to making them clearer and better understood without changing their meaning;
(4) the role of national Parliaments in the European architecture.

During the second semester of 2001, the then Belgian Presidency decided to work intensively in order to materialise these four questions and to establish a formal procedure which would be innovative enough to find bold solutions to these questions. It is the Belgian authorities, and in the first place the Prime Minister Guy Verhofstadt, who decided to push in favour of a 'Convention on the Future of Europe' and to give it a very vague but ambitious task consisting in inventing a new basic Treaty for the European Union.

One year after the 2000 Nice Declaration, in December 2001, the European Council adopted the 'Laeken Declaration'[14] (hereafter '2001 Laeken Declaration', named after the castle of the King of the Belgians where the European Council held its meeting). This Declaration was

---

[14] See Annex 1 to Presidency Conclusions of the European Council, Laeken, 14 and 15 December 2001, doc. SN 300/1/01 REV 1 (reproduced below as Annex 1).

adopted against the background of a decreasing interest of public opinion in the Member States for European integration. It contained a
number of statements such as 'The Union needs to become more
democratic, more transparent and more efficient' and that it should
resolve 'three basic challenges' which are 'how to bring citizens . . . closer
to the European design', 'how to organise . . . the European political area
in an enlarged Union and how to develop the Union into a stabilising
factor and a model in the new, multipolar world'.

The Declaration went on to list several questions such as 'how to
clarify, simplify and adjust the division of competence between the
Union and the Member States', 'whether the Union's various instruments
should not be better defined and whether their number should not be
reduced', how to 'increase the democratic legitimacy and transparency of
the institutions', how to simplify and reorganise the existing Treaties
without changing their content and whether this 'might not lead in the
long run to the adoption of a constitutional text in the Union'.

Some of the elements of the 2001 Laeken Declaration reflected the
concerns that had been worrying political leaders and European institutions for several years already, which were that European integration
was being seen with less enthusiasm by European citizens. Over the years,
the turnout trends for the European Parliament elections[15] showed, and
still show, a worrying steady decline from 63% in 1979 for the first direct
elections to 45.7% in 2004,[16] with record lows in new Member States
such as 17% in Slovakia and 20.9% in Poland.[17] The 'No' votes of 1993
in Denmark to the Maastricht Treaty had been a wake-up call and was
still in everyone's memory. The 'No' vote of June 2001 in Ireland to the
Nice Treaty and, to a certain extent, the 'No' vote of September 2000 in
Denmark and of September 2003 in Sweden on joining the euro, were to
be stark reminders of this public disaffection.

In addition, the usual method of negotiating amendments to the
Treaties, in diplomatic conferences between representatives of the Governments of the Member States, was denounced in some quarters
(notably in the European Parliament) as being too secretive and elitist,
keeping the citizens away from the debate and not taking into account

---

[15] Source: internet site of the European Parliament on [http://elections2004.eu.int]. See also
Chapter I above.
[16] About 42% turnout in 2004 if one discounts the four Member States where voting is
obligatory.
[17] About 31% turnout on average in the eight new Central and Eastern Member States.

their needs and their wishes. However, the form of an Intergovernmental Conference (IGC) was unavoidable, as it is legally required by Article 48 of the EU Treaty.

Therefore, the European Council decided that the traditional IGC would be preceded and prepared for by a 'Convention', a new type of body that had already been successfully used in 1999–2000 for the drafting of the EU Charter of Fundamental Rights, a text which was agreed upon by the European Council in Nice in December 2000. A Convention would involve democratically elected representatives of all Member States which would work together. Moreover, they would debate in public, hopefully attracting the attention of the media in their debates, and that might help to reconnect with the people.

Section 3: The European Convention which proposed the draft Constitution

The European Council decided that the 'Convention on the Future of Europe'[18] would be composed of representatives from the Member States' Heads of State or Government, from national parliaments, from the European Parliament and from the Commission. It would be chaired by the former French President, Mr Valéry Giscard d'Estaing, and vice-chaired by former Heads of Italian and Belgian governments, respectively Mr Giuliano Amato and Mr Jean-Luc Dehaene.

The ten acceding States and the three candidate States were also represented and fully involved in the proceedings. All in all, including the alternates and the observers from different Committees and social partners, the Convention numbered 220 persons, out of which about two-thirds were elected parliamentarians (51% from national parliaments and

---

[18] The work of the Convention has been the subject of a large number of books and articles, and it will not be developed here. For an interesting analysis, see G. Milton and J. Keller-Noëllet, with A. Bartol-Saurel, *The European Constitution: its Origins, Negotiation and Meaning* (John Harper Publishing, 2005).

See also, among others: P. Magnette and K. Nicolaïdis, 'The European Convention: Bargaining in the Shadow of Rhetoric' (2004) vol. 27, no. 3 *West European Politics* 381–404; R. Smith, 'Constitutionalising the European Union' (Bristol, *Working Paper Series of the School for Policy Studies*, no. 6, 2003), http://www.bris.ac.uk/sps/downloads/working_papers/sps06_rs.pdf; J. Jarlebring, 'Taking Stock of the European Convention: What Added Value does the Convention bring to the Process of Treaty Revision?' (2003) 8 *German Law Journal*, European & International Law; P. Norman, *The Accidental Constitution: the Making of Europe's Constitutional Treaty* (Brussels, EuroComment, 2005); A. Lamassoure, *Histoire secrète de la Convention européenne* (Paris, Albin Michel éd., 2004).

14% from the European Parliament) and a quarter were appointed by governments (see box 2.3).

Box 2.3   Composition of the European Convention

The European Convention brought together 220 persons:

- 1 Chairman and 2 Vice-Chairmen;
- 15 representatives of the Heads of State or Government of the Member States[19] (one from each Member State), plus 15 alternates;
- 10 representatives of the Heads of State or Government of the Acceding States[20] (one from each Acceding State), plus 10 alternates;
- 3 representatives of the Heads of State or Government of the Candidate States[21] (one from each Candidate State), plus 3 alternates;
- 30 representatives of the national parliaments of the Member States (two from each Member State), plus 30 alternates;
- 20 representatives of the national parliaments of the Acceding States (two from each Acceding State), plus 20 alternates;
- 6 representatives of the national parliaments of the Candidate States (two from each Candidate State), plus 6 alternates;
- 16 representatives of the European Parliament, plus 16 alternates;
- 2 representatives of the Commission, plus 2 alternates;

  and, as observers:

- 3 representatives of the Economic and Social Committee
- 3 representatives of the European Social Partners;
- 6 representatives of the Committee of the Regions;
- the European Ombudsman.

---

[19] The 15 Member States at that time were: Austria, Belgium, Denmark, Finland, France, Germany, Greece, Ireland, Italy, Luxembourg, the Netherlands, Portugal, Spain, Sweden and the United Kingdom.

[20] The ten Acceding States at that time were: Cyprus, the Czech Republic, Estonia, Hungary, Latvia, Lithuania, Malta, Poland, Slovakia and Slovenia.

[21] The three Candidate States at that time were: Bulgaria, Romania and Turkey. Since June 2004, Croatia has also become a Candidate State (see Presidency Conclusions, European Council of 17 and 18 June 2004, para. 33).

The mandate of the Convention in the 2001 Laeken Declaration was rather vague. It was 'to consider the key issues arising for the Union's future development and try to identify the various possible responses' and to 'draw up a final document which may comprise either different options . . . or recommendations if consensus is achieved'. This final document was to 'provide a starting point for discussions in the Inter-governmental Conference, which [would] take the ultimate decisions'.

The Convention started in February 2002 and completed its work a year and a half later, in July 2003 with a 'draft Treaty establishing a Constitution for Europe'. It created 11 working groups and three 'discussion circles'.[22] Interestingly enough, no working group was established on institutional questions, thus stressing the will of the Praesidium or of its President to keep these delicate questions under their control. All the meetings of the Convention itself or of its bodies were public, as well as its documents.[23] The work was prepared by a steering board, called the Praesidium, which was composed of 12 members plus one 'invitee' from the acceding States.[24] This body had a crucial role in preparing the documents and draft legal texts that would be submitted to the plenary sessions of the Convention. Contrary to the Convention, the Praesidium did not work in public at all, attendance at

---

[22] The Working Groups held hearings with senior experts, in particular from universities and from the EU institutions. For instance, I was heard by Working Group I 'Subsidiarity' (see doc. WG I-WD 4 of 27 June 2002), Working Group II 'Incorporation of the Charter/Accession to the ECHR' (see doc. WG II-WD 13 of 5 September 2002), Working Group III 'Legal Personality' (see doc. WG III-WD 26 of 18 September 2002), Working Group V 'Complementary Competences' about the subject of the *acquis communautaire* (see summary of the meeting in doc. CONV 251/02 of 9 September 2002) and Working Group IX on 'Simplification' (see doc. WG IX-WD 06 of 6 November 2002). The General Secretariat of the Council also replied to questions from the President of Working Group IV 'Role of National Parliaments' about the implementation of the Protocol on national parliaments, COSAC and openness of the Council (see doc. WG IV-WD 33, of 8 October 2002). I had also contacts with Mr Vitorino, in his capacity as Chairman of the 'Discussion Circle on the Court of Justice'.

[23] The address of the internet site of the Convention is http://european-convention.eu.int.

[24] The Praesidium was composed of the Chairman and two Vice-Chairmen, three representatives from the rotating Council Presidency (Spanish, Danish and Greek presidencies), two representatives from national parliaments, two from the European Parliament and two from the Commission. In terms of nationalities, there were two French, two Spaniards, one Briton, one German, one Italian, one Belgian, one Portuguese, one Irish, one Danish, one Greek and one Slovenian (the invitee). This means that five nationalities out of the then 15 Member States were not present (the Netherlands, Austria, Sweden, Finland and Luxembourg). This created some bitterness on the part of these Member States.

its meetings was strictly restricted and only short procedural summaries of its proceedings were made public.

The Convention and its Praesidium was supported by a Secretariat of about 20 people, whose Secretary-General was Sir John Kerr (now Lord Kerr of Kinlochard), a former UK Permanent Representative to the EU.[25] There was however no Legal Adviser or Legal Service to assist in the drafting of texts and no drafting or legal committee had been established by the Convention or its Praesidium. Towards the end of the Convention's work only, a small group of six legal experts designated by the Legal Services of the European Parliament, the Council and the Commission, helped at the request of the Praesidium of the Convention, and with a very strict mandate, by quickly reviewing the adaptations made to the provisions of Part III on EU competences which had mostly been recopied from the existing provisions of the Treaty.[26]

Following an initial so-called 'listening' phase which lasted quite long (six to seven months), the Convention was presented by its President in October 2002 with a draft table of contents of what Mr Giscard d'Estaing was already proposing to call a 'Constitutional Treaty'. This Treaty would merge the EC and EU Treaties into a single text, resulting in a new 'European Union' with a single legal personality. The first set of draft provisions prepared by the Praesidium was presented in February 2003. From then on, the process greatly accelerated. Hundreds of amendments were tabled by Convention members, which were then discussed in the

---

[25] The other members of the Convention Secretariat were: Annalisa Giannella (Deputy Secretary-General), Marta Arpio Santacruz, Agnieszka Bartol, Hervé Bribosia, Nicole Buchet, Elisabeth Gateau, Clemens Ladenburger, María José Martínez Iglesias, Nikolaus Meyer-Landrut, Guy Milton, Ricardo Passos, Kristin de Peyron, Alain Pilette, Alan Piotrowski, Etienne de Poncins, Alessandra Schiavo, Walpurga Speckbacher, Maryem van den Heuvel and Anne Walter.

[26] The Praesidium on 29 January 2003 asked the Legal Services from the European Parliament, the Council and the Commission to designate two experts each who would help in the technical and legal adaptations to be made in the drafting of the future Part III (at the time it was called Part II) of the Constitution, i.e. the part on EU competences which mostly takes over existing Treaty provisions. The Group was not authorised to look at the rest of the draft text or at the institutional provisions. Most of the mandates and reports of this Group (composed of Christian Pennera and Kieran Bradley from the Legal Service of the European Parliament, Thérèse Blanchet and Emer Finnegan from the Legal Service of the Council and Alain van Solinge and Paolo Stancanelli from the Legal Service of the Commission) may be found in documents CONV 529/03, CONV 618/03 (+ ADD 1), CONV 682/03 and CONV 729/03 on the internet site of the Convention. Some of the work of this group of experts was not published in Convention documents by the secretariat of the Convention and is therefore not available on the site.

Praesidium and, accompanied by the Praesidium's suggestions, submitted to the next plenary session. Progressively, further sets of provisions were presented and amended, until a first 'complete' draft Treaty establishing a Constitution for Europe was submitted to the Convention at the end of May 2003 and then presented by the Convention's President to the Heads of State or Government on 20 June 2003 in Thessaloniki (Greece). The draft text was completed afterwards and was approved by an overwhelming majority (which its President determined to be 'a consensus') of the Convention at its last plenary session on 10 July 2003 and officially transmitted to the President of the European Council on 18 July 2003.[27]

This draft prepared by the Convention served as the basis for the work of the IGC which, pursuant to Article 48 of the EU Treaty, was convened by the Italian Presidency of the Council in a letter of 30 September 2003.

Section 4: The Intergovernmental Conference which approved the Constitution

The IGC held its first meeting on 4 October 2003 in Rome. It was composed of the representatives of the governments of the Member States and of the ten acceding States at the level of Foreign Minister. Two representatives from the Commission and two from the European Parliament also participated, as well as observers from the candidate countries Bulgaria, Romania and Turkey. As had been the case in previous IGCs, the Secretariat of the IGC was provided by a task force from the General Secretariat of the Council.[28] After a first unsuccessful attempt in December 2003, the IGC reached an agreement on the Constitution in June 2004.

At the outset, it was decided that the IGC would only meet at the level of Prime Ministers or Heads of State (who held five meetings), with preparation at the level of Ministers for Foreign Affairs (who held nine meetings). No meeting was scheduled at the level of civil servants, despite the wishes of some delegations, notably the Nordic ones. The

---

[27] See doc. CONV 850/03 of 18 July 2003, on the internet site of the Convention. A minority of the Convention ('Euro-sceptics') expressed its disagreement. The representatives of the Spanish and Polish Governments also expressed reservations, in particular on the QMV system.

[28] This task force was headed by Jean-Claude Piris. Jacques Keller-Noëllet, Giorgio Maganza, Marta Arpio, Martin Bauer, Agnieszka Bartol, Thérèse Blanchet, Emer Finnegan, Jan-Peter Hix and Guy Milton participated in its work.

German delegation insisted very much on the fact that the draft approved by the European Convention should be adopted as such, 'without any modifications'. It therefore stressed that it would not accept any meeting at the level of civil servants. In reality, two informal meetings of diplomats took place in Rome, during the Italian presidency, under the chairmanship of Rocco Cangelosi,[29] who had been directly involved in previous IGCs and later became the Italian Permanent Representative to the EU. One informal meeting took place in Dublin, during the Irish presidency, which was chaired by Bobby Mc Donagh, who had also been involved in previous IGCs and at the end of June 2005 has become the Irish Permanent Representative to the EU. These informal meetings were called 'Focal Points Meetings' and were supposed to be a forum for exchanging views and not for negotiations.

The IGC did not hold its meetings in public. However, all its documents, as well as the contributions by the Presidency, the delegations and the IGC Secretariat, were made public on its internet site.[30]

The text agreed upon by the IGC in June 2004 did not fundamentally modify the essential features of the draft proposed by the Convention. The IGC concentrated on those institutional issues which had not commanded a consensus in the Convention such as the definition of qualified majority voting (QMV) in the Council, the composition of the Commission and the new organisation of the Presidency of the Council. It also discussed the policy on defence, the scope of QMV in certain fields, notably justice and home affairs, it revised the budgetary procedure and introduced a simplified revision procedure for the Constitution.

Moreover, the IGC established a working group of legal experts to review the legal drafting of the text of the Constitution as proposed by the Convention and approved the legal or drafting improvements proposed by this group.

The Working Party of Legal Experts of the IGC

From a legal and drafting point of view, the text of the Constitution as drafted by the Convention was not very good: it contained inconsistent provisions, lacunae, incorrect legal drafting or ambiguities which had to

---

[29] See the article he wrote on the IGC: R. Cangelosi, 'Il progetto di Trattato Costituzionale, la Presidenza italiana e la Conferenza intergovernativa. Da Roma a Bruxelles: cronaca di un negoziato' (2003) 4 *La Comunità Internazionale* 533–560.

[30] The 2003–2004 IGC documents are accessible on the internet site of the Council, under 'documents' and 'IGC'.

be corrected for reasons of legal certainty. This was understandable, given the fact that the Convention only had a month and a half (end of May to 10 July 2003) to look at the entire draft text of 300 pages! Moreover, save for the small group of six legal experts referred to above, it had never been assisted by a Legal Service or by a drafting committee!

Member States quickly realised that a serious technical/legal review of the text was necessary. Therefore, in planning the conduct of the IGC, the Italian Presidency proposed to the IGC in September 2003[31] that a Working Party of Legal Experts should be officially established to carry out a 'legal verification' of the draft Treaty establishing a Constitution for Europe drawn up by the European Convention. This Working Party was to be the only group of civil servants officially set up by the IGC. In order to stress the purely legal/technical character of its mandate, the Working Party would not be chaired by the usual six-monthly rotating presidency, but by myself, Legal Counsel to the IGC (Director-General of the Council Legal Service) and in my absence by Mr Giorgio Maganza, Director in the Council Legal Service. This particular way of proceeding, which had never been used in previous IGCs, was also followed by the Irish Presidency in the first semester of 2004.

The Working Party was composed of representatives from the 25 Member States (including the ten which would join the European Union on 1 May 2004), from the three candidate States (Bulgaria, Romania and Turkey), from the Commission and from the European Parliament.[32]

The Group worked on the basis of documents drafted in French by members of the Council's Legal Service working for the IGC Secretariat[33] (with help from the Commission's Services as regards the existing Protocols and Acts of Accession). These documents[34] contained detailed

---

[31] Letter of 29 September 2003 from Mr Frattini, Italian Foreign Minister, to his colleagues and to the European Parliament and the Commission (see internet site of the Council, under 'documents', 'IGC' and 'preparatory documents'). The Working Party became known as 'the Piris Group'.

[32] The European Parliament was represented by its Legal Counsel, Gregorio Garzòn Clariana, and the Commission was represented by the Director-General of its Legal Service, Michel Petite.

[33] These were Marta Arpio, Martin Bauer, Thérèse Blanchet, Emer Finnegan and Jan-Peter Hix, of the Council's Legal Service. Alain van Solinge, Paolo Stancanelli and Hervé Bribosia, from the Commission Services, also played a major role in preparing drafts with regard to the 36 existing Protocols, of which 26 would be taken over in the Constitution, and the five Accession Acts.

[34] For the draft Constitution and its five Protocols, see doc. CIG 4/03 of 6 October 2003 and CIG 49/03 of 17 November 2003 (on the Euratom Protocol). For the Protocols,

drafting suggestions (with explanations for those suggestions) from a technical/legal perspective. All the drafting amendments suggested and agreed by the Group were clearly marked in bold and strike-out characters. In order to be retained, drafting suggestions had to be agreed by all participants.

The Group started its work during the week following the launch of the IGC on 4 October 2003 and held a total of 23 meetings until April 2004. The work took place in two phases. During a first phase, from October to December 2003, the Group concentrated on the text of the Constitution and its five Protocols, as well as on the necessary adaptations to be made to the existing 36 Protocols and Annexes I and II to the present Treaties, which had not been examined at all by the Convention.

During a second phase, from February to April 2004, the Group concentrated on the drafting of three new Protocols which were considered necessary to preserve certain other provisions of primary law, notably two protocols consolidating the provisions of the five Accession Treaties and Acts of Accession which were still in force. This was a particularly difficult task from a political point of view, given that the last Accession Treaty, which had been signed in Athens on 16 April 2003, was not yet in force; negotiating its repeal was not an easy task for the representatives of the ten new Member States!

During the first phase, the Group firstly agreed to suggest legal and drafting improvements to most articles of the Constitution as drawn up by the Convention. The aims were, in particular, to achieve legal and editorial consistency between the different parts of the draft Constitution through greater legal consistency in provisions, the rectification of some omissions, and the correction of legal inaccuracies. The Group also agreed to suggest the total recasting of most of the final provisions

---

see doc. CIG 8/03 of 13 October 2003 (which lists all the 36 Protocols to the existing Treaties and the 82 Protocols to the four Acts of Accession), CIG 41/03 of 3 November 2003 (on 34 existing Protocols, leaving aside the EIB Protocol and the Protocol on the position of Denmark which was dealt with by the IGC itself) and CIG 48/03 of 17 November 2003 (on the EIB Protocol). For the preserved and repealed primary law provisions and the Acts of Accession, see doc. CIG 68/04 of 18 February 2004 (on the repealing of certain primary law provisions and the adaptation of others), CIG 54/03 of 24 November 2003 (on the methodology for the adjustment of the Acts of Accession), CIG 66/04 of 4 February 2004 (on the first four Acts of Accession) and CIG 71/04 of 26 March 2004 (on the last Act of Accession). These documents, like all the 2003–2004 IGC documents, are accessible on the internet site of the Council, under 'documents' and 'IGC'.

contained in Part IV, more specifically the provisions entailed by the repeal of the existing Treaties. It accordingly suggested the addition, in the preamble, of a reference to succession between Treaties and to legal continuity of the 'acquis communautaire', as well as the combining, in a single Protocol, of the various transitional provisions which had been scattered throughout the draft Constitution, and the addition of transitional provisions which had not been drawn up by the Convention. Some of these required major legal redrafting of texts, in particular the one on transitional provisions relating to the institutions. For instance, if the text as drafted by the Convention had been kept unchanged, the Commission would have legally 'disappeared' upon entry into force of the Constitution, due to the absence of proper transitional provisions.

The Group also agreed improvements to the other Protocols which had been drafted by the Convention. This was notably the case for the Protocol amending the Euratom Treaty (which would remain in force as a separate Treaty). The purpose of this work was to adapt that Treaty to the new rules laid down by the draft Constitution, in particular in the institutional and financial fields; it was one of the most delicate tasks of the Group. Finally, the Group agreed drafting adaptations to the 36 Protocols and Annexes I and II to the Treaties; these texts had not been examined by the Convention. The Group agreed to repeal nine of these Protocols, either because these Protocols were replaced by new ones or because there was agreement in the Group that they were obsolete.

The first report of 25 November 2003 from the Chairman of the Group also drew the Conference's attention to four areas where amendments to the text had not been possible to agree in the Group, but which were considered necessary by the Chairman if the text was not to remain legally incorrect.[35] Solutions were subsequently agreed in these four areas in the context of the overall agreement; these solutions closely corresponded to the suggestions originally made to the Group.[36]

---

[35] See doc. CIG 51/03 of 25 November 2003. These four areas concerned the last recital of the preamble to the Charter of Fundamental Rights; the legal basis allowing the adoption of specific measures for the euro area; the rule on non-interference between CFSP procedures and procedures for other policies, and the rules on access to documents of the European Investment Bank.

[36] See the final text of the last recital to the Charter's preamble, of Art. III-194 on the euro area, of Art. III-308 on CFSP and other procedures, and Art. III-399 on access to EIB documents.

During the second phase, in the early part of 2004, the Group approved the text of three new Protocols: the Protocol on the acts and treaties which have supplemented or amended the EC and EU Treaties, and two Protocols taking over the substantive contents still in force of the previous four Accession Treaties (1972, 1979, 1985 and 1994)[37] and the latest Accession Treaty (2003) respectively. It was necessary to preserve explicitly those elements of these acts and treaties which had to remain in force, because the acts and treaties themselves are otherwise repealed pursuant to Part IV of the draft Constitution. The task was less difficult in relation to the four older Accession Treaties, as many of their provisions were already out of date. However, the 2003 Accession Treaty, which was not even in force when the work began, contained many more provisions whose effects had to be preserved; but the aim was of course to shorten as much as possible the length of the Protocol which consolidated those provisions.

It was also important to make the necessary technical adjustments to all the provisions of these Treaties and Acts of Accession remaining in force, in order to bring them into line with the draft Constitution, without altering their legal effect. The Protocols to the Accession Treaties and Acts which were still in force were transformed into articles of the two Protocols (nos. 8 and 9) on the Acts of Accession. The preambles to these Protocols to the Accession Treaties and Acts which were considered politically important by delegations were transformed into Declarations in the Final Act of the IGC which adopted the Constitution.[38]

As regards the numbering of the Articles of the draft Constitution, the Group considered that it would be preferable, both for legal certainty and for transparency, as well as simplicity and ease of use, to use continuous Arabic numbering for the entire text of the Constitution. For political reasons, some delegations asked that the Arabic numeral be accompanied by the Roman numeral indicating the relevant Part (I, II, III and IV), in order to preserve a distinction between the four Parts of the Constitution. This suggestion, like all others, was unanimously approved by the IGC, and the renumbering was carried out during the

---

[37] In approving that Protocol, the Working Party agreed that it was advisable to retain certain provisions as historical references, although its Chairman noted that, since the expiry of the deadlines specified therein, those provisions no longer had legal effect.

[38] See Declarations nos. 31 to 41 to the Final Act of the Conference.

revision of the text by the Council's legal/linguistic experts before signature of the Constitution.

The outcome of the proceedings of the Group as a whole[39] was set out in document CIG 50/03, which was adopted by the IGC as its sole basic working document. All the amendments subsequently agreed by the IGC were to be incorporated into this basic document.[40]

The Constitution restructures and simplifies the existing Treaties, streamlines their structure and procedures, and enhances the powers of the EU institutions. With the exception of the chapters on the Common Foreign and Security Policy (CFSP) and Justice and Home Affairs (JHA), i.e. the present second and third 'pillars', no fundamental changes are made to the substantive content of the present text of the Treaties. In order to examine in a systematic way the changes made by the Constitution, they may be classified into three broad categories:

1. Structures and procedures: many simplifications (see Chapter III);
2. Institutions: some important reforms (see Chapter IV);
3. Substance: not many changes, except in the fields of CFSP and JHA (see Chapter V).

---

[39] The three reports from the Chairman of the Group to the IGC may be found in doc. CIG 51/03, CIG 63/03 and CIG 74/04.

[40] CIG 50/03 (+ COR 1 to 5) contained the draft Treaty establishing a Constitution for Europe. Its Addendum 1 (+ COR 1 to 3) contained the Protocols agreed on during 2003, Addendum 2 contained the three new Protocols on which agreement was reached in April 2004, and Addendum 3 contained the new Declarations relating to the two Protocols on the Accession Treaties which were to be annexed to the Final Act of the IGC. The text of several other new declarations (three of which had been initially proposed by the Convention) was agreed later at political level.

III

Changes in structures and procedures

The Constitution will restructure the existing texts of the Treaties, streamline legal instruments and procedures and codify long-standing principles and rules, so as to try and make these texts more consistent and easier to read for the users.

Up to the Constitution, the original Treaties from 1957 had been amended 15 times. As a result, there are at present about 2800 pages of primary law contained in 17 Treaties or Acts, three legal personalities,[1] three so-called 'pillars', 15 types of different legal instruments and several types of decision-making procedures. Restructuring all this and trying to make it more readable was long-needed.[2]

---

[1] Without taking into account the EC or the EU Agencies, which are often given separate legal personalities for the purpose of their functioning.

[2] See the article I wrote in 1995, before the Amsterdam IGC, under the pseudonym 'Justus Lipsius': 'The 1996 Intergovernmental Conference' (1995) 20 *European Law Review* 235–267: 'The ideal would be to replace the present Treaties (EU, EC, ECSC, EAEC, Merger Treaty, Single European Act, plus the Treaties amending budgetary and financial provisions) by a single Treaty Charter. This is technically feasible but entails political choices which will sometimes be difficult . . . It is legally and politically feasible for the 1996 IGC to agree on the merger into one entity of the three existing Communities and of the Union, the new entity being a European Union which should be given legal personality and treaty-making power. This will in no way prevent the IGC from deciding that the decision-making process will be completely different in one or other of the areas pertaining to Union competence, in, for instance, CFSP or co-operation in justice and home affairs, and that the Court of Justice will have a different role or no role at all regarding these last areas, etc. These are separate questions, which can be solved technically while avoiding a legal architecture which is of such complexity that nobody can understand. That being said . . . the single Treaty would still remain too long and too complex if the exercise was limited to merging all the provisions of the present Treaties into a single consolidated text. Therefore, the best solution would be to draft, on the one hand, a "Treaty-Charter", as short and readable as possible, dealing with principles, competence and institutional matters, and, on the other hand, a number of protocols annexed to it, dealing in detail with specific matters, such as the Internal Market . . . Of course, particular attention should be given to the brevity and quality of drafting of these protocols' (pp. 265–266).

This restructuring is the most visible and, in a way, the most revolutionary work achieved by the Convention and the IGC. The choice was made to repeal all existing Treaties[3] and to replace them by the single, restructured, text of the Constitution. This choice entails the re-ratification by Member States of all those existing, and often old, provisions which have been recopied without any substantial changes for the Rome Treaty into the Constitution. This re-ratification opens the political opportunity for Euro-sceptics of all kinds to criticise one or other provision of the present Treaties, claiming that it confers a new competence on the Union, whereas in reality it has been existing for a long time and has been already ratified in the past.

Section 1: Simplifying the structures of the Union

What the Constitution will do in terms of structure could be summarised as: One Treaty, One Legal Personality, One Pillar. Indeed, one of the greatest advantages of the Constitution as compared with the present situation is the merging of most primary law, now spread over 17 Treaties and Acts, into one single document, the merging of the two legal personalities of the EC and the EU into one and, subject to some specificities as explained below, the removal of the pillar structure.

One Treaty

There are at present three basic treaties, the Treaty establishing the European Community (EC), the Treaty on European Union (EU) and the Treaty establishing the European Atomic Energy Community (Euratom), with in all 36 Protocols annexed to them. There are in addition nine amending or supplementing Treaties and five Accession Treaties, all of these containing provisions still in force. All of these represent about 2800 pages of primary law.

The Constitution merges the two main Treaties, i.e. the EC and EU Treaties, into one single document. It repeals all the previous Treaties and protocols,[4] save for the Euratom Treaty which remains

---

[3] Apart from the Euratom Treaty (see below under 'One Treaty').

[4] See Art. IV-437 and the Protocol on the Acts and Treaties which supplemented or amended the Treaty establishing the European Community and the Treaty on European Union. Ten existing protocols were repealed by the IGC (i.e. Protocols nos. 9, 10, 12, 13, 19, 23, 24, 30, 33 and 35 from the list of Protocols in the consolidated version of the

separate.[5] 36 Protocols and two Annexes are annexed to the Constitution. The number of pages of primary law diminishes considerably from 2800 pages to 560 pages (including the Euratom Treaty), the Constitution as such being only 200 pages (400 pages with its 36 protocols).

The Constitution is structured in four parts:[6]

- Part I lays down, in about 30 pages (60 Articles), the main elements of the EU: its values and objectives, the citizens' rights, the Union's competences, its institutions, its legal instruments, its finances and its membership. This Part is meant to be the most 'user friendly' part, a sort of 'reader's digest' of what the Union is, what it does and how. This is the part on which the Convention spent most of its time between February and May 2003. If one adds to it the six pages of Part IV, it is in these 36 pages where most of the totally new provisions of the Constitution may be found (about 20), as compared with the existing Treaties.[7]
- Part II, with 54 Articles, in about ten pages, reproduces almost exactly the EU Charter of Fundamental Rights adopted in Nice in December 2000.
- Part III, with 322 Articles, in about 130 pages, contains the details of internal and external 'policies', or rather of the competences conferred on the Union. It contains all the enabling clauses, or 'legal bases'. These provisions set out exactly what, and how much, competence is conferred on the Union by the Member States and what powers the institutions have to exercise these competences, as well as the details of institutional and financial provisions. This part is largely a copy of the present provisions of the EC and EU Treaties, albeit reorganised

Treaties in OJ No. C325, 24 December 2002, pp. 37–38) but ten new protocols were added by the IGC (i.e. Protocols nos. 1, 2, 8, 9, 12, 23, 32, 33, 34 and 36 from the list of Protocols in the Constitution, OJ No. C310, 16 December 2004).

[5] See the Protocol (no. 36) amending the Treaty establishing the European Atomic Energy Community. As regards the two protocols annexed to the Euratom Treaty, one had already been repealed by the Treaty of Amsterdam (see Art. 8, point III(2) of that Treaty) and the other one, on the Statute of the Court of Justice, had been repealed and replaced by the new Statute contained in the Treaty of Nice (see Art. 7 of that Treaty).

[6] For a table of equivalence between the provisions of the Constitution and the provisions of the existing EU and EC Treaties, see Annex 6.

[7] Part I of the Constitution together with Part IV could have been the short 'Treaty-Charter' which I was contemplating in 1995, Part III being put in a Protocol (see footnote 2 above).

and amended to fit the new context. It also contains certain new provisions in some existing domains such as Justice and Home Affairs, the euro zone, the Common Foreign and Security Policy and defence. It contains as well some new legal bases in matters such as space policy, energy policy, tourism, sport or civil protection, which mostly make explicit and codify the existing powers to act which the EU institutions already have.

- Part IV, with 12 Articles, in six pages, contains the general and final provisions, including new provisions on the repeal of the present Treaties, succession and legal continuity, as well as transitional provisions relating to the institutions and revision procedures. This part was almost entirely drafted by the Group of Legal Experts of the IGC.

With 448 Articles and 36 protocols, the Constitution runs to 400 pages, thus rather far from the pocket-sized Constitution that some had expected. However, given the specificity and the inherent complexity of the multi-layered EU construction, a founding Treaty the size of the US Constitution (34 Articles, divided into sometimes long sections) or of the constitution of other federal States (e.g. the German Constitution with about 150 Articles or the Belgian Constitution with about 200 Articles) will certainly never be possible for the Union. The Union is a very peculiar and unique legal construction which, although it is not a State, uses certain federal tools. Therefore, its founding Treaty needs to define precisely, for each area of action, what the EU's competences are in order not to encroach unduly on national competences.[8] The Member States, authors of the Treaty, want it detailed, because they want to control exactly how much competence they give to the EU and how much power they give to its institutions to exercise these competences.

---

[8] See my article 'The European Union: Towards A New Form of Federalism?' (2003) in Basil Markesinis and Jörg Fedtke (eds.), *Patterns of Regionalism and Federalism: Lessons for the UK* (Oxford, Hart Publishing, forthcoming), which is based on a lecture I gave in London on 7 November 2003 in a Conference on 'Patterns of Federalism and Regionalism: Lessons for the UK' organised by the Institute of Transnational Law of the University of Texas (Austin) and the Institute of Global Law of University College London. See also J. Straw, UK's Foreign Secretary: 'Were it a superstate, writing its constitution would be easy, and the result short. You would declare that power resided in its parliament, government and supreme court, and leave those institutions to make and enforce the law. It is precisely because the EU is not a superstate that it needs a more complicated rule-book spelling out, policy by policy, the areas of its competence. This is what gives the document its length . . .', *The Economist*, 10 July 2004, p. 30.

The drafting of these elaborate provisions is the result of long negotiations in the successive IGCs.

This explains why Part III of the Constitution, which describes in detail all the competences conferred on the Union and the limits of these competences, is the longest of the four Parts of the Constitution (more than 70% of the total number of Articles). In Part III, about 215 Articles concern internal and external competences, together with the procedures for exercising them, the other 100 Articles being institutional and financial provisions. This proportion, with about half of the Articles concerning competences, is the same as in the Swiss Constitution (83 Articles on competences out of a total of 197).

The experience of the debate which preceded the referendum in France shows that the particular nature of Part III, the fact that this Part does not actually describe 'policies', as was often claimed due to its misleading title, but rather the detailed list of competences which the Member States have decided to confer on the Union, was particularly difficult to explain. People used to living in a unitary State like France, where State authorities are omni-competent and where, therefore, the national Constitution is normally quite short and lean, limiting itself to setting up the State authorities without entering into the details of different policy areas, have difficulties in understanding why a federal-like legal system which creates a multi-layered legal order needs to describe in its Constitution, for it to be able to function, the competences which are conferred on the different layers.

In view of this inherent complexity, Part I, with its user-friendly character, brings real added value in terms of readability, although it duplicates some of the Articles from other Parts of the Constitution. There is however no hierarchy between the four Parts of the Constitution. Part I in particular needs to be read in the light of the detailed competences and powers set out in Part III.

One legal personality

There are at present two separate legal personalities: the European Community (Article 281 EC Treaty) and the European Union (through its treaty-making power under Article 24 EU Treaty).[9] Euratom also has

---

[9] The existence of an EU legal personality has been denied by some authors, as there is no provision in the EU Treaty expressly conferring such personality on it. However, practice has shown that the Council has repeatedly used Art. 24 EU Treaty, which gives it a treaty-making power, and that third countries have agreed to consider the EU as an active

a separate legal personality (Article 184 Euratom Treaty), but it is only a sectoral Treaty. The Constitution merges the two legal personalities of the EC and of the EU into one single new EU legal personality. The Euratom legal personality remains separate.

Article I-7 of the Constitution (hereafter abbreviated 'Cst') states that 'The Union shall have legal personality' and Article III-426 Cst states that 'In each of the Member States, the Union shall enjoy the most extensive legal capacity accorded to legal persons under their laws; it may, in particular, acquire or dispose of movable and immovable property and may be a party to legal proceedings'.[10]

The creation of one single legal personality enabled the drafters of the Constitution to provide for one single procedure to negotiate and conclude international agreements. This procedure is contained in Article III-325 Cst. It replaces the two procedures under the EC and EU Treaties (Article 300 EC Treaty and Article 24 EU Treaty). However, some variations will apply in this procedure, depending on the subject-matter of the agreement:

- Article III-325(3) Cst will give the Council the choice of the negotiator, either the Commission or the EU Minister for Foreign Affairs, depending on the subject-matter of the agreement envisaged;
- Article III-325(6) Cst will increase the powers of the European Parliament as compared with Article 300(3) of the EC Treaty, in that it provides for the consent of the European Parliament with regard to all agreements covering fields where codecision applies internally;
- agreements will be concluded by the Council using qualified majority voting (QMV), save for cases where the agreement covers a field for which unanimity is required for the adoption of an EU act (Article III-325(8) Cst);

subject of international law. The Union fulfils all the criteria set out by the International Court of Justice in the Hague, in its Advisory Opinion of 11 April 1949 on the international personality of the United Nations (see Case *Reparation for injuries suffered in the service of the United Nations* [http://www.icj-cij.org)...]. On the issue of the legal personality of the Union, see S. Marquardt, 'The Conclusion of International Agreements under Article 24 of the Treaty on European Union', Chapter 16 in *The European Union and the International Legal Order: Discord or Harmony?* (The Hague, ed. Vincent Kronenberger, T. M. C. Asser Instituut, 2001) 333–349; updated after the Nice Treaty in 'La capacité de l'Union européenne de conclure des accords internationaux dans le domaine de la coopération policière et judiciaire en matière pénale, in G. de Kerchove and A. Weyembergh (eds), *Sécurité et justice: enjeu de la politique extérieure de l'Union européenne* (Institut d'Etudes Européennes, Université de Bruxelles, 2003) 179–194.

[10] Art. III-426 Cst corresponds to Art. 282 EC Treaty.

- agreements concluded under the Constitution will be 'binding on the institutions of the Union and on its Member States' (Article III-323(2) Cst), as is the case with those presently concluded on the basis of the EC Treaty. The Constitution will thus remove the existing particularity in CFSP where, pursuant to Article 24(5) of the EU Treaty, 'no agreement shall be binding on a Member State whose representative in the Council states that it has to comply with the requirements of its own constitutional procedure'. However, all the CFSP decisions to be taken by the Council in such a process (from the authorisation to open negotiations to the decision to conclude agreements) will be taken by unanimity (Articles III-325(8), 2nd subparagraph and III-300(1) Cst). This includes the system of 'constructive abstention' under which 'when abstaining in a vote, any member of the Council may qualify its abstention' in which case 'it shall not be obliged to apply the European decision, but shall accept that the latter commits the Union'. Up to now, this mechanism has never been applied.[11]
- Article III-315 Cst, which takes over Article 133 of the EC Treaty, contains specific provisions concerning the common commercial policy (Commission as sole negotiator and QMV as a general rule save for certain matters where unanimity will still be required[12]).

One pillar

The Constitution removes the pillar structure, although it keeps specific procedures, notably for CFSP.

---

[11] For an analysis and suggestions made at the time of the Convention, see my contribution of 18 September 2002 to Mr Amato, President of Working Group III 'Legal Personality' set up by the Convention, in Working Document 26 (WG III-WD 26), page 6, of 18 September 2002 (available on the internet site of the Convention).

[12] Unanimity will still be required for the following agreements:

- trade in services, commercial aspects of intellectual property and foreign direct investments if unanimity is required for the adoption of internal rules;
- trade in cultural and audiovisual services, where they risk prejudicing the EU's cultural and linguistic diversity (unanimity in these fields was especially requested by France);
- trade in social, education and health services if they risk seriously disturbing the national organisation of such services and prejudicing the responsibility of Member States to deliver them (unanimity in these fields was especially requested by Finland and Sweden).

The existing 'pillar structure' of the Treaties

Following the Maastricht Treaty's entry into force, the existing Treaties establish a so-called 'three pillars' structure. Each of these 'pillars' has its own specific procedures, legal instruments and scope of jurisdiction of the Court of Justice. This structure is placed under the common umbrella of the Union as stated in Article 1 of the EU Treaty, according to which 'The Union shall be founded on the European Communities, supplemented by the policies and forms of cooperation established by this Treaty' and 'be served by a single institutional framework' (Article 3 EU Treaty).

The so-called 'first pillar' is the European Community (EC) as established by the 1957 Rome Treaty and modified by successive amending Treaties, notably the Single European Act in 1986. It is the most integrated pillar, where all the institutions play their full role. The Commission has an almost exclusive right of initiative.[13] The European Parliament is generally associated with the adoption of legislative acts by the Council, either through mandatory consultation or through codecision together with the Council. The EC institutions may adopt regulations, directives and decisions. The Treaty defines three types of voting rule for the Council: unanimity (with the possibility of abstaining, which does not prevent the adoption of a decision), qualified majority (whereby each Council member has a vote carrying a different weight depending on the Member State which it represents) or simple majority (one vote per Council member). Each legal basis specifies the voting rule to be used in the Council.

The European Court of Justice has full jurisdiction to interpret and review the legality of EC acts.[14] This 'complete system of legal remedies and procedures designed to permit the Court of Justice to review the legality of measures adopted by the institutions', including for the benefit of individuals, makes the EC a 'Community based on the rule of law' or, in French, 'Communauté de droit', by reference to the expression *Etat*

---

[13] Apart from some specific cases where procedural or institutional decisions are taken by an institution without a proposal from the Commission.

[14] See in the EC Treaty: Arts. 226 and 227 (infringement procedures), 228 (penalties), 230 (annulment), 232 (failure to act), 234 (preliminary rulings), 235 (damages) and 241 (plea of illegality). However, the jurisdiction of the Court is subject to a number of limitations in Title IV, Part three, of the EC Treaty concerning visas, asylum, immigration and other policies (see Art. 68 EC Treaty).

de droit.[15] The Court has developed an extensive case-law stating that the EC must respect fundamental rights[16] and laying down such founding principles as the primacy[17] and the direct effect of EC law.[18]

The so-called 'second pillar' is the Common Foreign and Security Policy (CFSP), which includes the European Security and Defence Policy (ESDP). It is based on Title V of the EU Treaty (adopted in 1992 in Maastricht). Although, thanks to the 'single institutional framework' of the EU (Article 3 EU Treaty), the CFSP is served by the same institutions, their respective powers are not the same as in the EC. The Council exercises its powers through the adoption, generally by unanimity, of joint actions, common positions and decisions. It is assisted in this task by a High Representative for the CFSP, at present Mr Javier Solana, whose office was introduced by the Amsterdam Treaty in 1997 (Articles 18 and 26 EU Treaty). The policy is implemented by the Council's six-monthly rotating Presidency, which also represents the EU externally (Article 18 EU Treaty). The Commission is 'fully associated' with the work carried out in the CFSP field (Article 27 EU Treaty). It also has a

---

[15] Judgment of 23 April 1986, Case 294/83, *Les Verts v. Parliament*, [1986] ECR p. 1365, para. 23: 'the Community is a Community based on the rule of law, inasmuch as neither its Member States nor its institutions can avoid a review of the question whether the measures adopted by them are in conformity with the basic constitutional charter, the Treaty'.

[16] Judgment of 12 November 1969, Case 29/69, *Stauder*, [1969] ECR p. 425, para. 7. See also Opinion 2/94 of 28 March 1996, *Accession of the EC to the European Convention on Human Rights*, [1996] ECR, p. I-1759, paras. 33 and 34: 'Respect for human rights is . . . a condition of the lawfulness of Community acts'.

[17] The leading case-law is the judgment of 15 July 1964, Case 6/64 *Costa v. ENEL* [1964] ECR, para. on pp. 593 and 594, in which the Court derives from the specificities of the EC which it lists that it is 'impossible for the States, as a corollary, to accord precedence to a unilateral and subsequent measure over a legal system accepted by them on a basis of reciprocity . . . The executive force of Community law cannot vary from one State to another in deference to subsequent domestic laws, without jeopardizing the attainment of the objectives of the Treaty set out in Article 5(2) and giving rise to the discrimination prohibited by Article 7.' See also the judgment of 9 March 1978, Case 106/77, *Simmenthal*, [1978] ECR p. 629, paras. 17 and 21.

[18] The leading case-law is the judgment of 5 February 1963, Case 26/62, *van Gend & Loos*, ECR [1963] pp. 23–25: 'The Community constitutes a new legal order . . . the subjects of which comprise not only Member States but also their nationals. . . . Community law therefore not only imposes obligations on individuals but is also intended to confer upon them rights which become part of their legal heritage.' See also the judgment of 4 December 1974, Case 41/74, *van Duyn*, [1974] ECR p. 1337, para. 12. Under this case-law, a provision of the Treaty or of an act adopted on the basis thereof may have a direct effect, i.e. may be invoked by an individual, if this provision is sufficiently clear and unconditional. On the EC legal order, see J.-V. Louis and T. Ronse, *L'ordre juridique de l'Union européenne* (Brussels, Bruylantéd, 2005).

right of initiative, parallel to the right of initiative of the Member States (Article 22 EU Treaty). The European Parliament is consulted only 'on the main aspects and the basic choices' of the CFSP and is 'kept regularly informed' of the development of the policy (Article 21 EU Treaty).

The Court of Justice, according to Article 46(d) of the EU Treaty, has no jurisdiction over CFSP. However, it ensures that the institutions respect the 'non-affectation' rule set out in Article 47 of the EU Treaty, according to which CFSP acts must not, in the words of the case-law, 'encroach upon the powers conferred by the EC Treaty on the Community'.[19]

The so-called 'third pillar' covers Police and Judicial Cooperation in criminal matters (commonly known as 'Justice and Home Affairs' (JHA)) and is provided for by Title VI of the EU Treaty. Here again, the respective functions of the institutions are not the same as in the EC, although the Amsterdam Treaty gave the Commission and the European Parliament a more Community-like role. The Commission has a right of initiative, but not an exclusive one, as the Member States also have a right of initiative (Article 34(2) EU Treaty). The consultation of the European Parliament on legal acts is mandatory (decisions, framework decisions and conventions and their implementing measures) before the Council adopts them (Article 39(1) EU Treaty), but its power remains advisory.

The Amsterdam Treaty enlarged the scope of judicial review by the Court, although this scope remains more limited than in the EC. Under Article 35 of the EU Treaty, the Court may review the legality of JHA acts at the request of a Member State or the Commission. It may also rule on disputes between Member States regarding the interpretation or the application of JHA acts or on any dispute between Member States and the Commission regarding the interpretation or the application of JHA conventions. However, contrary to the situation in the EC, the Court's power to give preliminary rulings on the validity and interpretation of JHA legislative acts and on the interpretation of JHA conventions is limited. It exists only if the Member State concerned has accepted such jurisdiction by making a declaration to that effect.[20] Furthermore, the

---

[19] See the judgment of 12 May 1998, Case C-170/96, *Commission v. Council* (on airport transit visas) [1998] ECR p. I-2763, para. 16.

[20] By September 2005, 14 Member States out of 25 had accepted the jurisdiction of the Court to deliver preliminary rulings. UK, Ireland and Denmark had not accepted it. As to the new Member States, the Czech Republic made a declaration at the time of Accession by which it accepted the Court's jurisdiction in JHA (see declaration no. 26, OJ 2003 No. L236, 23 September 2003, p. 980) and Hungary made a declaration to the same effect in July 2004. The other new Member States have not yet accepted the Court's jurisdiction.

Court has no jurisdiction either to rule on infringements of JHA rules by Member States, or on a failure to act by institutions, and individuals have no right to bring actions for annulment against JHA acts, nor applications for compensation or pleas of illegality. Finally, according to Article 35(5) of the EU Treaty, 'The Court of Justice shall have no jurisdiction to review the validity or proportionality of operations carried out by the police or other law enforcement services of a Member State or the exercise of the responsibilities incumbent upon Member States with regard to the maintenance of law and order and the safeguarding of internal security.'

The effects of the removal of the 'pillar structure' by the Constitution

The Constitution will remove the pillar structure. However, specific procedures will remain applicable, in particular in the field of CFSP. The removal of the pillar structure means that one single set of binding legal instruments called laws, framework laws, regulations and decisions, as well as the general rules and principles, will apply to all chapters of the Constitution, unless expressly excluded. This will reverse the existing legal situation whereby none of the EC's rules applies automatically to the CFSP and JHA pillars,[21] and vice versa, unless that is expressly specified. Pursuant to the Constitution, all these rules will apply unless expressly excluded. It will also (hopefully) remove the word 'pillar' from the 'euro-speak' jargon, which is incomprehensible for outsiders.

However, contrary to what is sometimes claimed, the removal of the pillar structure does not mean that everything will be put under the EC pillar. Not all matters (by far) will be governed by the 'Community method', i.e. a combination of exclusive initiative by the Commission, qualified majority voting in the Council and codecision with the European Parliament. Actually, this method is not a general rule anyway. The Constitution will not make it a general rule either. A number of variations in procedures will still exist, in particular with regard to the field of CFSP. In addition, several 'opt-out' protocols[22] will continue to cause their share of legal headaches.

---

[21] In the present Treaties, those EC provisions which are made applicable to the CFSP and JHA pillars are exhaustively listed in Arts. 28 and 41 EU Treaty.

[22] UK and Ireland have an 'opt-out' from the so-called Schengen area composed of 13 Member States within which internal border controls on persons have been abolished. They also have an opt-out protocol from policies in respect of border controls, asylum

The removal of the pillar structure has the automatic effect of making the following provisions and principles applicable to all sectors, save for certain exceptions which are expressly provided for and therefore easier to spot for the reader.

The jurisdiction of the Court of Justice

The Court's jurisdiction will be extended to cover the whole JHA sector. Therefore, preliminary ruling procedures, infringement procedures and actions brought by individuals will apply. The only limitation for JHA is that, with regard to judicial cooperation in criminal matters and police cooperation, the Court is still barred from reviewing 'the validity or proportionality of operations carried out by the police or other law-enforcement services of a Member State or the exercise of the responsibilities incumbent upon Member States with regard to the maintenance of law and order and the safeguarding of internal security' (Article III-377 Cst).[23]

The Court will continue to have no jurisdiction with respect to CFSP and defence provisions (Article III-376, 1st subparagraph, Cst), except that it will have the power, as now, to review compliance with the non-affectation clause (Article III-308 Cst). However, a novelty is that the Court will have the power to review the legality of Council decisions providing for restrictive measures against natural or legal persons adopted on the basis of the CFSP Chapter (Article III-376, 2nd subparagraph, Cst).

The application of the basic principles of EU law

The basic principles relating to the relationship between EU law and national law (primacy, Article I-6 Cst), the delimitation of EU competences (conferral, Article I-11(2) Cst) and of institutions' powers

---

and immigration, judicial cooperation in civil matters and police cooperation. Denmark has an opt-out protocol from the whole Chapter on the area of freedom, security and justice (policies on border checks, asylum and immigration, judicial cooperation in civil and criminal matters and police cooperation), with the exception of certain aspects of visa policy. Denmark also has an opt-out from the whole defence policy (ESDP). Finally, UK and Denmark both have an opt-out from the euro. Conversely, third countries participate as quasi-members of the Schengen area: Iceland and Norway (Agreement signed on 18 May 1999, OJ No. L176, 10 July 1999, p. 35, which entered into force on 26 June 2000) and Switzerland (Agreement signed in October 2004).

[23] Such a limitation also exists in the present EC Treaty with regard to the rules on the crossing of internal borders (Art. 68(2) EC Treaty), but it will no longer exist in the Constitution.

(conferred powers, Article I-19(2) Cst), the principles governing the use
of such competences (subsidiarity and proportionality, Articles I-11(3)
and I-11(4) Cst), the principle of loyalty between the Union and the
Member States and between the institutions (sincere cooperation, Articles I-5(2) and I-19(2) Cst), as well as the principle of 'indirect administration' whereby the responsibility for implementing and applying EU
law belongs primarily to the Member States (Articles I-5(2), 2nd subparagraph and I-37(1) Cst), will apply throughout all sectors of EU
activity. All these principles already exist at present, either because they
are expressly laid down in the Treaties or because they have been
developed in the case-law. However, some of them presently apply only
to the Community and within its fields of competence, and do not apply,
at least expressly, to the Union.[24]

The so-called 'flexibility clause'

Article I-18 Cst[25] is a legal basis enabling the Council to adopt a measure
when action is necessary to attain one of the Union's objectives, but the
Constitution has not provided the necessary powers. The scope of this
'flexibility clause' will be extended to cover all EU sectors, including JHA
and CFSP, whereas now it applies only to the EC pillar. This clause
corresponds to the present Article 308 of the EC Treaty (ex-Article 235
EC Treaty) and has given rise to controversies in the past.[26]

---

[24] For instance:

  – the primacy principle developed in the EC case-law since 1964 (see cases 6/64, *Costa v. ENEL*,
    and 106/77, *Simmenthal*). The fact that the Constitution codifies and extends this principle
    to the EU might give rise to political controversy in some Member States;
  – the proportionality principle mentioned in Art. 5 EC Treaty, is not expressly referred to in
    Art. 2, 2nd subpara., of the EU Treaty, which mentions only the subsidiarity principle.

[25] Art. I-18 Cst reads: '1. If action by the Union should prove necessary, within the
    framework of the policies defined in Part III, to attain one of the objectives set out in the
    Constitution, and the Constitution has not provided the necessary powers, the Council
    of Ministers, acting unanimously on a proposal from the European Commission and
    after obtaining the consent of the European Parliament, shall adopt the appropriate
    measures . . . 3. Measures based on this Article shall not entail harmonisation of Member
    States' laws or regulations in cases where the Constitution excludes such harmonisation.'

[26] In its Opinion 2/94, *Accession of the EC to the European Convention on Human Rights*
    (ECHR), the Court stated that 'Article 235 [now 308] is designed to fill the gap where no
    specific provisions of the Treaty confer on the Community institutions express or
    implied powers to act, if such powers appear nonetheless to be necessary to enable the
    Community to carry out its functions with a view to attaining one of the objectives laid

The protection of personal data

The right to the protection of personal data stated in Article I-51(1) Cst, as well as the Community rules adopted to protect individuals regarding the processing of such data, will apply to all EU sectors of activity, including JHA and CFSP, and will no longer be limited to the EC pillar (Article 286 EC Treaty).

The powers of the European Ombudsman

The scope of the powers of the European Ombudsman under Articles I-49 and III-335 Cst to enquire into complaints about maladministration will cover activities of EU institutions and bodies in all EU sectors, including CFSP, and will no longer be limited to the EC and JHA pillars (Article 195 EC Treaty and Articles 28(1) and 41(1) EU Treaty).

The temporary enquiry committees set up by the European Parliament

The European Parliament will be allowed to set up temporary enquiry committees under Article III-333 Cst in order to enquire into alleged contraventions or maladministration in the implementation of Union law in all EU sectors, including JHA and CFSP, and not only in the EC pillar (Article 193 EC Treaty).

The territorial scope of the Constitution

At present, there is no provision on the territorial scope of the EU Treaty, which is the case in the EC Treaty (Article 299). Article IV-440 Cst reproduces Article 299 of the EC Treaty, with the addition of elements contained in the Accession Treaties. The present territorial scope of the EC will thus expressly apply to all EU matters.

---

down in the Treaty . . . That provision, being an integral part of an institutional system based on the principle of conferred powers, cannot serve as a basis for widening the scope of Community powers beyond the general framework created by the provisions of the Treaty as a whole and, in particular, by those that define the tasks and the activities of the Community. On any view, Article 235 cannot be used as a basis for the adoption of provisions whose effect would, in substance, be to amend the Treaty without following the procedure which it provides for that purpose' (paras. 29 and 30). See also the judgment of the Supreme Court of Denmark of 6 April 1998, in Case *Carlsen v. Prime Minister*, on the Maastricht Treaty (I 361/1997, UfR 1998, 800) and more specifically on Art. 235 EC Treaty (now Art. 308). For a commentary on this case, see K. Høegh, 'The Danish Maastricht Judgment' (1999) 24 *European Law Review*, 80–90.

Privileges and immunities

At present, the protocol on privileges and immunities is annexed to the EC Treaty and applies to the EC (and therefore to the agencies set up on the basis of the EC Treaty), but it does not apply to the EU. This has obliged the Member States to conclude specific privileges and immunities agreements to cover agencies set up under the EU Treaty,[27] such agreements having to be ratified by each of the 25 Member States. The removal of the pillar structure will result in the new EU being wholly covered by these provisions, thus doing away with a lengthy ratification procedure when establishing a new agency in the JHA or CFSP fields.

Section 2: Streamlining the instruments and the procedures of the Union

Another achievement of the Constitution is the streamlining of instruments and decision-making procedures which the EU institutions have to use to exercise their powers. The Constitution reduces the number of different types of legal instruments. It introduces a distinction between legislative and non-legislative procedures and a hierarchy between legislative and non-legislative acts. Drawing a logical conclusion from this distinction, it provides for full openness of Council meetings when acting in a legislative capacity. The Constitution also streamlines the different decision-making procedures.

Streamlining the legal instruments adopted by the EU institutions

The Constitution will replace the present 15 different types of legal instruments with six legal instruments.

---

[27] There are at present three agencies set up under the EU Treaty:

- the EU Institute for Security Studies (Council Joint Action 2001/554/CFSP of 20 July 2001, OJ No. L200, 25 July 2001, p. 1);
- the EU Satellite Centre (Council Joint Action 2001/555/CFSP of 20 July 2001, OJ No. L200, 25 July 2001, p. 5);
- the European Defence Agency (Council Joint Action 2004/551/CFSP of 12 July 2004, OJ No. L245, 17 July 2004, p. 17).

These 'EU agencies' should not be confused with the numerous agencies set up under the EC Treaty, which are automatically covered by the Protocol on privileges and immunities annexed to that Treaty.

The 15 existing types of legal instruments

The present Treaties provide for 15 different types of legal instruments with different legal effects, albeit minor in some instances:[28]

- the regulation (which is binding and directly applicable);
- the directive (which is binding as to the results to be achieved but leaves to national authorities the choice of form and methods);
- four types of decisions (EC, CFSP, JHA and 'sui generis', which all have binding force);
- the recommendation and the opinion (which have no binding force);
- the framework decision (similar to a directive);
- the convention between Member States (i.e. the traditional agreement existing under international law, used in EC seldom and JHA);
- principles and general guidelines (listed among CFSP instruments, though not a legal act);
- the common strategy (CFSP);
- two types of common positions (CFSP and JHA, which both have binding force); and
- the joint action (CFSP, which also has binding force).[29]

While the original Rome Treaty of 1957 provided for only five legal instruments, the addition of the second and third pillars (CFSP and JHA) in the nineties and the political will to differentiate these new sectors resulted in a proliferation of legal instruments, which sometimes had similar names but different legal effects or, conversely, different names but similar legal effects. This phenomenon did not particularly contribute to enhancing the readability of the Treaties.

The six types of legal instruments in the Constitution

The Constitution reduces the number of legal instruments to six, i.e. two legislative instruments, two non-legislative instruments and two non-binding ones (Article I-33 Cst):

---

[28] See Arts. 249 and 293 EC Treaty, Arts. 12 to 15 EU Treaty and Arts. 34 and 37 EU Treaty.

[29] For an analysis and suggestions made at the time of the Convention, see my contribution of 17 October 2002 to the Working Group IX 'Simplification' set up by the Convention, in Working Document 06 (WG IX-WD 06), of 6 November 2002 (available on the internet site of the Convention). On this issue, see also T. Blanchet, 'Les instruments juridiques de l'Union européenne et la rédaction des bases juridiques: situation actuelle et rationalisation dans la Constitution' (2005) 2 *Revue trimestrielle de droit européen* 319–343.

- the European law, which is 'a legislative act of general application. It shall be binding in its entirety and directly applicable in all Member States' (same legal effects as an EC regulation);
- the European framework law, which is 'a legislative act binding, as to the result to be achieved, upon each Member State to which it is addressed, but shall leave to the national authorities the choice of form and methods' (same legal effects as an EC directive);
- the European regulation, which is a non-legislative act which may be of two types, i.e. either have the same legal effects as an EC regulation or have the same legal effects as an EC directive. One may think that this 'dual nature' will entail the risk of creating some confusion and difficulties when drafting such a possibly 'hybrid' legal act;
- the European decision, which is 'a non-legislative act, binding in its entirety. A decision which specifies those to whom it is addressed shall be binding only on them';[30]
- the recommendation and the opinion, which have no binding force.

The difference in name for acts which in reality have the same legal effects (a law and a framework law have the same legal effects as, respectively, the above two types of regulation) not only allowed differentiation, in the constitution, between legislative and non-legislative acts, but also allowed to introduce a hierarchy between the legislative level and the delegated, or executive, level (see below). In addition to satisfying the Euro-enthusiasts with its symbolism, the use of the name 'law' or 'framework law' in the different legal bases allows one to identify immediately the cases where legislative powers are granted to the EU institutions. These cases are those where the principle of full transparency of proceedings,[31] as well as the specific procedures provided for by the protocols on national parliaments and on the application of the principles of subsidiarity and proportionality, will apply.

Moreover, the drafting of the legal bases in the Constitution has been streamlined so as to follow a consistent pattern. Most of them now indicate the type of legal act which may be adopted. When the legal basis starts with the wording 'European laws shall . . .' or 'European framework laws shall . . .', without specifying which institution(s) is/are to be the author of the law, it means that this law or framework law will be adopted, as a default rule, in codecision by the European Parliament and the Council. This procedure is

---

[30] Decisions are the only type of acts which the Council may adopt under the CFSP Chapter of the Constitution (see Arts. I-40(3), III-294(b) and III-295(2) Cst).
[31] See Arts. I-24(6) and I-50(2) Cst.

called the 'ordinary legislative procedure' (Article I-34(1) Cst). Conversely, the procedure is called a 'special legislative procedure' when the author is specified in the legal basis, such as 'a European law of the Council shall. . .' (Article I-34(2) Cst).

Streamlining the procedures followed by the institutions of the Union

Streamlining instruments also helped to streamline procedures. It enabled the drafters of the Constitution to distinguish between legislative and non-legislative procedures, and thus to introduce a hierarchy between legislative acts, on the one hand, and delegated and implementing acts, on the other.

Trying to transpose to the EU a ready-made State model would not suit its legal and institutional uniqueness. Therefore, introducing a strict Montesquieu-like division of powers between the Legislature and the Executive would not make sense in the EU. However, introducing some logic and clarity into the famous 'comitology' procedures set up to monitor the implementing powers conferred on the Commission by the EU legislature was needed. This is done in Articles I-36 and I-37 Cst.

The present rules on implementing powers ('comitology')

At present, Article 202 of the EC Treaty provides that the Council may 'confer on the Commission, in the acts which the Council adopts, powers for the implementation of the rules which the Council lays down'. Practice to date under the expression 'implementing powers' has combined two types of power which are different in nature: the power to adopt a normative act which amends or supplements the basic legislative act itself,[32] on the one hand, and the power to implement, or to execute at EC level, all or part of a legislative act, on the other hand.

The latter is an exception to the basic principle of 'indirect administration', whereby the responsibility for implementing and applying EC law belongs to the Member States, under the control of the Commission,

---

[32] For example, where the Commission is authorised by the legislature to adapt a legislative act to technical progress or to international standards, to amend a date or a figure, to lay down additional and more detailed rules for application by the Member States of the legislative act, etc. Sometimes, the mere fact of amending or setting a figure (e.g. a percentage) may have very significant implications affecting the very essence of the legislative act (e.g. the definition of chocolate according to the percentage of a particular type of fat).

the national courts and the Court of Justice.[33] Indirect administration reflects the fact that Member States do not wish to endow the EC with the huge administrative infrastructure which would be necessary to enable it to implement EC legislation. They want to keep the Commission as a small administration. However, in specific cases, the EC legislature may consider it necessary to entrust the Commission with adopting, at EC level, implementing rules or measures to ensure the uniform application of an EC legislative act in order to avoid distortion of competition or discrimination between economic operators.[34]

Irrespective of the type of implementing power, whether it consists in amending or supplementing the legislative act itself or whether it consists in applying the act at EC level instead of at the Member States' level, the system of control over the exercise of such powers is presently the same. It is in the hands of committees of representatives of the Member States (the so-called 'comitology'). In some instances, a system of 'referral' or 'call-back' brings the dossier to the Council in case of deadlock at the committee level. Therefore, even when the implementing power given to the Commission allows it to amend a legislative act adopted in codecision, only Member States and the Council may control the exercise of such power, not the European Parliament (which is only informed and may adopt a resolution on the draft implementing measures). Of course, this has been for years a matter of fierce criticism by the European Parliament, despite the few improvements made in the last 1999 Comitology Decision as compared with the previous one of 1987 (see box 3.1).[35]

---

[33] Art. 10, 1st subpara., EC Treaty obliges Member States to take 'all appropriate measures, whether general or particular, to ensure fulfilment of the obligations arising out of the . . . Treaty or resulting from action taken by the institutions'. This principle of indirect administration (also known as 'implementing federalism'), which is based on the rationale of subsidiarity, already existed in the original Rome Treaty of 1957 but had often been denied by the Commission. Its services claimed, basing themselves on the wording of Art. 202, 3rd indent, EC Treaty, that the Council was obliged to confer all implementing powers on the Commission. The principle of indirect administration, which is now clearly stated in Arts. I-5(2), 2nd subpara., and I-37(1) Cst, may be compared with Art. 83 of the German Constitution which reads: 'Except as otherwise provided or permitted by this Basic Law, the Länder shall execute federal law under their own powers.'

[34] In some cases, the Commission has been entrusted with the task of directly applying a given policy (competition law, the centralised issuing of authorisations for placing products on the market or of EC intellectual property rights, managing various support or incentive programmes).

[35] See Council Decision of 28 June 1999 laying down the procedures for the exercise of implementing powers conferred on the Commission (OJ No. L184, 17 July 1999, p. 23). The previous Decision was of 13 July 1987 (OJ No. L197, 18 July 1987, p. 33).

Box 3.1 The present 'Comitology' system (1999)

The present 'Comitology' system, i.e. the system by which committees composed of Member States' representatives, meeting outside the Council structure, control the exercise by the Commission of implementing powers conferred on it by the EU legislature pursuant to Article 202 of the EC Treaty, is set out in a Council Decision of June 1999. The Decision provides for three types of committees, all composed of Member States' representatives and chaired by a Commission representative, which differ by the effects of the opinion they deliver:

- advisory committees, which deliver a purely consultative opinion on the draft measures submitted to it by the Commission, the Commission having to 'take the utmost account of the opinion' in the measures it will adopt;
- management committees, which also deliver an opinion. If the measures adopted by the Commission are not in accordance with the Committee's opinion, these measures must be communicated by the Commission to the Council, in which case the Commission may defer the application of the measures for a maximum period of three months, during which the Council may take a different opinion by QMV;
- regulatory committees, which also deliver an opinion. However, if the draft measures are not in accordance with the Committee's opinion or if no opinion is delivered, the Commission must submit to the Council a proposal relating to the measures and must inform the European Parliament. The Council must act by QMV within a maximum of three months, in view of the position taken by the European Parliament if the basic act was an act adopted in codecision. If the Council opposes the proposal, the Commission will have to re-examine it. If the Council does not oppose or has not adopted the proposed act, the Commission will automatically adopt the implementing act.

The choice of the type of committee is left to the legislature, which is to be guided by certain non-binding criteria[36] set out in Article 1 of the Decision. The European Parliament has to be informed by the

---

[36] See however judgment of 21 January 2003, Case C-378/00, *Commission v. Council* (LIFE), [2003] ECR p. I-937, in which the Court stated that 'when the Community legislature

Commission of committee proceedings on a regular basis. If the European Parliament adopts a resolution indicating that draft implementing measures for a basic act adopted in codecision would exceed the implementing powers provided for in this basic act, the Commission is obliged to re-examine the draft measures and inform the European Parliament of the action it intends to take on the latter's resolution. The Commission has to publish a list of all the Comitology committees as well as an annual report on their working.[1]

Note: [1] See the list in OJ No. C225, 8 August 2000, p. 2.

The new system of delegated and implementing powers in the Constitution

The Constitution resolves this unsatisfactory situation by providing for two separate control procedures:[37]

- one in Article I-36 Cst, with regard to delegated regulations, under which either branch of the legislature, the European Parliament or the Council, can control how the Commission exercises its delegated powers to supplement or amend non-essential elements of a legislative act, powers which normally would have been exercised by the legislature itself;
- and one in Article I-37 Cst, with regard to implementing acts, under which the Member States control the Commission's exercise of implementing powers which normally, by virtue of the principle of indirect administration, would have been exercised by Member States, but which were entrusted to the Commission because uniform implementation conditions were needed.

New rules by default in legislative matters and other streamlining of procedures

The decision-making procedures will be streamlined in various ways, notably through the streamlining of instruments. The number of

departs, in the choice of committee procedure, from the criteria which are laid down in Art. 2 of the second comitology decision, it must state the reasons for that choice.' (para. 55).

[37] For suggestions made to the Convention, see pp. 20–23 of my contribution of 17 October 2002 to the Working Group IX 'Simplification' (WG IX-WD 06 of 6 November 2002).

procedures will be reduced by removing the 'cooperation procedure' (Article 252 EC Treaty) which was the predecessor of the codecision procedure, and which had survived only in the monetary policy sector.

Codecision becomes the 'ordinary legislative procedure' (Articles I-34 (1) and III-396 Cst) whereby laws and framework laws are adopted by the European Parliament and the Council, acting by QMV, on a proposal from the Commission.[38]

The other procedure under which laws or framework laws may be adopted is called the 'special legislative procedure'. It covers cases where laws or framework laws are adopted either by the Council with the participation of the European Parliament (through consultation or consent) or by the European Parliament with the consent of the Council.[39] Other institutions, such as the Commission or the European Central Bank, may also have to be consulted.

The present situation, in which most legislative acts are adopted on a proposal from the Commission, is codified in Article I-26(2) Cst[40] and becomes the rule by default. Likewise, the present situation under which the Council acts by QMV in most policy areas is codified in Article I-23(3) Cst and becomes the rule by default.[41] These two default rules enabled the drafters to avoid repeating in all relevant legal bases that the legislature shall act on a proposal from the Commission or that the Council shall act by a qualified majority. It is only exceptions to this general rule which are specified. That is better drafting.

---

[38] As indicated in Arts. I-34(3) and III-396(15) Cst, there are some cases where the ordinary legislative procedure is not triggered by a Commission proposal but by an initiative of a group of Member States (at least a quarter of the Member States) in the JHA field (see Arts. I-42(3) and III-264 Cst), by a recommendation from the European Central Bank (see Art. III-187(3)(b) Cst) or at the request of the Court of Justice (see Arts. III-359(1) and III-381 Cst).

[39] The European Parliament may adopt laws in three instances: Art. III-330(2) Cst on the Statute of MEPs, with the consent of the Council, Art. III-333 Cst on committees of inquiry, with the consent of the Council and the Commission, and Art. III-335(4) Cst on the Ombudsman, with the consent of the Council.

[40] Art. I-26(2) Cst reads: 'Union legislative acts may be adopted only on the basis of a Commission proposal, except where the Constitution provides otherwise. Other acts shall be adopted on the basis of a Commission proposal where the Constitution so provides.'

[41] Art. I-23(3) reads: 'The Council shall act by a qualified majority except where the Constitution provides otherwise.' This is in lieu of the present rule by default which is a simple majority, and which is, in reality, the least common of the voting procedures, save for procedural decisions (Art. 205(1) EC Treaty).

Apart from legislative procedures, there are procedures for adopting non-legislative acts. The European Council may adopt decisions, but this new 'institution' is not allowed to adopt legislative acts (Article I-21(1) Cst). The European Parliament, the Council and the European Central Bank may adopt regulations and decisions, as well as recommendations (Article I-35). The legal basis specifies in each case which procedure is to be followed.

In the CSFP field, the only kind of act which may be adopted is a decision, and the European Council or the Council will act either on an initiative from a Member State, or on a proposal from the Minister for Foreign Affairs, or on a proposal from the Minister with the Commission's support (Articles I-40(6) and III-299 Cst).

Section 3: Codifying existing rules and principles of EU law

Rather than inventing new principles of law or new categories of competences, the Constitution codifies principles and categories of competences which had been already identified by the Court of Justice or had been codified in the present Treaties. The Constitution puts them into a more coherent order.

Classifying EU competences into three categories

The Constitution lists and defines three categories of EU competences (Article I-12 Cst):[42]

- exclusive competences, where only the EU may legislate; the Member States are allowed to do so only if they are specifically empowered by the EU, or of course when they need to legislate for ensuring the proper implementation of EU acts;
- shared competences, where both the EU and Member States may legislate, but the Member States may exercise their competences only to the extent that the EU has not exercised its competence;

---

[42] These categories had already been identified either by the Court in its case-law (see e.g. as regards exclusive competences, Opinion 2/91 of 19 March 1993, *ILO*, ECR p. I-1061, para. 19) or mentioned in the Treaties (e.g. in Art. 43(d) EU Treaty, in Art. 5 EC Treaty or in Art. 133(6), 2nd subpara., EC Treaty).

- supporting competences, where the EU may support, coordinate or supplement actions of the Member States, but without being allowed to adopt legislative harmonisation rules.

The Constitution lists the policy areas in which the EU has exclusive, shared and supporting competences (respectively Articles I-13, I-14 and I-17 Cst) (see table 3.1). As can be seen from these lists, and contrary to what is sometimes thought, the number of areas of exclusive competences is very limited (only five), while the list of shared and supporting competences is much longer.

Although the classification of these areas into the three categories of competences defined by the Constitution did not in all cases follow a purely Cartesian logic, the new Articles on competences have the merit of codifying and clarifying the existing delimitation of competences between the Union and the Member States. They do not change the present balance and preserve a margin of flexibility. They also establish a mechanism which allows for more effective control of respect for the subsidiarity principle by the EU institutions.

The debate on the issue of division of competences and the solutions found

The issue of the division of competences was one of the four items listed in the 2000 Nice Declaration on the future of the Union: 'how to establish and monitor a more precise delimitation of powers between the European Union and the Member States, reflecting the principle of subsidiarity'. It was included at the request of the German Government, whose Länder had criticised a lack of clarity in the delimitation of these competences. It was argued that this lack of clarity made it very difficult for the citizen to understand 'who does what in Europe' and allowed a 'creeping' increase in the powers of the EU.

In the Convention, the idea of establishing a precise and rigid catalogue of competences was quickly abandoned: it was found too difficult to establish and, in any case, inappropriate given the characteristics of the EU.[43] Discussions focused on:

[43] See my article 'The 1996 Intergovernmental Conference' (footnote 2 above).

Table 3.1. *The division of competences between the European Union and its Member States*

Exclusive competences	Shared competences	Supporting competences
– customs union – establishment of the competition rules necessary for the functioning of the internal market – monetary policy for the Member States whose currency is the euro – conservation of marine biological resources (fisheries policy) – common commercial policy	– internal market – social policy, for the aspects defined in Part III of the Constitution – economic, social and territorial cohesion – agriculture and fisheries (except conservation of marine biological resources) – environment – consumer protection – transport – trans-European networks – energy – area of freedom, security and justice – common safety concerns in public health matters, for the aspects defined in Part III of the Constitution	– protection and improvement of human health – industry – culture – tourism – education, youth, sport and vocational training – civil protection – administrative cooperation

Specific cases
- coordination of economic and employment policies
- common foreign and security policy (CFSP)
- research, technological development and space
- development cooperation and humanitarian aid

- devising a new mechanism in order to ensure strict respect for the principles of subsidiarity and proportionality by the institutions;
- defining the different categories of competences.

Reaching a consensus on the definition of the different categories of EU competences and on the listing of the areas belonging to each category was not an easy task. The wish to preserve some flexibility in the system, the fact that the EU's competences evolve and that in most areas these competences are shared with the Member States, made it difficult to establish closed lists of areas of competences in all cases. Therefore, while the lists of areas of exclusive and supporting competences are exhaustive, the list of areas of shared competences is not exhaustive. It starts with the sentence 'The Union shall share competence with the Member States where the Constitution confers on it a competence which does not relate to the areas referred to in Article I-13 and I-17.' It implies, therefore, that the list of areas which follows in paragraph 2 might not be exhaustive and that Article I-15 on coordination of economic and employment policies and Article I-16 on CFSP belong to the category of shared competences.

That was also the way to solve the difficulty caused by the fact that the classification made in the Constitution did not fit exactly with the variety of competences of the EC and the EU. Areas such as research and development, development cooperation and humanitarian aid, found themselves in between shared and supporting competences (Article I-14(3) and (4) Cst), with legal bases showing that the EU has neither a shared nor a supporting competence, but a complementary competence of its own in addition to the Member States' competence.

With regard to economic and employment policies (Article I-15 Cst), the EU has only a competence of coordination, while the Member States retain the competence on substance. This area could thus have been classified as a 'complementary' competence and not as a 'shared' one. Nevertheless, it was decided politically that the importance of the coordination done by the EU in this area made it difficult to classify it as a mere 'complementary' competence.

With regard to CFSP (Article I-16 Cst), it was considered that the specificity of the EU competence in this area, where both the EU and the Member States are competent, made it difficult to include this area in one of the three general categories of competences.

The classification of the internal market was also subject to discussion, because, in this area, the Union has a functional competence of harmonisation (which logically can only be done by the Union) but, as long as the Union has not exercised its competence, Member States keep their power to legislate.

In any case, the inclusion of an area in one or other category cannot modify the substance of the competences as they are defined precisely in Part III of the Constitution, given that, according to paragraph 6 of Article I-12, 'the scope of and arrangements for exercising the Union's competences shall be determined by the provisions relating to each area in Part III'.

Codifying long-standing principles of EU law

The Constitution codifies long-standing legal principles which either were already defined in the text of the Treaties or had already been developed by the Court of Justice. All these principles are regrouped in the same part, Part I, at the beginning of the Constitution.

The principle of primacy of EU law

Article I-6 Cst reflects the principle that EC law has supremacy over national law: 'The Constitution and law adopted by the institutions of the Union in exercising competences conferred on it shall have primacy over the law of the Member States' (Article I-6 Cst).

A Declaration (no. 1) to the Final Act of the IGC 'notes that Article I-6 reflects existing case-law of the Court of Justice'. This principle had indeed already been affirmed in 1964 by the EC Court of Justice in its landmark judgment *Costa v. ENEL*: 'The executive force of Community law cannot vary from one State to another in deference to subsequent domestic laws, without jeopardizing the attainment of the objectives of the Treaty set out in Article 5(2) (renumbered 10) and giving rise to the discrimination prohibited by Article 7 (renumbered 12).'[44]

---

[44] See Case 6/64, *Costa v. ENEL*. See also Case 106/77, *Simmenthal* in which the Court stated that 'in accordance with the principle of the precedence of Community law, the relationship between provisions of the Treaty and directly applicable measures of the institutions on the one hand and the national law of the Member States on the other is such that those provisions and measures not only by their entry into force render automatically inapplicable any conflicting provision of current national law but – in so far as they are an integral part of, and take precedence in, the legal order applicable in the territory of each of the Member States – also preclude the valid adoption of new national legislative measures to the extent to which they would be incompatible with Community provisions' (para. 17) and 'every national Court must, in a case within its jurisdiction, apply Community law in its entirety and protect rights which the latter confers on individuals and must accordingly set aside any provision of national law which may conflict with it, whether prior or subsequent to the Community rule' (para. 21).

See also judgment of 17 December 1970, Case 11/70, *International Handelsgesellschaft*, [1970], ECR 1125 in which the Court stated that 'In fact, the law stemming from the Treaty, an independent source of law, cannot because of its very nature be overridden by rules of national law, however framed, without being deprived of its character as Community law and without the legal basis of the Community itself being called in

Actually, this case-law had already been codified, although not so clearly for non-specialists, in paragraph 2 of the Protocol on the application of the principles of subsidiarity and proportionality, annexed to the EC Treaty by the Treaty of Amsterdam, which reads 'The application of the principles of subsidiarity and proportionality . . . shall not affect the principles developed by the Court of Justice regarding the relationship between national and Community law.'

The primacy rule is a classic principle in multi-layered legal orders such as federal States.[45] In the EU, it is also a consequence of the international law principle *pacta sunt servanda* (Article 27 of the Vienna Convention on the Law of Treaties). The primacy of EU law over national law is essential to the Union's ability to function. Without it, legislation validly adopted by the EU institutions could be ignored by a Member State whenever it was contrary to the latter's economic or political interests. In the absence of primacy, 'the legal basis of the Community itself [would be] called in question' (as the Court stated in *Simmenthal*), and the internal market and all the basic policies of the EU could not function.

The objective pursued by the drafters of the Constitution, both in the Convention and in the IGC, was to codify this basic principle explicitly and in a readable manner. Despite some mixed reactions from a few Member States, especially the UK, this has been done. The legal effect this will have is that the primacy rule will now cover Union law as well as Community law. It remains the case, however, that the EU Court of Justice will have no jurisdiction in CFSP or ESDP matters. Moreover, the Constitution itself recognises that the EU is bound to respect 'national identities' of Member States, 'inherent in their fundamental structures, political and constitutional, inclusive of regional and local self-government' and that 'it shall respect their essential State

---

question. Therefore the validity of a Community measure or its effect within a Member State cannot be affected by allegations that it runs counter to either fundamental rights as formulated by the Constitution of that State or the principles of a national constitutional structure' (para. 3).

[45] See for instance Cl. 2 of Art. VI of the US Constitution: 'This Constitution, and the Laws of the United States which shall be made in Pursuance thereof; and all Treaties made, or which shall be made, under the Authority of the United States, shall be the supreme Law of the Land; and the Judges in every State shall be bound thereby, any Thing in the Constitution or Laws of any State to the Contrary notwithstanding'; Art. 31 of the German Constitution: 'Federal law shall have primacy over Land law'; and Art. 49 of the Swiss Constitution: 'Federal law shall have primacy over contrary cantonal law.'

functions, including ensuring the territorial integrity of the State, maintaining law and order and safeguarding national security' (Article I-5 (1) Cst).

Two Constitutional Courts (the French *Conseil constitutionnel*[46] and the Spanish *Tribunal Constitucional*[47]) have examined this new provision. They both found that it reflected a principle which already existed and that it did not require a modification of the national Constitution.

The principle of conferral of competences

Article I-11(2) Cst provides that '. . . the Union shall act within the limits of the competences conferred upon it by the Member States in the Constitution to attain the objectives set out in the Constitution. Competences not conferred upon the Union in the Constitution remain with the Member States.' This rule is known as the principle of conferral of competences on the Union.

Its twin principle, as regards the powers of the EU institutions, is the principle of conferred powers set out in Article I-19(2) Cst under which 'Each institution shall act within the limits of the powers conferred on it in the Constitution and in conformity with the procedures and conditions set out in it (. . .)'.

These two principles are already set out in Article 5, 1st subparagraph, and in Article 7(1), 1st subparagraph, of the EC Treaty. They are also a classic principle in the Constitutions of federal states.[48]

---

[46] Decision of the *Conseil constitutionnel* no. 2004-505 DC of 19 November 2004. In its decision, the *Conseil constitutionnel* clearly puts the French Constitution outside the EU legal order and, therefore, not bound by EU law (http://www.conseil-constitutionnel.fr/decision/2004/2004505/2004505dc.pdf). See J.-E. Schoettl, 'La ratification du "Traité établissant une Constitution pour l'Europe" appelle-t-elle une révision de la Constitution française?' (2004) vol. 393, no. 238 *Les Petites Affiches* 3–25.

[47] Decision of the *Tribunal Constitucional* no. DTC 1/2004 of 13 December 2004 (http://www.tribunalconstitucional.es/Stc2004/DTC2004-001.htm).

[48] Compare with 10th Amendment to the US Constitution: 'The powers not delegated to the United States by the Constitution, nor prohibited by it to the States, are reserved to the States respectively, or to the people'; Art. 30 of the German Constitution: 'Except as otherwise provided or permitted by this Basic Law, the exercise of state powers and the discharge of state functions is a matter for the Länder'; and Arts. 3 and 42, para. 1, of the Swiss Constitution: 'The cantons are sovereign insofar as their sovereignty is not limited by the Federal Constitution; they exercise all rights which are not delegated to the Confederation' and 'The Confederation shall accomplish the tasks which are attributed to it by the Constitution.'

The Constitution also makes clear in Article I-1(1) that it is the Member States which confer competences on the EU, not the Constitution itself.[49]

The principle of subsidiarity

Article I-11(3) Cst provides that '(. . .) in areas which do not fall within its exclusive competence the Union shall act only if and insofar as the objectives of the intended action cannot be sufficiently achieved by the Member States, either at central level or at regional and local level, but can rather, by reason of the scale or effects of the proposed action, be better achieved at Union level'.

This principle is already set out in Article 5, 2nd subparagraph, of the EC Treaty and referred to in Article 2, 2nd subparagraph, of the EU Treaty.

The principle of proportionality

Article I-11(4) Cst provides that '(. . .) the content and form of Union action shall not exceed what is necessary to achieve the objectives of the Constitution'.

This principle is already set out in Article 5, 3rd subparagraph, of the EC Treaty.

The principle of sincere cooperation

Article I-5(2) Cst provides that '. . . the Union and the Member States shall, in full mutual respect, assist each other in carrying out tasks which flow from the Constitution . . . The Member States shall facilitate the achievement of the Union's tasks and refrain from any measure which could jeopardise the attainment of the Union's objectives.' Article I-19(2) Cst provides that 'the institutions shall practise mutual sincere cooperation'.

This principle is already set out in Article 10 of the EC Treaty which provides that '[Member States] shall facilitate the achievement of the Community's tasks. They shall abstain from any measure which could jeopardise the attainment of the objectives of this Treaty.'

It has been interpreted by the Court as also applying to the relations between EU institutions.[50]

---

[49] This specific formulation was approved by the Convention as a result of a discussion on this very issue.

[50] See judgment of 30 March 1995, Case 65/93, *European Parliament v. Council*, [1995] ECR p. I-643, para. 23.

The principle of indirect administration

Article I-5(2), 2nd subparagraph, Cst provides that 'the Member States shall take any appropriate measure, general or particular, to ensure fulfilment of the obligations arising out of the Constitution or resulting from the acts of the institutions of the Union' and Article I-37(1) Cst provides that 'Member States shall adopt all measures of national law necessary to implement legally binding Union acts.'

There will even be a new legal basis enabling the Union 'to support the efforts of Member States to improve their administrative capacity to implement Union law' (Article III-285 Cst).

This principle is already set out in Article 10, 1st subparagraph, of the EC Treaty, under which 'Member States shall take all appropriate measures, whether general or particular, to ensure fulfilment of the obligations arising out of the . . . Treaty or resulting from action taken by the institutions', but the Constitution sets it out in more explicit terms.[51]

The principle of equality of Member States before the Constitution

Some delegations (Portugal in particular) asked that the Constitution should establish a 'principle of equality between Member States of the Union'. This appeared to be unacceptable for a number of delegations (including those of the larger Member States), which stressed that such a principle did not exist within the Union legal order. Actually, the Constitution itself differentiates between Member States, according to certain objective criteria. The final compromise was to refer to the 'equality of Member States before the Constitution' (Article I-5 Cst), which is a formulation already used by the Court of Justice in its case-law and which, therefore, did not give rise to any legal concern.[52]

---

[51] For explanations on the system of 'indirect administration', see above under 'The present rules on implementing powers ("comitology")'.

[52] The Court has referred to 'the principle of equality of Member States before Community law' in a case concerning the elimination of quantitative restrictions on agricultural products, in connection with the UK's accession in 1973 (see judgment 29 March 1979, Case 231/78, *Commission v. UK* (potatoes), [1979] ECR, p. 1447, para. 17). See also judgments of 7 February 1979, Case 128/78, *Commission v. UK* (tachographs), [1979] ECR, p. I-419, para. 12, and judgment of 7 February 1973, Case 39/72, *Commission v. Italy* (premiums for slaughtering cows), [1973] ECR p. 101, para. 24).

IV

Changes in the institutions

Besides the Treaties' structure, the second most visible changes brought about by the Constitution are of an institutional nature.

These reforms concern the number of institutions and their respective powers, composition or internal functioning.

They also give increased rights to political actors other than the EU institutions, such as the national Parliaments, the Committee of the Regions and the citizens themselves.

They establish a number of 'facilitating' mechanisms in order to allow for more flexibility in the functioning of an enlarged EU: 'enhanced cooperation' among some of the Member States, pre-established cases of 'inbuilt closer cooperation', simplified revision procedures for amending the Constitution and an express right for a Member State to withdraw voluntarily from the EU.

Section 1: Adapting the institutions to an enlarged EU

The number of EU institutions is increased from five to seven, by the addition of the European Council and of the European Central Bank. Their respective powers are somewhat reshuffled through a widening of the scope of the codecision procedure, an increase in the number of cases where a (redefined) QMV in the Council will apply, the creation of the new offices of a full-time European Council President and of a Union Minister for Foreign Affairs, the formal mentioning of the Eurogroup which will be chaired by a President elected by his peers and, finally, a reduced number of Commissioners as from 2014.

Two more institutions: the European Council and the European Central Bank

By adding the European Council and the European Central Bank (ECB) to the present five institutions,[1] the Constitution brings them within the

---

[1] The present five institutions are the European Parliament, the Council, the Commission, the Court of Justice and the Court of Auditors (see Art. 7 EC Treaty). In the

scope of all the general provisions and rules that are applicable to the EU and its institutions, including provisions concerning the review by the Court of Justice of the legality of their acts. Each time a provision uses the term 'institutions' without specifying an exception, it will also include these two new institutions.

Legal consequences of the European Council becoming an institution

With regard to the European Council, the change, while not revolutionary, is substantial. At present, the European Council, composed of the Heads of State or Government and of the President of the Commission, is mentioned in Article 4 of the EU Treaty as a body which, through political conclusions or declarations, 'shall provide the Union with the necessary impetus for its development and shall define the general political guidelines thereof'; but it is not an institution, although it may, in some rare cases, take decisions.[2]

Under the Constitution, the European Council will continue to fulfil this 'impetus' role and, in doing so, it will act by consensus, which is not a voting rule (Article I-21(4) Cst).

However, since it will be an institution, this means that whenever it adopts legally binding acts, the relevant legal basis will identify in each case the relevant procedure to be followed (type of legal instrument to be adopted, applicable voting rule, etc.) and the European Council will be obliged to respect these rules. The Constitution specifies that the President of the European Council and the Commission's President will not have the right to vote (Article I-25(4) Cst) and that the European Council will be barred from exercising 'legislative functions' (Article I-21(1) Cst). In order to regulate its new functioning as an EU

Constitution, the list of institutions is divided between those (five) which are part of the 'institutional framework' (Art. I-19 Cst) and the other two institutions, the ECB and the Court of Auditors (Articles I-30 and I-31 Cst), which are not part of this framework.

[2] See 'common strategies' in CFSP (Art. 13(2) EU Treaty), 'decision' on a common defence (Art. 17(1) EU Treaty) or 'conclusion' on the broad economic guidelines (Art. 99(2) EC Treaty). However, in all other cases where members of the European Council adopt legal acts, the Treaties entrust this power to the Council 'meeting in the composition of the Heads of State or Government' (see for instance Art. 7(2) EU Treaty on the determination of the existence of a serious and persistent breach of the founding EU principles mentioned in Art. 6(1) EU Treaty, or Art. 214(2) EC Treaty on the nomination of the person intended to be appointed as President of the Commission).

decision-making body, the European Council will have to adopt its own Rules of Procedure (Article III-341(3) Cst).

Likewise, as was suggested by the Working Party of Legal Experts of the IGC, the European Council has been expressly added to the list of institutions against which an action for annulment or an action for failure to act may be brought before the Court of Justice (Articles III-365(1) and III-367 Cst). It has also been specifically included, albeit together with the Council, in the list of separate sections of the budget (Article III-406 Cst).

Legal consequences of the European Central Bank becoming an institution

For the ECB, becoming an institution will not really change its political or legal situation, as its independence from the other institutions will still be guaranteed (Articles I-30(3) and III-188 Cst) and as the jurisdiction of the Court to review the legality of its acts was already provided for in the EC Treaty and in the Protocol on the Statute of the ECB.[3]

The institutions' powers and functioning

Each of the five 'core' institutions listed by the Constitution as part of the EU 'institutional framework' will see its powers increase, either through a widening of their scope, or through a change in its internal functioning likely to bring about more efficiency in its work and

---

[3] Arts. 230, 232, 237(d) and 241 EC Treaty and Art. 35 of the ECB Statute. On the question of whether or not the ECB is part of the Community structure and falls within EC law, see R. Torrent, 'Whom is the European Central Bank the Central Bank of? Reaction to Zilioli and Selmayr' (1999) vol. XXXVI *Common Market Law Review* 1229–1241. See also C. Zilioli and M. Selmayr, 'The External Relations of the Euro Area: Legal Aspects' (1999) vol. XXXVI *Common Market Law Review* 273–349, as well as 'The European Central Bank: an Independent Specialized Organization of Community Law' (2000) vol. XXXVII *Common Market Law Review* 591–644. The issue has been clarified by the Court of Justice in its judgment of 10 July 2003, Case C-11/00, *Commission v. ECB* (on OLAF Regulation) [2003] ECR p. I-7147, paras. 91 and 135: '91. . . . the fact that a body, office or agency owes its existence to the EC Treaty suggests that it was intended to contribute towards the attainment of the European Community's objectives and places it within the framework of the Community . . . 135. . . . recognition that the ECB has such independence does not have the consequence of separating it entirely from the European Community and exempting it from every rule of Community law. . . . Finally, it is evident that it was not the intention of the Treaty draftsmen to shield the ECB from any kind of legislative action taken by the Community legislature.'

decision-making and therefore to increase (or at least to maintain) its powers.

The European Parliament: more powers

The scope of the European Parliament's powers will increase through an extension in the scope of the codecision procedure, but also in other cases. Moreover, its composition will change.

Extension in the scope of codecision   Codecision will become the ordinary legislative procedure and its scope will be extended to about 40 more cases than at present.[4] The most noticeable sectors of extension are JHA, coordination of social security for migrant workers, culture, measures necessary for the use of the euro, the establishment at EU level of intellectual property rights and other centralised regimes, common organisation of the markets and general objectives in agriculture, definition of the framework for implementing the common commercial policy, amendments to the Statute of the Court and rules on 'comitology'.

Other cases of increase in the European Parliament's powers   The European Parliament will have the right to elect the President of the Commission proposed by the European Council, whose proposal should take into account the results of the elections to the European Parliament (Article I-27 Cst).[5]

The new budget procedure will also increase the European Parliament's powers (although the IGC modified the Convention's draft in

---

[4] See in Annex 2 the list of about 30 existing cases which will be switched to codecision. To this should be added the 11 new legal bases which provide for the codecision procedure. See in Annex 4 the list of new legal bases, of which there are 23 cases where QMV in the Council will apply, for 13 of which codecision will also apply.

[5] As events in the Autumn of 2004 relating to the nomination of the Commission headed by Mr Barroso have shown, the European Parliament is quite ready to make full use of the powers it is granted by the Treaty to approve the Commission President and the college of Commissioners. It has even, for some time already and going beyond what is laid down in the Treaty, developed a practice of hearing each Commissioner-designate individually before taking its decision of approval on the whole Commission. It was during this procedure of hearings in September 2004 that some of the Parliamentary Committees responsible for such hearings expressed concerns about some of the Commissioners-designate. The risk of a negative vote by the European Parliament on 27 October 2004 led President Barroso to withdraw his team from the approval vote and reconstitute and reshuffle it before submitting it to a successful vote of approval on 18 November 2004.

order to give more balanced powers to the Council) because there will no longer be so-called 'compulsory expenditure' (on which at present the Council has the last word), as opposed to 'non-compulsory expenditure' (on which at present the European Parliament has the last word) (Article III-404 Cst). Under the Constitution, the European Parliament will 'co-decide' with the Council on all expenditure.

Moreover, the scope of the procedures requiring, in some instances, the consent of the European Parliament and, in other instances, its mandatory consultation before the conclusion of an international agreement will both be enlarged (Article III-325(6) Cst).

Finally, the European Parliament will be allowed to propose a revision of the Constitution, either in the ordinary procedure for revision or in the simplified procedure (Articles IV-443(1) and IV-445(1) Cst). This was a long-standing request from the European Parliament, which up to now had been rejected by the Member States.

The composition of the European Parliament According to Article I-20(2) and (3) Cst 'the European Parliament shall be composed of representatives of the Union's citizens . . . elected for a term of five years by direct universal suffrage in a free and secret ballot'.

The number of the members of the European Parliament 'shall not exceed seven hundred and fifty' and 'Representation of citizens shall be degressively proportional, with a minimum of six members per Member State. No Member State shall be allocated more than ninety-six seats.' (Article I-20(2) Cst).

These criteria for the Parliament's composition (degressively proportional, with an upper limit of 96 seats for a given Member State and a lower limit of six) will not be sufficient to give automatically a single ready-made solution for the number of seats for each of the Member States. Therefore, the Constitution provides that the European Council will have to adopt by unanimity, on the initiative of the European Parliament and with its consent, a decision establishing the future composition of the European Parliament, in accordance with these criteria. This decision will have to be adopted in due time before the elections of 2009.

The minimum number of seats per Member State was hotly debated until the end of the IGC. The more populated States wanted a minimum number of four, the less populated ones a minimum of six. The final result, which provides for a minimum of six seats, is favourable to the smaller Member States. It was part of a package which included the reduction of the number of Commissioners, which had been something very difficult to accept for these States.

The European Council: a strengthened role

Apart from making it an institution, the main novelty brought about by the Constitution is that the European Council will no longer be chaired by a part-time and six-monthly rotating President. It will elect by QMV a full-time President for a mandate of two and a half years, renewable once (Article I-22 Cst). Besides its traditional role in giving political impetus, the European Council will also be in charge of all 'quasi-constitutional' functions.[6]

The European Council and its President will be assisted by the General Secretariat of the Council (Article III-341(4) Cst).[7] This was important in order to avoid the creation of a new bureaucracy and to avoid divergences of opinion between the existing Council's Secretariat and another Secretariat to be established which would have served the European Council.

These new provisions will make the role of the European Council in the institutional architecture clearer and more coherent. They will probably strengthen its function in establishing the political direction and priorities of the European Union and in providing it with the necessary impetus for its development.

The new office of President of the European Council   At present, pursuant to Article 4, 2nd subparagraph, of the EU Treaty, the European Council is chaired by the Head of State or Government of the Member State which holds the six-monthly rotating Presidency of the Council. This situation attracts from some quarters the same criticisms as those directed at the rotating system for the Council Presidency, i.e. difficulties

---

[6] Such as, for instance, the appointment of the Commission (Art. I-27 Cst), the appointment of the Union Minister for Foreign Affairs (Art. I-28(1) Cst), the decision to move to a common defence (Art. I-41(2) Cst), the decision to suspend certain rights resulting from Union membership in case of breach of EU fundamental values (Art. I-59 (3) Cst), the decision on a Member State's withdrawal from the Union (Art. I-60 Cst), the assessment of the fulfilment of criteria for becoming party to the euro zone (Art. III-198 (2) Cst), the 'emergency brakes' in social security, JHA and CFSP (Arts. III-136(2), III-270 (3), III-271(3) and III-300(2) 2nd subpara., Cst) and the Treaty revision procedures (Arts. IV-443, III-444 and III-445 Cst).

[7] The Heads of State or Government meeting on 29 June 2004 decided that Mr Pierre de Boissieu, current Deputy Secretary-General of the Council, will be appointed as the Secretary-General of the Council, when the Constitution enters into force, for the remainder of his present term of office.

in ensuring consistency and continuity in the work of the Council; changes of priorities in the EU's work every six months; lack of leadership; lack of time of the President to prepare the sessions of the European Council properly, given that this task comes on top of his or her normal tasks as Head of State or Government, etc.

Therefore, providing for a more stable Presidency of the European Council soon appeared as one of the main institutional issues during the Convention. The larger Member States were generally in favour of a President elected for a renewable period of two and a half years. The Commission and a number of the smaller Member States, which often prefer the six-monthly rotating Presidency as being more 'egalitarian', were opposed to this idea. They argued that it would undermine the position of the President of the Commission and that it would promote 'intergovernmentalism' at the expense of the Commission. As a consequence, the debate concentrated on the definition of the role of the President of the European Council. Should he or she be a real 'President' or only a 'Chairman' without any substantial power?

In the end, those in favour of having a stable President of the European Council were obliged to give up on their wish of entrusting him or her, in addition, with the chair of the General Affairs Council as well as with the task of coordinating the work of the different configurations of the Council. They were obliged to accept, instead, a rather vague job description and, at the same time, the establishment of a new so-called 'double-hatted' Union Minister for Foreign Affairs who would be a member of the Commission. This delicate balance was obtained thanks to a compromise between France (which was in favour of a strong President of the European Council but not enthusiastic about the concept of a 'double-hatted' Foreign Minister) and Germany (which was of the opposite view on both issues). This delicate balance will have to be kept in mind when implementing these particular provisions of the Constitution.

Under the Constitution, the European Council will elect its President, by QMV, for a term of two and a half years renewable once. This possible five years' duration corresponds to the duration of the mandates of the European Parliament and the Commission (including the Union Minister for Foreign Affairs) (Articles I-20(3) and I-26(3) Cst).[8] The President

---

[8] However, one has to remember that the European Parliament can adopt a censure motion on the Commission as a whole (including the Union Minister for Foreign Affairs as a Commission Member) (Arts. III-26(8) and III-340 Cst).

may not hold a national office at the same time (Article I-22(1) and (3) Cst).

The President's tasks will be (Article I-22(2) Cst):

- to chair the European Council and drive forward its work;
- to ensure the preparation and continuity of the work of the European Council in cooperation with the President of the Commission, and on the basis of the work of the General Affairs Council;
- to endeavour to facilitate cohesion and consensus within the European Council;
- to present a report to the European Parliament after each of the meetings of the European Council;
- to ensure, at his or her level and in that capacity, the external representation of the Union on issues concerning its common foreign and security policy, without prejudice to the powers of the Union Minister for Foreign Affairs.

Although the role of the President of the European Council in ensuring the external representation of the Union at his or her level will be 'without prejudice' to the powers of the Union Minister for Foreign Affairs, one may suppose that, in practice, it will not be easy to delimit their respective powers, as well as those of the Commission in external affairs.

The Council: more legitimate decision-making and a Minister for Foreign Affairs

The Constitution includes provisions designed to improve efficiency in the role and functioning of the Council. The main measure to improve its efficiency will of course be the increase in the number of legal bases where the Council acts by QMV. This, being coupled with a new QMV system designed to make it more legitimate and, in principle, simpler, should facilitate the decision-taking in an enlarged EU.

The other measure to improve the Council's efficiency is the change made to the Council's six-monthly rotating Presidency, notably through the creation of the new office of Union Minister for Foreign Affairs.

Extension in the coverage of Qualified Majority Voting (QMV) The coverage of QMV will be extended to about 40 more cases than at present.[9] The most notable sectors of extension are JHA, the accession

---

[9] This will be the case in more than 20 instances as compared with the present Treaties, to which should be added about 20 new legal bases where QMV will apply. See in Annex 3

to the European Convention on Human Rights,[10] the coordination of social security for migrant workers, the establishment of a permanent structured cooperation in defence and the definition of the EU Defence Agency's statute, seat and operational rules,[11] the unified representation of the euro on the international scene, culture, the diplomatic and consular protection of EU citizens abroad and the establishment at the EU level of intellectual property rights and other centralised regimes. The Council may also use QMV for concluding an agreement of withdrawal from the EU with a Member State, for amending the six-monthly rotation system of Council Presidency and for adopting the rules on 'comitology'.

However, it should be stressed that measures in a number of important sectors (about 60 legal bases) will continue to be adopted by unanimity, such as taxation, social security and social policy, measures on passports and identity cards, operational police cooperation, the establishment of an EU Public Prosecutor, own resources of the EU and the multiannual financial framework, the conclusion of trade agreements in certain sensitive fields, as well as most of the measures in CFSP including defence.[12] These issues are obviously very important and this is precisely the reason why unanimity there will remain the rule.

A new QMV method   A new QMV method has been agreed upon by the IGC, based on, but modifying, the approach proposed by the Convention on which the 'consensus' noted by its President had been rather weak, given the strong opposition of the representatives of the Governments of Poland and Spain. Under this new method, QMV will no longer be based on weighted votes attributed to each Member State, as has been the case since 1957. It will be based on a 'double majority'

the list of 24 existing legal bases which will be switched to QMV and in Annex 4 the list of new legal bases, in 23 of which QMV in the Council will apply.

[10] However, as all EU Member States are also Contracting Parties to the European Convention on Human Rights and as this Convention will need to be amended in order to accommodate in particular the fact that the EU is not a State, each of the EU States will keep a veto right in that capacity (see Protocol (no. 32) relating to Art. I-9(2) Cst on the accession of the Union to the European Convention on the Protection of Human Rights and Fundamental Freedoms).

[11] This Agency has already been established (see below in chapter V, under 'The innovations brought about by the Constitution').

[12] See in Annexes 5 and 6 the list of 59 provisions where unanimity and common accord will apply or will continue to apply in the Council. To these should be added the approximately 20 cases where unanimity or consensus will apply at the level of the European Council.

with two thresholds: 55% of the number of Member States and 65% of the Union's population (Article I-25 Cst) (see box 4.1). This new rule will enter into force on 1 November 2009, until which the present QMV as defined by the Treaty of Nice will continue to apply.

Box 4.1   Article I-25 of the Constitution reads:

'Definition of qualified majority within the European Council and the Council

1. A qualified majority shall be defined as at least 55% of the members of the Council, comprising at least fifteen of them and representing Member States comprising at least 65% of the population of the Union.
   A blocking minority must include at least four Council members, failing which the qualified majority shall be deemed attained.
2. By way of derogation from paragraph 1, when the Council does not act on a proposal from the Commission or from the Union Minister for Foreign Affairs, the qualified majority shall be defined as at least 72% of the members of the Council, representing Member States comprising at least 65% of the population of the Union.
3. Paragraphs 1 and 2 shall apply to the European Council when it is acting by a qualified majority.
4. (. . .)'

The primary reason why this double majority system was chosen was because it was considered, rightly or wrongly, easier to understand for the public and closer to what was seen as the essential nature of the EU, a Union of States and a Union of citizens as reflected in the first Article of the Constitution, which starts with the words 'Reflecting the will of the citizens and States of Europe to build a common future . . .' The other reason was to keep the QMV threshold low enough to facilitate the adoption of acts in an enlarged Council. This latter aim will be achieved, whereas the first one may be considered as having been missed.

A short history of qualified majority voting in the Council   One of the major elements of the political and institutional architecture of the Union, as it has been painstakingly built up and finely tuned over the years, is the close attention which the Member States have always given to the sharing and balance of powers, i.e. not only between the EU institutions, but also in the respective weight given to each Member State in the decision-taking system.

Member States participate in the decision-taking in each of the three main institutions, either indirectly through the presence and the number of their nationals in the European Parliament and in the Commission, or directly through the weight carried by their vote in the Council.

In the original EC of six Member States in 1957, the system of weighted votes in the Council was based implicitly on a balance of demographic, economic and political elements. As shown in the table below (page 100), the system was characterised by three 'clusters' of Member States: the larger ones (with four votes each, regardless of the differences in their respective populations), the middle-sized ones (with two votes each, despite the fact that Belgium is less populated than the Netherlands) and the smallest one (one vote). This was done for political reasons, to show that the building of a reconciled Europe was a common endeavour, based in particular on the equal weight of Germany and France within the European institutions.[13]

At that time, the three larger Member States (France, Germany and Italy) together could outvote the other three Member States, which together could not block a decision, but nor could a large Member State alone. This situation would last for the first 15 years of existence of the Community, until the first enlargement in 1973.

In the original Rome Treaty, the relative weakness of the smaller Member States was regarded by them as compensated for by the direct and indirect powers which the Treaty gave to the Commission. This institution was established in order to act independently in the sole interest of the Community, regardless of the power or influence of particular Member States. Therefore, it was considered as a reassuring and counter-balancing element for the smaller or less powerful Member States. The three 'counter-balancing' powers of the Commission were: first, its exclusive right of initiative, second, the requirement for unanimity within the Council to amend a Commission proposal

---

[13] Together, the Netherlands and Belgium had a voting weight identical to a large Member State. This particular feature would remain untouched until the Treaty of Nice gave one vote more to the Netherlands (13) than Belgium (12), which together no longer equalled a large Member State as they had until then. Under the Nice Treaty, only the three Benelux countries together can reach the 29 votes equivalent to that of a large State.

against the latter's will and, third, the 'super qualified majority' required in the Council (12 positive votes, including four members in
favour) when it acted without a Commission proposal. These original
'counter-balancing' powers still exist at present and have been retained
in the Constitution.

These 'counter-balancing' powers of the Commission, aimed at
favouring the smaller Member States, were themselves 'rebalanced' in
favour of the larger Member States through the fact that these States had
two Commissioners each in the Commission, whereas the smaller States
had only one Commissioner each. In a body acting by a simple majority,
this meant that, together, the Commissioners from the larger Member
States could outvote the Commissioners from the smaller Member
States. This particular feature would remain the same until the 1995
enlargement, when the ten Commissioners from the five larger Member
States would no longer be able to outvote the ten Commissioners from
the other Member States.

As from the first enlargement in 1973 onwards, the larger Member
States could no longer outvote the other ones in the Council. At each
successive enlargement thereafter, the system of weighted votes in the
Council was merely extrapolated so as to keep roughly the same
characteristics:

- three 'clusters' of Member States (the cluster of the large ones, in the range
  of ten and eight votes, the cluster of the middle-sized ones, with five and
  four votes, and the cluster of the small ones, with three and two votes);
- a QMV threshold of about 70–71% of the votes;
- the simple majority of Council members automatically 'contained' in
  any given qualified majority.

However, an element which at each enlargement steadily changed was
the share of the total votes given to the larger Member States, which
eroded from 70% in 1954 to 55% in 1995, while they represented about
80% of the total EU population in 1995 (75% after the last 2004
enlargement). The wide difference between these two figures (55% of
the votes and 80% of the citizens) was considered too large by the most
populated States.

In addition, the biggest of them, Germany, reunified on 3 October
1990, started already during the Amsterdam IGC to request that the
increase in its population be reflected in its weight in the institutions.
This is why the 1995 Accession Act gave Germany 99 members in the
European Parliament ('MEPs'), while the three other large Member

States had only 87 each. Before that, the four large Member States had an equal number of MEPs, 81 each.

This, and the constant erosion of the large Member States' share in the total of the votes within the Council, explains why the population criterion became such a contentious issue. This is why, during the Amsterdam IGC, both the issues of the weighting of votes in the Council and of the composition of the Commission in view of the coming waves of enlargement were so inextricably linked, and continued to be so in the Nice IGC and in the IGC on the Constitution. For the larger Member States, and particularly for Spain, renouncing 'their' second Commissioner meant they had to be 'compensated' by their voting weight in the Council. Moreover, Germany wanted the fact that it has the largest population to be acknowledged.

The Nice Treaty made the first step towards giving more importance to the demographic element. A double majority system (50% of States and 50% of EU population) had been advocated during the Nice IGC by the small Member States, Germany and the Commission, but was opposed by the other larger Member States, particularly by France and Spain. In the end, the Nice Treaty retained the system of weighted votes, with four 'clusters' of Member States. As a result, Germany and France still had (at least in appearance) the same number of votes each (29), while Spain got 27 votes, a generous, and hard fought for, 'compensation' for the loss of 'its' second Commissioner. However, thanks to the population 'safety net' under which a Council member 'may request verification that the Member States constituting the qualified majority represent at least 62% of the total population of the Union' (Article 205 (4) EC Treaty), Germany has obtained in effect more weight as compared with the other large Member States. These new QMV rules have been applicable since 1 November 2004 (for an overview, see table 4.1)

Although the demographic element has given rise, in the last two IGCs, to sometimes fierce opposition between the larger and the smaller Member States, it should be underlined that, in real life, a coalition of 'big' versus 'small' never occurs in the Council (nor, it seems, within the Commission). Majorities vary very much and form around specific subject-matters between 'like minded' Council members (net contributors to or recipients from the EU budget, those that wish stricter environment-friendly rules, those that wish more labour protection rules, those that are wine, sugar or textile producers, etc.).

Each time a new method of calculating QMV is negotiated, Member States try their best to keep enough power to protect their national

Table 4.1. *Weight of Council members' votes since 1957*

Member States	EU-6 votes + % of votes		EU-9 votes + % of votes		EU-10 votes + % of votes		EU-12 votes + % of votes		EU-15 votes + % of votes		EU-25[1] votes + % of votes		Population[2]	Share in EU population[3]
Germany	4	23.5	10	17.2	10	15.9	10	13.2	10	11.5	29	9	82 531.7	18.00%
France	4	23.5	10	17.2	10	15.9	10	13.2	10	11.5	29	9	61 684.7	13.45%
UK			10	17.2	10	15.9	10	13.2	10	11.5	29	9	59 651.5	13.01%
Italy	4	23.5	10	17.2	10	15.9	10	13.2	10	11.5	29	9	57 888.2	12.62%
Spain							8	10.5	8	9.2	27	8.4	42 345.3	9.23%
Poland											27	8.4	38 190.6	8.33%
Netherlands	2	11.8	5	8.6	5	7.9	5	6.6	5	5.7	13	4	16 258.0	3.55%
Greece					5	7.9	5	6.6	5	5.7	12	3.7	11 041.1	2.41%
Portugal							5	6.6	5	5.7	12	3.7	10 474.7	2.28%
Belgium	2	11.8	5	8.6	5	7.9	5	6.6	5	5.7	12	3.7	10 396.4	2.27%
Czech Republ.											12	3.7	10 211.5	2.23%
Hungary											12	3.7	10 116.7	2.21%
Sweden									4	4.6	10	3.1	8 975.7	1.96%
Austria									4	4.6	10	3.1	8 114.0	1.77%
Denmark			3	5.2	3	4.8	3	3.9	3		7	2.9	5 397.6	1.18%
Slovakia											7	2.9	5 380.1	1.17%
Finland									3	3.4	7	2.9	5 219.7	1.14%
Ireland			3	5.2	3	4.8	3	3.9	3	3.4	7	2.9	4 027.5	0.88%
Lithuania											7	2.9	3 445.9	0.75%
Latvia											4	1.2	2 319.2	0.51%

Member State / Category													Population	
Slovenia											4	1.2	1 996.4	0.44%
Estonia											4	1.2	1 350.6	0.29%
Cyprus											4	1.2	730.4	0.16%
Luxembourg	1	5.9	2	3.4	2	3.2	2	2.6	2	2.3	4	1.2	451.6	0.10%
Malta											3	0.9	399.9	0.09%
Total	17		58		63		76		87		321		458 599.0	
QMV	12		41		54		62		62		232			
QMV threshold	70.6%		70.7%		71.4%		71%		71.3%		72.3%			
Blocking min.	6		18		19		23		26		90			
Share of large Member States	70.5% of votes		68.8% of votes		63.6% of votes		63.3% of votes		55.2% of votes		52.8% of votes		74.64% of EU population	

[1] As from 1 November 2004, date of application of the new provisions of the Nice Treaty (the weighted votes were different during the period between the entry into force of the Accession Act of the ten new Member States on 1 May 2004 and 31 October 2004).

[2] Figures for 2005 as published in Council Decision of 11 October 2004 (OJ No. L319, 20 October 2004, p. 15).

[3] And therefore share in the votes for the calculation of the 62% condition under Art. 205(4) EC Treaty and for the second element of the voting system (65% of EU population) under Art. I-25 Cst.

interests. All of them try to imagine any possible scenario in which they could be outvoted and try to calculate their 'blocking power' in such situations. They also study all theoretical possibilities available for constructing qualified majorities or blocking minorities with 'like minded' Member States. Diplomats try to turn themselves into mathematicians.[14]

The debate on QMV in the Convention and in the IGC   In the Convention, the debate focused on introducing a new system, which would depart from the traditional one of weighted votes, because the latter had been criticised as being too complicated to be understood by ordinary people. The Convention therefore recommenced the whole discussion about the so-called 'double majority' system which had already taken place during the Nice IGC.

The double majority thresholds finally proposed by the Convention (50% of the number of States and 60% of the EU population) were satisfactory neither for the small Member States, nor for Poland and Spain. The small Member States argued that the population threshold was too high when compared with the States' threshold. Poland and Spain opposed the population method as such and argued that, especially when compared with the weight they had obtained in the Nice Treaty, the population threshold was in any case too low.

As a consequence, the IGC had to renegotiate the figures suggested by the Convention, in order to make them acceptable both for Poland and Spain and for the small Member States. The resistance from Poland and Spain to the new QMV method was one of the main reasons for the failure of the IGC in December 2003. Then, following its change of government in March 2004, Spain agreed to continue the discussion on the basis of the new QMV method, but requested a population threshold of two-thirds (66.66%), in order to keep a 'blocking power' comparable to the one which it had obtained under the Nice Treaty. This new position resulted in the isolation of Poland, which concentrated its efforts on obtaining, in addition, a 'Ioannina-like' solution (see box 4.2, p. 104 about the 1994 'Ioannina decision').

---

[14] In June 2004, a group of mathematicians argued that the clearest way of ensuring respect for the basic democratic principle would have been to give each Member State a voting weight equivalent to the square root of its population (see paper by the 'Scientists for a democratic Europe' reproduced at http://www.ruhr-uni-bochum.de/mathphys/politik/eu/open-letter.htm).

At the end of the IGC in June 2004, as one could have foreseen, it was necessary to increase both thresholds: 55% for the threshold of States and 65% for the threshold of population. A first collateral damage of that was a raising of the QMV threshold, thus making the adoption of acts in the Council more difficult. In addition, the result would have allowed any three of the four largest Member States to form a blocking minority, which was unacceptable not only for the small Member States, but also for Spain, which would no longer have been instrumental in all such combinations of large Member States to form a blocking minority.

For these reasons, the IGC added a further requirement that a blocking minority must include at least four Council members, otherwise a QMV is deemed to be attained. This was a small facilitating mechanism for decision-making,[15] as well as a reassurance to Spain. At the last minute, at the request of Austria, the IGC also added a requirement that the 55% threshold of States should comprise at least 15 of them. This was a sweetener for the small Member States in order to reduce the gap between the two percentages which they always claimed should be as narrow as possible so as to keep a 'parity' between the two thresholds. Since, in a Union of 25, 15 States represent 60% of the Member States, this requirement has effectively resulted in increasing the threshold of States to 60%. In an EU of 27, however, i.e. as from when Bulgaria and Romania will have become members, this requirement will lose its significance as it will correspond to the 55% threshold of States.

Moreover, in order to accommodate the concerns of Poland, it was decided that, when the Constitution enters into force, the Council will adopt the 'decision relating to the implementation of Article I-25' which is contained in Declaration no. 5 to the Final Act of the IGC and which is inspired by the 'Ioannina decision' of 1994. The decision contained in Declaration no. 5 provides that even when a qualified majority is reached on a given dossier, a member of the Council may ask for the matter to be discussed further when the minority on that dossier is close to the blocking minority provided for in the Treaty (i.e. when the minority represents three-quarters of 35.01% of the population and/or

---

[15] Another effective facilitating mechanism had been proposed during the IGC. It consisted in not counting abstentions any more. However, due to the opposition of Germany, this proposal was not retained: 'Abstentions shall not be taken into account when counting the total number of Council members and of population' (see p. 7 of document CIG 83/ 04 of 18 June 2004). Consequently, as is the case today, an abstention will continue to be equal to a negative vote.

three-quarters of 45.01% of States).[16] This decision makes it look as if
the two thresholds in the double majority would be increased respectively to 66% of States and 74% of the population. That is the case in
theory. Therefore, Poland was quite happy to have obtained this result.
However, this will not be the case in reality, because the decision also
provides, as did the 'Ioannina' Decision of 1994, that the Council's Rules
of Procedure must always be respected. Since these Rules provide in their
Article 11(1) that a simple majority of the Council may request that
a vote (according to the normal Treaty rules) take place, the future
decision will probably have similar results to the 1994 Decision.

Box 4.2   The 'Ioannina Decision' of 1994

At the end of the accession negotiations with Austria, Finland and
Sweden in 1994, the issue of the adaptation of the weighting of votes
attributed to each member of the Council and of the QMV threshold
in the Council was a very acute problem and blocked the finalisation
of the negotiations. The mere extrapolation of the number of votes
attributed to each Member State, as had been done for the previous
accessions, appeared to give more weight to the States with less
population and to reduce the proportion of population represented
by a qualified majority. Two Member States in particular (UK and
Spain) denounced that as being unacceptable.

After very difficult negotiations, a solution was finally found at an
informal meeting of the 12 Foreign Ministers in Ioannina (Greece).
This solution took the form of a Decision of the Council.[1] Pursuant
to that Decision, if members of the Council representing 23 to 25
votes (i.e. close to the threshold of 26 votes required to form a
blocking minority) indicated their intention to vote against the adoption by the Council of an act by a qualified majority, the Council
would do its utmost to reach a satisfactory solution that could be

---

[16] Under Art. 1 of this draft decision 'if members of the Council, representing: (a) at least
three quarters of the population; or (b) at least three quarters of the number of Member
States, necessary to constitute a blocking minority resulting from the application of
Article I-25(1), first subparagraph, or Article I-25(2), indicate their opposition to the
Council adopting an act by a qualified majority, the Council shall discuss the issue'. Art. 4
states that the decision will 'take effect on 1 November 2009. It shall remain in force at
least until 2014. Thereafter the Council may adopt a European decision repealing it.' The
Council will act by QMV.

adopted by at least 65 votes (instead of the 62 votes which were legally sufficient for the adoption).

However, the Decision made clear that, during that period, the Council's Rules of Procedure would always have to be respected. As these Rules provide that a simple majority of the Council may ask for a vote to take place, it explains why the application of this compromise has very rarely been invoked, and why it has never involved delaying more than one day for the act to be adopted.

Note: [1] Council Decision of 29 March 1994 concerning the taking of decisions by qualified majority by the Council (OJ No. C105, 13 April 1994, p.1), amended on 1 January 1995 (OJ No. C1, 1 January 1995, p. 1).

Although these compromises had the major advantage of enabling Spain and Poland to present the IGC results as a political success for them, they caused further collateral damage to the supposed simplicity of the new QMV system, thus undermining one of the main arguments which were used to support the introduction of this system. One could even see the new system as less simple and less transparent than the classic weighted votes system, where the number of votes attributed to each Member State is clearly set out in a table which allows the reader to see immediately how many weighted votes each State has and how it compares with others.

Changes to the six-monthly rotating Presidency of the Council   Other measures which have been taken with the aim of increasing the efficiency of the functioning of the Council are the changes made to its six-monthly rotating Presidency. The Union Minister for Foreign Affairs, appointed for a five-year mandate, will chair the Foreign Affairs Council (Article I-28(3) Cst). Similarly, the Eurogroup, although not being transformed into a formal configuration of the Council, but remaining an informal meeting of the finance ministers of the euro zone, will be chaired by a President elected by his peers, by a simple majority, for two and a half years.[17] Combined with an elected President of the European Council, these stabilising measures for the Presidency of the Council should increase the consistency and the efficiency of its functioning.

[17] See Art. 2 of the Protocol (no.12) on the Eurogroup. At its meeting on 10 and 11 September 2004, the Eurogroup had already chosen Mr Jean-Claude Juncker, Prime Minister and Finance Minister of Luxembourg, as President of the Eurogroup for two years as from 1 January 2005.

However, the other Council configurations[18] will be chaired by pre-established groups of three Member States (so-called 'team Presidencies') for a period of 18 months, constituted on the basis of equal rotation (for the list of future presidencies until 2020, see box 4.3). These groups of three will cooperate on the basis of a programme established in common for a duration of 18 months. Given that, unless they decide an alternative arrangement among themselves, each member of such a group will in turn chair for six months all configurations of the Council (except the Foreign Affairs one), the six-monthly Presidency will, in effect, continue more or less as at present.[19]

However, contrary to the situation under the present Treaty where a formal amendment to Article 203 of the EC Treaty, involving ratification by the Member States, would be required to change the rotating presidency system for the Council,[20] the European Council will be able to directly change the system by QMV (Article I-24(7) Cst).

It remains to be seen whether and how a proper coordination of these configurations will be ensured. The Constitution provides that the General Affairs Council will be in charge of ensuring 'consistency in the work of the different Council configurations' and that it will 'prepare and ensure the follow-up to meetings of the European Council, in liaison with the President of the European Council and the Commission'

---

[18] At present, the Council, although indivisible, meets in nine different configurations, depending on the subject matters on its agenda (Environment, JHA, Finance and budget, etc.; see Art. 2 of the Council's Rules of Procedure and the list of configurations in Annex I to these Rules, OJ No. L106, 15 April 2004, p. 22, amended by Council Decision of 11 October 2004, OJ No. L319, 20 October 2004, p. 15). This situation is acknowledged in Art. I-24 Cst. The number of these configurations may be amended at present by a simple majority decision of the 'General Affairs' Council (Art. 2(1) of the Rules of Procedure). Under the Constitution, this list will be established by a QMV decision of the European Council (Art. I-24(4) Cst).

[19] See the draft European Council Decision on the exercise of the Presidency of the Council contained in Declaration no. 4 to the Final Act of the IGC. At present, the Council's Rules of Procedure already provide for close cooperation between the two Presidencies of a given year, which have to establish an annual work programme for the Council, based on a three-year strategic work programme adopted by the European Council. They also provide for the chairing of meetings dealing with the EC annual budget by the Presidency of the second semester and for cooperation between the two successive Presidencies (see Arts. 2(4) and (5), 19(5) and (6) and 20(2) of the Council's Rules of Procedure).

[20] However, at present, Art. 19(4) of the Council's Rules of Procedure enables the Council to decide, by simple majority, that a committee created by the Treaty (other than Coreper) be chaired by another president than the ordinary six-monthly rotating presidency. Coreper may also take such a decision, by simple majority, with regard to the chairmanship of other committees and working groups of the Council.

(Article I-24(2) Cst). The President of the European Council and the President of the Commission could also play important roles in that respect.

Box 4.3   The rotation of Council Presidencies from 2005 to 2020[1]

The IGC agreed upon a draft Decision of the European Council concerning the exercise of the Presidency of the Council (which is contained in Declaration no. 4 to the Final Act of the Conference). This Declaration also provided that the Council was to prepare, within six months from the signature of the Constitution, a draft implementing decision, which it did on 13 December 2004.[2] The list of the six-monthly rotating presidencies until 2020 is as follows:

Under the existing Decision of 1995[3]

Luxembourg	January–June 2005
United Kingdom	July–December 2005
Austria	January–June 2006
Finland	July–December 2006

Under the draft Decision of December 2004

Germany	January–June 2007
Portugal	July–December
Slovenia	January–June 2008
France	July–December
Czech Republic	January–June 2009
Sweden	July–December
Spain	January–June 2010
Belgium	July–December
Hungary	January–June 2011
Poland	July–December
Denmark	January–June 2012
Cyprus	July–December
Ireland	January–June 2013
Lithuania	July–December
Greece	January–June 2014
Italy	July–December

Latvia	January–June 2015
Luxembourg	July–December
Netherlands	January–June 2016
Slovakia	July–December
Malta	January–June 2017
United Kingdom	July–December
Estonia	January–June 2018
Bulgaria	July–December
Austria	January–June 2019
Romania	July–December
Finland	January–June 2020

Note: [1] Until the entry into force of the Constitution, this list will be valid, but the European Council and the Foreign Affairs Council will continue to be chaired by the representative of the Member State holding the six-monthly rotating Presidency.
[2] See Council documents nos. 15865/04 and 15866/04, accessible on the Council's Registry of documents [http://register.consilium.eu.int].
[3] See Council Decision of 1 January 1995 determining the order in which the office of President of the Council shall be held (OJ No. L1, 1 January 1995, p. 220), amended by Council Decision of 28 January 2002 (OJ No. L39, 9 February 2002, p. 17).

The new office of Union Minister for Foreign Affairs A further measure designed to increase the efficiency of the Council is the new office of Union Minister for Foreign Affairs, who will be at the same time a member (Vice-President) of the Commission. This stable figure will be in charge of CFSP in lieu of the six-monthly rotating Presidency of the Council and of the present High Representative for CFSP (for more details on CFSP and the Minister, see below under Chapter V, Section 2, under 'Foreign policy').[21]

The Union Minister will conduct the Union's CFSP, a task which he will carry out 'as mandated by the Council' and, at the same time, he will

[21] At present, the six-monthly rotating Presidency is in charge of chairing the 'External Affairs' Council, representing the EU abroad, implementing CFSP decisions and negotiating international agreements in CFSP matters (see Arts. 18 and 24 EU Treaty). Under the Constitution, all these functions will be dealt with by the Union Minister for Foreign Affairs. The Heads of State or Government, meeting on 29 June 2004, decided that Mr Javier Solana, the present Secretary-General of the Council, High Representative for CFSP, will be appointed as the future first Union Minister for Foreign Affairs, when the Constitution enters into force.

'be responsible within the Commission for responsibilities incumbent on it in external relations' for which he will be bound by Commission procedures (Article I-28 Cst). The purpose of this peculiar construction is to try and enhance the consistency of the EU's external action, i.e. between its present CFSP and EC pillars. In performing his mandate, the Minister will be assisted by a 'European External Action Service' (Article III-296(3) Cst), which will be a kind of European Diplomatic Service.

It has already been agreed that a member of this Service will chair the Political and Security Committee. It would also be logical that members of the Service should chair the Council working groups directly linked to CFSP and ESDP. This seems to follow implicitly from the text of Article 2 of the draft European Council decision on the exercise of the Presidency of the Council contained in Declaration no. 4 to the Final Act.[22]

The Convention's failed attempt to create a 'legislative Council' The Convention, in Article 23(1) of its draft Constitution, had proposed the creation of a 'Legislative Council' which, according to some of its supporters, would have been the sole 'counterpart' of the European Parliament for adopting, in codecision, all legislative acts. This idea had originally been advocated by the representatives of the Commission and of the European Parliament in the Convention. They wanted this new configuration of the Council to have the monopoly of adopting legislative acts on the Council's side, instead of the present system, where the dossiers are dispatched to different Council configurations depending on the subject-matter. This would have symbolised for them the fact that the Council is the second chamber of the legislature in the Union, the first chamber, directly elected by the citizens, being the European Parliament. They found a forceful ally in the person of one of the two deputy-Presidents of the Convention, Giuliano Amato, former President of the Council of the Italian Republic.

---

[22] The second and third subparas. of this Article read: 'The Chair of the Political and Security Committee shall be held by a representative of the Union Minister for Foreign Affairs. The chair of the preparatory bodies of the various Council configurations, with the exception of the Foreign Affairs configuration, shall fall to the member of the group chairing the relevant configuration, unless decided otherwise in accordance with Article 4.'

This suggestion from the Convention was the first which the IGC agreed to dismiss in order to stick to the present, and more flexible, system of Council configurations which best suits the organisational needs of the Council and of the Member States. A 'Legislative Council' would have virtually forced each Member State to designate one minister (or 'super-minister') to represent its government in this particular configuration, thus creating problems in 'coalition' governments. It would also have cut off the sectoral ministers from the legislative items which their ministries would have to implement afterwards. Alternatively, it would have resulted in a queue of impatient and frustrated sectoral ministers waiting in the corridors for their item on the agenda to be discussed. Moreover, the legislative items would no longer have been discussed by the same configuration as their corresponding non-legislative items, thus creating inconsistencies in policy making.[23] Finally, the Council's freedom to organise its proceedings and to exploit fully the flexible arrangements of its Rules of Procedure would have been curtailed.[24]

Keeping the present system of configurations did not prevent the IGC from providing for full publicity of the deliberations of the Council when it discusses and votes on legislative acts, which is quite logical. To that end, the Council's agendas will be divided into a legislative part, for which it will meet in public (through audio-visual means), and a non-legislative part, for which the meetings will not be public but the current rules on access to documents and other transparency rules will continue to apply (see Article I-24(6) Cst).

The Commission: streamlined and more efficient

Together with the new QMV, the issue of the size and composition of the Commission was one of the most passionately debated, both in the Convention and in the IGC.

---

[23] For instance, the 'Legislative Council' would have debated and adopted the law on 'taxation of savings' whereas the 'Ecofin' Council, composed of Ministers for Economic Affairs and Finance, would have negotiated corresponding agreements with relevant third countries; the 'Environment Council' would have negotiated the 'Kyoto' Protocol on climate change whereas the 'Legislative Council' would have adopted the internal EU laws to implement it within the EU.

[24] Such as the use of the so-called 'A items' system which enables any Council configuration, regardless of the subject-matter at stake, to adopt an item in the 'A part' of its agenda, i.e. the part reserved for items to be adopted without discussion because they have already been resolved either by another Council configuration or in the preparatory bodies of the Council (see Art. 3(6) of the Council's Rules of Procedure).

The most important measure designed to increase the efficiency of the Commission, i.e. the reduction of the number of Commissioners from one per Member State to two-thirds of the number of Member States, with a system of equal rotation, will be applied only as from 2014 (Article I-26(6) Cst).

However, according to the transitional rules in the Constitution (Article I-26(5) Cst), i.e. until 2014, the Commission will be composed of one national per Member State. This composition runs the risk of the Commission falling into a sort of intergovernmentalism. Why? Because Member States have a tendency to identify sometimes 'their' Commissioner as 'their representative' in the Commission, to defend 'their' interests. This runs contrary to the spirit and the letter of the Treaties which state the independence of the Commission members from governments.[25] It is also to be recalled that all the decisions of the Commission are adopted by a simple majority, with one vote per Commissioner. Therefore, this 'intergovermentalist' tendency could jeopardise the legitimacy of the Commission's decisions, since these decisions could be taken by a majority of 13 Commissioners 'representing' only 10.4% of the EU population. Such a majority could easily outvote the six Commissioners who are nationals of the largest Member States having 75% of the EU population. This of course is completely theoretical. However, the argument might be used in order to weaken the legitimacy of the Commission's decisions when it deals with politically sensitive dossiers (notably in the field of competition, merger control or State aid). This being said, others are of the opinion that only a commission composed of one commissioner per Member State is legitimate.

It should anyway be remembered that if the Constitution does not enter into force before 1 November 2009, the Nice Treaty will apply to that next Commission. According to Article 4(2) of the Protocol on the enlargement of the European Union adopted at Nice, 'as from the date on which the first Commission following the date of accession of the 27th Member State of the Union takes up its duties', which is 1 November 2009, 'the number of Members of the Commission shall be less than the number of Member States'. They are to be chosen 'according to a rotation system based on the principle of equality, the implementation arrangement for which shall be adopted by the Council acting unanimously' and 'the number of Members of the Commission shall be set by the Council, acting unanimously'.

---

[25] See Art. 213(2) EC Treaty, repeated in Arts. I-26(7) and III-347 Cst.

As the Constitution was set to enter into force on 1 November 2006, i.e. before the date provided for the entry into force of the Accession Treaty with Bulgaria and Romania (which should enter into force on 1 January 2007, or on 1 January 2008 at the latest, if the safeguard clause referred to in Article 4(2), 3rd subparagraph, of that Treaty is triggered by the Council), the reduction of the number of Commissioners provided for in the Nice Treaty would not have applied. However, if the Accession Treaty enters into force before the Constitution, this reduction will apply and the Council will have to adopt, in due time before the beginning of the next mandate of the Commission, the necessary decisions (i.e. set out the number of Commissioners and the rotation rules). One may think that the solutions found in Article I-26(6) Cst might help in that respect.

The debate on the size and composition of the Commission in the Convention and in the IGC   The smaller Member States have always insisted on the need to be 'represented' by one of their nationals in the Commission in order for the Commission to be more legitimate. Not without reason, they argue that, even if one of the largest Member States did not have one of its nationals as a member of the Commission, its interests could not and would not be ignored, but that the same would not be true for the smaller Member States. The larger Member States, for their part, insisted that the size of the Commission should be reduced, arguing that a Commission with 25 and more members would not function effectively, that its members are not there to represent the interests of the Member States and that a Commission reduced in size would be more collegial.

This is why, trying to square the circle, the Convention suggested a strange and complicated formula. According to that formula, each Member State would have had one of its nationals being a 'member of the Commission'. However, only some of these 'members' (called 'the European Commissioners') would have had the right to vote in the Commission. The other 'members' (called 'the Commissioners') would have participated in Commission meetings, but without the right to vote (see Article 25(3) of the draft text as submitted by the Convention to the President of the European Council on 18 July 2003).

Not surprisingly, this formula was rejected by all Member States during the IGC.

After long discussions, a compromise was finally found, based on three elements:

- equality between States: the rotation between the Commissioners will apply on a strictly equal footing, regardless of the size of the population of the Member States. Each Member State will have one of its nationals appointed as a Commissioner for two out of three mandates of the Commission. This system of equal rotation will be established by a unanimous decision of the European Council, in due time before 2014. Each successive Commission will be composed so as to reflect satisfactorily the demographic and geographical range of all the Member States;
- progressivity: the new system will only apply to the Commission which will be appointed in 2014 and not for the first Commission to be appointed after the foreseen entry into force of the Constitution (whose mandate will start in 2009);
- package deal with the composition of the European Parliament: the less populated Member States obtained the guarantee that each State, whatever its population, will have a minimum of six seats in the European Parliament.

Additional powers of the President of the Commission   Due to the fact that the Foreign Minister will also be a Vice-President of the Commission, the agreement of the President of the Commission will be required before his appointment by the European Council (Article I-28(1) Cst). The Commission's President, the Minister and the other members of the Commission will be subject, as a body, to a vote of consent by the European Parliament (Article I-27(2), 2nd subparagraph, Cst).

Conversely, if a motion of censure on the Commission is tabled before the European Parliament and adopted, the members of the Commission will have to resign as a body and the Minister will 'resign from the duties that he or she carries out in the Commission' (Articles I-26(8) and III-340 Cst). If the Commission's President asks the Minister to resign as a member of the Commission, the Minister will have to resign 'in accordance with the procedure set out in Article I-28(1)' which states that the European Council may end the Minister's mandate by QMV, with the agreement of the Commission's President.

The Court of Justice: an extended jurisdiction

The jurisdiction of the Court of Justice will be increased in three areas:

- first, the Court's jurisdiction will cover the whole area of JHA, an area which is at present partially excluded from its competence. This is

good news for the rule of law, the uniform application of EU law and
the protection of individual rights;

- secondly, despite the fact that CFSP will remain outside the Court's
  jurisdiction, the Court will have the power to review the legality of
  decisions providing for restrictive measures against natural or legal
  persons (Article III-376 Cst);
- thirdly, the scope of actions for annulment brought by individuals
  against EU regulatory acts will be increased by removing the
  condition that the act in question should be of individual concern
  to the individual. Pursuant to Article III-365(4) Cst, it will be
  sufficient that the EU regulatory act 'is of direct concern to him or her
  and does not entail implementing measures', whereas the present
  Article 230, 4th subparagraph, of the EC Treaty requires that the act
  be 'of direct and individual concern' to the individual.[26] During the
  review of the drafting of the text in the Working Party of Legal
  Experts of the IGC, it was suggested that the words 'a regulatory act',
  which occur only in Article III-365(4) Cst and are not defined, be
  replaced by the words 'a regulation or decision having no addressees',
  thus making it clear that the act in question is a non-legislative one
  and, if it is a decision, that it is the normative type of decision (i.e.
  without addressees) and not the individual type. However, this
  suggestion was not taken on board.

In addition, Article III-365(1) provides expressly that actions for annulment may also be brought against 'acts of bodies, offices or agencies of
the Union' (which is an improvement as compared with the present
scope of actions for annulment under Article 230 EC Treaty).

---

[26] The new wording in the Constitution responds to the latest case-law of the Court of
Justice which interpreted the limits of Art. 230 EC Treaty: 'according to the system for
judicial review of legality established by the Treaty, a natural or legal person can bring an
action challenging a regulation only if it is concerned both directly and individually.
Although this last condition must be interpreted in the light of the principle of effective
judicial protection by taking account of the various circumstances that may distinguish
an applicant individually . . . such an interpretation cannot have the effect of setting aside
the condition in question, expressly laid down in the Treaty, without going beyond the
jurisdiction conferred by the Treaty on the Community Courts . . . While it is,
admittedly, possible to envisage a system of judicial review of the legality of Community
measures of general application different from that established by the founding Treaty
and never amended as to its principles, it is for the Member States, if necessary, in
accordance with Article 48 EU, to reform the system currently in force' (see judgment of
25 July 2002, Case 50/00 P, *Union de Pequeños agricultores*, [2002] ECR, p. I-6719, paras.
44 and 45).

Furthermore, the name of the EU judicial institution as a whole will become 'Court of Justice of the European Union', which will comprise several bodies, each with its own area of jurisdiction: 'the Court of Justice', 'the General Court' (instead of the present 'Court of First Instance') and 'specialised courts' attached to the General Court (instead of the present 'judicial panels'). Choosing this single name for the Court as an institution allowed for the drafting of the provisions on the Court to be more precise, using the full name of the institution in all the general provisions and the specific name of its different bodies only in those provisions dealing with such bodies.

The Constitution will also improve the procedure for appointing judges as compared to the present system whereby each Member State communicates the name of the candidate of its choice,[27] who, in practice, is then automatically appointed. Pursuant to Article III-357 Cst, there will be a panel of seven persons chosen from among former judges from the Court of Justice, national supreme courts and lawyers of recognised competence, who will give an opinion on the candidates' suitability to perform the duties of Judge and Advocate-General. On the basis of this opinion, the judges will then be appointed by common accord of the governments of the Member States.[28]

Finally, the procedure for amending the Statute of the Court (by a law in codecision with QMV in the Council) will make it easier for the Court of Justice to adapt itself to new challenges (Article III-381 Cst).[29]

Section 2: More democracy: conferring increased rights on actors other than the EU institutions

The Constitution will confer increased rights on some actors other than the EU institutions: the national Parliaments, the Committee of the Regions and the EU's citizens. These increased rights are an additional

---

[27] In a few Member States, this choice is subject to an internal selection procedure.
[28] A similar procedure, with a Selection Committee, has already been used for the appointment of the judges to the recently created EU Civil Service Tribunal (see Council Decision of 2 November 2004 establishing the European Union Civil Service Tribunal, OJ No. L333, 9 November 2004, p. 7; Council Decision of 18 January 2005 concerning the conditions and arrangements governing the submission and processing of applications for appointment as a judge of the European Union Civil Service Tribunal, OJ No. L50, 23 February 2005, p. 7; and Council Decision of 22 July 2005 appointing Judges of the European Union Civil Service Tribunal, OJ No. L197, 28 July 2005, p. 28).
[29] For a more detailed analysis, see L. W. Gormley, 'The Judicial Architecture of the European Union in the Constitution' in Peter G. Xuereb (ed.), *The Constitution for Europe: An Evaluation* (EDRC, Medial Centre Print, Malta, 2005) pp. 57–72.

attempt to bring in the people, to try to give them other channels than
the European Parliament (directly elected) and the Council (composed
of members of governments responsible to their people) through which
to express their wishes and concerns.

The national Parliaments

Members of national Parliaments had requested for years, notably
through their meetings in the 'COSAC',[30] that the EU institutions should
take into account their opinions, in particular when drafting and
adopting legislative acts. The Constitution will give national Parliaments
the right to receive information directly from the EU institutions (i.e.
not through their national government) and a direct role in controlling
respect for the principle of subsidiarity (Article I-11(3) Cst),[31] as well as
in different evaluation and monitoring mechanisms in the field of JHA
(Article I-42(2) Cst) and in a new simplified revision procedure of the
Constitution (Article IV-444 Cst).

A right of direct information from the EU institutions and a direct role in controlling respect for the principle of subsidiarity

The Protocol on the role of national Parliaments in the EU and the
Protocol on the application of the principles of subsidiarity and proportionality will provide for direct relationships between EU institutions
and national Parliaments. Such a direct link is an innovation as compared with the present situation where information has to go via national governments. Not only all draft EU legislative acts, but also EU

---

[30] The present Protocol on the role of national Parliaments in the European Union
provides, in Part II under paras. 4 to 7, that the Conference of European Affairs
Committees of national Parliaments 'may make any contribution it deems appropriate
for the attention of the institutions of the European Union'. This Conference was
established in November 1989. Its name 'COSAC' is an acronym from its full name in
French: 'Conférence des organes spécialisés dans les affaires communautaires et
européennes des parlements de l'Union européenne' (www.cosac.org).

[31] For an analysis and suggestions made at the time of the Convention, see my contribution
of 25 June 2002 to the Working Group I 'Subsidiarity' set up by the Convention,
in Working document 4 (WG I-WD 4), of 27 June 2002 (available on the internet site of
the Convention). See also doc. WG IV-WD 33, of 8 October 2002, on the
implementation of the Protocol on national parliaments, COSAC and openness in the
Council.

legislative programmes, as well as consultation documents from the Commission on legislative matters, Council minutes of its deliberations on legislative acts and the annual report of the Court of Auditors will be forwarded directly by the EU institutions concerned to the national Parliaments for scrutiny and comments.

As is already the case now,[32] legislative acts may not be adopted by EU institutions before a six-week period has elapsed from the transmission of the draft act to national Parliaments. The Protocol makes clear that 'where the national Parliamentary system is not unicameral [the provisions] shall apply to the component chambers'.[33]

A national Parliament may send, within six weeks from such transmission, a reasoned opinion to the EU institutions stating why it considers that the draft legislative act does not comply with the principle of subsidiarity.[34] Such reasoned opinion must be taken into account by the authors of the draft legislative act.

A further step, nicknamed the 'yellow card' system after soccer vocabulary,[35] provides that, if a reasoned opinion is expressed by one-third of the total number of votes allocated to national Parliaments for such purposes (or one-fourth in the field of JHA), the draft must be reviewed (each national Parliament or chamber thereof is allocated one vote).[36]

Finally, the jurisdiction of the Court of Justice to review the legality of EU legislative acts on grounds of infringement of the principle of subsidiarity in an action for annulment brought by a Member State is restated, with the addition of a possible action 'notified by [Member States] in accordance with their legal order on behalf of their national Parliament or a chamber of it'.[37]

---

[32] See para. 3 of the existing Protocol on the role of national Parliaments in the European Union.

[33] See Arts. 1, 2, 4, 5, 7 and 8 of the Protocol on the role of national Parliaments in the Union. Belgium has made a unilateral Declaration to the Final Act of the IGC according to which, in accordance with its constitutional law, it is not only parliament chambers at the federal level which are component chambers, but parliamentary assemblies of the Communities and Regions also act as components of the national parliamentary system (see Declaration no. 49).

[34] See Art. 6 of the Protocol on the application of the principles of subsidiarity and proportionality (subsidiarity Protocol).

[35] As opposed to a 'red card' system which would have allowed national Parliaments to put a halt directly to the EU legislative process.

[36] See Art. 7 of the subsidiarity Protocol.

[37] See Art. 8 of the subsidiarity Protocol.

Evaluation and scrutiny of certain activities in the field of Justice and Home Affairs

In the field of JHA, the national Parliaments are to be informed, as is the case for the European Parliament, of the content and results of the evaluation system of the implementation of JHA policies by Member States. This system is to be put in place by the Council (Article III-260 Cst). The national Parliaments will also participate, together with the European Parliament, in a scrutiny procedure of Europol's activities to be laid down by a law in codecision (Article III-276(2), 3rd subparagraph, Cst). The same will apply to their involvement in the evaluation of Eurojust's activities (Article III-273(1), 3rd subparagraph, Cst).

Active role in the simplified revision procedure of the Constitution

The national Parliaments will take an active part in the application of the simplified procedure established to modify certain provisions of the Constitution, called the general 'passerelle' or 'bridge' (Article IV-444 Cst). This allows the European Council to decide by unanimity, with the consent of the European Parliament, to switch a legal basis from unanimity to QMV (with the exception of defence) or from a special legislative procedure to the ordinary legislative procedure (codecision). The European Council must notify its intention to the national Parliaments, which will have six months to notify any opposition. It is a 'silence procedure': if no objection is made, the decision may be adopted. Therefore, each national Parliament will have a right of veto.

These different measures introduced by the Constitution to increase the role of national Parliaments within the EU political game are quite innovative and will have some consequences, at least in certain Member States, for the relationship between the two chambers of the national Parliament (where such chambers exist) and between the Parliament and the government (particularly in the case of a minority government).

The Committee of the Regions

The Committee of the Regions is composed of representatives of regional and local bodies who hold local electoral mandates or are accountable to an elected assembly. It will gain the right to bring actions before the Court of Justice for the annulment of EU legislative acts for infringement of the subsidiarity principle, in cases where its consultation is mandatory under the relevant legal basis.[38] The Committee of the Regions will obtain also the right to bring actions for annulment in order to protect its own prerogatives (Article III-365(3) Cst).

The EU's citizens

For the first time, EU citizens themselves will be given, in addition to the other rights they already have to influence the EU process, a direct right to bring a so-called 'citizens' initiative' signed by 'not less than one million citizens who are nationals of a significant number of Member States'. Through such an initiative, they will be able to invite the Commission, within the framework of its powers, to submit appropriate proposals on matters for which they consider that a legal act of the EU is required (Article I-47(4) Cst). The details of this new right will have to be provided for in a law to be adopted in codecision (such as the minimum number of Member States from which such citizens must come, the minimum number of signatories per Member State, what definition to give to the word 'citizen' in this context, procedural questions, control of signatures, etc.).

This provision is very innovative and symbolic. One million signatures out of 450 million people is a rather easy target to reach and different groups and NGOs are already preparing draft 'citizens' initiatives'. Although the Commission will not be legally obliged to follow up on any such initiative, the political weight of it will, in practice, force the Commission to engage in serious work following the receipt of an initiative.

This novelty is to be added to the rights of citizens which already exist and which are designed to enable them to influence the EU process, such as the right to vote in the European Parliament elections, the right to petition the European Parliament, the right to apply to the European Ombudsman, the right to address the institutions in any of the Constitution's languages and to obtain a reply in that language (Articles I-10(2) (d), III-334 and III-335 Cst), etc.

In addition, Part I of the Constitution has been drafted in a manner that highlights everything related to the rights of citizens, whether it be the right to move and reside freely within the EU, the right to vote and to

[38] See Art. I-32(2) Cst and Art. 8, 2nd subpara., of the subsidiarity Protocol.

stand as candidates in elections to the European Parliament and in municipal elections in their Member State of residence, the right to enjoy diplomatic and consular protection from any Member State and the right to address the EU institutions in any of the Constitution's languages (Article I-10 Cst). There is also in Part I a whole Title VI on the democratic life of the Union which states the principles of the equality of citizens, of representative democracy, of participatory democracy and refers also to the dialogue with social partners, to the right to complain to the Ombudsman, to the transparency of the Union's proceedings, to the right of access to EU documents and to the protection of personal data.

Finally, the IGC decided to introduce a second paragraph in Article IV-448 of the Constitution on the languages into which the Constitution may be translated (in addition to the usual provision on the languages in which the text is authentic, which corresponds to the present Articles 53 of the EU Treaty and 314 of the EC Treaty). Under this new paragraph, the Constitution 'may also be translated into any other languages as determined by Member States among those which, in accordance with their constitutional order, enjoy official status in all or part of their territory. A certified copy of such translation shall be provided by the Member States concerned to be deposited in the archives of the Council.' The translations into these languages would therefore not be 'authentic texts' within the meaning of the first paragraph of Article IV-448 Cst, but only translations for the benefit of those EU citizens which use these languages.[39]

---

[39] At the time of writing (September 2005), three Member States had made use of this possibility and deposited in the Council's archives translations of the Constitution in other languages than those listed in Art. IV-448(1) Cst: Spain, which deposited translations into the Catalan/Valencian, Basque and Galician languages, the Netherlands which deposited a translation into the Frisian language and the UK which deposited a translation into the Welsh language. In the meantime, the Irish language was added to the list of official languages and working languages of the EU institutions, the number of official languages therefore being 22 (to which Bulgarian and Romanian will be added) (OJ No. L156, 18 June 2005, p. 3). As regards languages, other than those listed in the above-mentioned list, whose status is recognised by the Constitution of a Member State on all or part of its territory or the use of which as a national language is authorised by law, the Council may, through an administrative arrangement with the Member State concerned and upon request from that State, authorise the use of such languages under certain conditions (e.g. that the costs incurred be borne by the requesting State) (see Conclusions of the General Affairs Council of 13 June 2005, accessible on the internet site of the Council (press release no. 9499/05)).

Section 3: Establishing 'facilitating' mechanisms for a more flexible functioning of the EU

The last type of institutional changes brought about by the Constitution are a number of 'facilitating' mechanisms that are designed to allow for more flexibility in the functioning of an enlarged EU. These changes are the following:

- a modified 'enhanced cooperation' procedure;
- an additional case of 'inbuilt closer cooperation';
- different kinds of 'passerelles', both general and specific, allowing for the adoption of amendments to the Constitution through lighter procedures than the ordinary one;
- a general simplified revision procedure to amend Title III of Part III of the Constitution on internal policies and competences;
- specific simplified revision procedures to amend certain provisions of the Constitution; and
- an express right for a Member State to withdraw voluntarily from the EU.

With regard to the different procedures which allow for amending the provisions of the Constitution without having to follow the full ordinary procedure, they still require, as is the case under the present Treaties, unanimity of the Governments of the Member States. While the ordinary revision procedure involves ratification in each Member State (Article IV-443 Cst), the 'passerelles' use a lighter, but still unanimous, procedure, as do the few specific procedures which allow the Council to amend a particular Article of the Constitution.[40]

Therefore, contrary to what has been said in certain quarters, the Constitution is not 'cast in bronze or in marble'. It is not more difficult to amend than the present Treaties. Actually, it is quite the opposite, thanks to the new general and specific 'passerelles' which have been introduced into the text.

---

[40] Only two Articles allow the Council to amend, by QMV and in codecision with the European Parliament, certain provisions of Protocols, i.e. the Protocol on the Statute of the European Central Bank (see Art. III-187(3) Cst, corresponding to Art. 107 EC which already provides for QMV) and the Protocol on the Statute of the Court (see Art. III-381 Cst, corresponding to Art. 245 EC which, at present, provides for unanimity).

A modified 'enhanced cooperation' procedure

Enhanced cooperation, which was designed to allow some Member States, using the EU structure, to cooperate further between themselves in cases where the others do not wish to do so, has existed on paper ever since 1997 (Amsterdam Treaty).[41] However, perhaps due to political reasons (avoiding a 'two-speed Europe'), perhaps due to the strict conditions attached to launching it, the procedure has never been used so far, despite the fact that the Nice Treaty provided for QMV in order to make it easier to launch.

The Constitution regroups all the enhanced cooperation provisions from four sets of rules in the existing Treaties (due to the pillar structure) into one set of rules set out in Parts I (for the generalities, Article I-44 Cst) and III (for the details, Article III-423 Cst). It will make only slight improvements as compared with the existing procedure:

• it will widen its scope to cover the whole CFSP field, including defence, whereas at present it only covers the implementation of a CFSP action which has already been decided upon;
• it will remove the so-called 'emergency brake' procedure, which at present allows a Council member to request that the question of an authorisation for enhanced cooperation be referred to the European Council;
• it will provide for a new 'passerelle' that will allow participants in an enhanced cooperation to switch from unanimity to QMV (except in defence) and from a special legislative procedure to the ordinary legislative procedure (codecision).

However, the effect of these slight improvements will be somewhat reduced by:

• the increase in the minimum number of participants from eight at present to one-third of Member States under the Constitution (which in an EU of 27 makes nine, rising to ten in an EU of 28);
• the requirement of unanimity in the Council for authorising any kind of enhanced cooperation in CFSP, without any exception for an enhanced cooperation that would aim at implementing CFSP decisions which have already been adopted (whereas at present it is QMV in such cases);

[41] Originally, the idea was launched by a common letter from Chancellor Schröder and President Chirac at the end of 1995.

- the requirement of the consent of the European Parliament (where MEPs from all Member States will have a right to vote) for launching an enhanced cooperation, even for cases where the codecision procedure does not apply (whereas at present the European Parliament is only consulted in cases other than codecision);
- the requirement of a Commission proposal (decided, as in all cases, by a simple majority of Commissioners from all Member States) for triggering an enhanced cooperation in matters other than CFSP.

Finally, the existing preconditions for the launching of an enhanced cooperation will remain mostly the same as at present under Article 43 of the EU Treaty: no undermining of the internal market, no barrier to or discrimination in trade between Member States, no distortion of competition and no enhanced cooperation in areas of exclusive EU competence.

Cases of 'inbuilt closer cooperation'

In the present Treaties, there are already cases of what could be called 'inbuilt closer cooperation' which result either from specific conditions on the participation of Member States in certain EU policies and/or from the fact that some Member States have requested and obtained 'opt-outs' from certain EU policies. These particular situations also constitute tools for flexibility which the Constitution takes over and to which it adds a 'permanent structured cooperation' in the field of defence.

The existing cases

The two existing cases of 'inbuilt closer cooperation', not modified by the Constitution, are the euro zone and the Schengen area, in which, at present (September 2005), respectively 12 and 13 Member States participate. Participation in these areas is subject to criteria which have to be fulfilled by the Member States concerned.

Participation in the euro zone is subject to fulfilling, amongst other conditions, the 'convergence criteria' relating to price stability, a low budget deficit and the durability of limited fluctuation margins within the exchange-rate mechanism (Article III-198 Cst and the Protocol on the convergence criteria).

Participation in the core of the Schengen area (i.e. the removal of checks on persons at internal borders and access to the Schengen Information System (SIS) which is a computerised data-base and exchange of information system between the competent authorities of Member States) is subject to a State having successfully undergone an evaluation procedure concerning in particular the quality and level of controls at the external borders, as well as to a Council decision by unanimity of the Schengen Member States.[42]

Actually, the defence policy could already also be considered now as a case of 'inbuilt closer cooperation' among 24 Member States, since Denmark 'does not participate in the elaboration and the implementation of decisions and actions of the Union which have defence implications' (Article 5, 1st subparagraph, of the Protocol on the position of Denmark).

The new case added by the Constitution: the 'permanent structured cooperation' in the field of defence

The Constitution adds to the above cases a new case of 'inbuilt closer cooperation' which is the 'permanent structured cooperation' in the field of defence (Articles I-41(6) and III-312 Cst). This cooperation is open to Member States 'whose military capabilities fulfil higher criteria and which have made more binding commitments to one another in this area with a view to the most demanding missions'. The criteria concerning military capabilities to be fulfilled are set out in a Protocol (no. 23) on permanent structured cooperation. The Council will decide on the establishment of such cooperation by QMV, which is quite remarkable, as it will make the launching of such a cooperation easier than the launching of a classic 'enhanced cooperation' in the field of CFSP where unanimity is required (Article III-419(2), 2nd subparagraph Cst) (for further details on the permanent structured cooperation, see below in chapter V, under 'Defence').

With the so-called 'battlegroups' provided for under the 'Headline Goal 2010' having been endorsed by the European Council at its meeting on 17 and 18 June 2004, which are aimed at improving the capabilities of the EU Member States so that they will be able to respond to the whole spectrum of crisis management operations covered by the EU Treaty, Member States have already put in place measures which, to a certain extent, prefigure this permanent structured cooperation.

---

[42] See Art. 3(2) of the Protocol (no. 9) on the Treaty and the Act of Accession of the ten new Member States annexed to the Constitution.

General and sectoral 'passerelles' to amend the Constitution

As a result of the debate which took place both during the Convention and in the IGC, on whether to switch several provisions to QMV and/or codecision, or whether to allow for a simplified procedure for amending certain provisions or parts of the Constitution, a number of so-called 'passerelles' were agreed. These 'passerelles' allow either the European Council or the Council to decide by unanimity to switch a legal basis from unanimity to QMV or from a special legislative procedure to the ordinary legislative procedure (codecision), without having to follow the full ordinary procedure for revising the Constitution.

Some 'passerelles' had already been inserted in the Treaties at previous IGCs. They were often what remained of unsuccessful attempts in these IGCs to switch from unanimity to QMV, a consolation prize to those who had pleaded in favour of QMV.

The experience so far with the existing 'passerelles' has shown that they have rarely been used. But at least they do exist, and the sectoral ones provide for a less heavy procedure (consent required neither from the European Parliament nor from the national Parliaments). If the political will is there, and shared by all members of the Council, 'passerelles' are a simple way to amend the Constitution.

The existing 'passerelles' in the EU and EC Treaties

Some 'passerelles' already exist in the present Treaties. The only case where a 'passerelle' has been used so far is the decision in November 2004 by the European Council, within the framework of the new pluriannual JHA programme (called 'The Hague Programme'), whereby it requested the Council to adopt a decision, based on Article 67(2), 2nd indent, of the EC Treaty, to apply the codecision procedure (thus including QMV in the Council) to provisions on border crossing, visas, asylum and immigration policy, except for legal migration.[43]

The 'passerelles' provided for in the present Treaties are the following:

- Article 42 of the EU Treaty, which allows the Council, by unanimity, to 'communitarise' the whole or parts of the JHA pillar. Such a decision will then have to be ratified by all Member States in accordance with their respective constitutional requirements;

---

[43] The Decision was adopted by the Council on 22 December 2004 and has made codecision applicable as from 1 January 2005 (OJ No. L396, 31 December 2004, p. 45).

- Article 67(2), 2nd indent, of the EC Treaty, which allows the Council, by unanimity and without a ratification procedure in the Member States, to switch the whole or parts of the Title on visas, asylum and immigration to codecision, and to adapt the provisions on the Court's jurisdiction in the same Title;
- Article 137(2), 2nd subparagraph, of the EC Treaty, which allows the Council, by unanimity and without ratification by Member States, to switch to QMV and codecision for adopting certain measures in the social chapter (protection of workers in case of termination of their employment contract, the representation and collective defence of workers and conditions of employment of third-country nationals);
- Article 175(2), 2nd subparagraph, of the EC Treaty, which allows the Council, by unanimity and without ratification by Member States, to switch to QMV for those environment matters which are still subject to unanimity (provisions primarily of a fiscal nature, measures affecting town and country planning, management of water resources and land use).

The new general 'passerelle' in the Constitution

The Constitution provides for a general 'passerelle' in Article IV-444, under which the European Council may decide by unanimity, with the consent of the European Parliament and if no national Parliament opposes it within six months, to switch a legal basis from unanimity to QMV (with the exception of defence) or from a special legislative procedure to the ordinary legislative procedure (codecision).[44]

Such a general 'passerelle' will not be applicable to the whole Constitution, but only to policies and competences in Part III, whether internal or external, in those cases where a switch to QMV or to codecision was not agreed during the IGC (such as in the sensitive fields of taxation or social policy). However, it will not enable a legal basis which is placed wholly in Part I (such as the legal basis for the EU's own resources in Article I-54) to be switched to QMV or codecision.

The sectoral 'passerelles' in the Constitution

In addition to this general 'passerelle', the Constitution contains six sectoral 'passerelles' which, in Part III, are *lex specialis* with respect to the general one. The Constitution retains two of the existing 'passerelles'

---

[44] For an overview of all 'passerelles' and provisions on a simplified revision procedure, see Annex 7.

in the social policy and environment fields (Articles III-210(3), 2nd subparagraph, and III-234(2), 2nd subparagraph, Cst).

The Constitution adds four new sectoral 'passerelles': one enabling a switch to QMV in CFSP, except for decisions having military or defence implications (Articles I-40(7) and III-300(3)and (4) Cst), one enabling a switch to QMV for the adoption of the multiannual financial framework (Article I-55(4) Cst), one enabling to switch to codecision in family law with cross-border implications (Article III-269(3) 2nd subparagraph, Cst) and one enabling a switch to QMV or codecision for adopting acts within an enhanced cooperation (with the exception of military or defence matters) (Article III-422 Cst).

A general simplified revision procedure to amend Title III of Part III of the Constitution (on internal policies and competences)

The same debate on a facilitated amendment procedure of the Constitution as the one that resulted in the 'passerelles' gave rise to an attempt to provide for a simplified revision procedure of Title III of Part III of the Constitution, the Title which contains the details of all the EU internal policies and competences. This simplified procedure is set out in Article IV-445 Cst. However, any such revision may 'not increase the competences conferred on the Union in [the Constitution]'.

As compared with the ordinary revision procedure, the simplification consists in dispensing with both the convening of a Convention and of an IGC, allowing the amendments to be agreed by a decision of the European Council, acting by unanimity after consulting the European Parliament and the Commission.[45] However, this decision will come into force only once it has been approved by all Member States in accordance with their respective constitutional requirements.

Specific simplified revision procedure to amend certain provisions of the Constitution

There are also twelve specific clauses which will allow the Council to amend the scope of a given legal basis or the provisions of a protocol annexed to the Constitution:

- Article III-129, 2nd subparagraph, Cst will enable the Council, by unanimity with the consent of the European Parliament and after

---

[45] And the European Central Bank in cases of institutional changes in the monetary area.

approval by Member States in accordance with their respective constitutional requirements, to 'add to the rights' of the EU citizens as laid down in Article I-10 Cst. This Article contains the list of citizens' rights, such as the right to move freely within the Union, the right to vote and the right to stand as candidates in elections to the European Parliament and in municipal elections, etc.. This possibility of adding to the list of citizens' rights already exists under the present EC Treaty (Article 22, 2nd subparagraph, EC Treaty);

- in two cases, in the JHA field, the Council, by unanimity and with the consent of the European Parliament, but without the need for ratification procedures in Member States, will be allowed to extend the scope of a provision. It can extend the list of areas of crime where minimum rules concerning the definition of criminal offences and sanctions may be established (Article III-271(1), 3rd subparagraph, Cst), and it can extend the powers of the European Public Prosecutor's Office (Article III-274(4) Cst);

- four provisions will allow the Council to amend, totally or in part, the provisions of certain protocols. Article III-184(13) Cst allows the Council, by unanimity and after consulting the European Parliament and the European Central Bank, to replace the Protocol on the excessive deficit procedure (no. 10).[46] The same goes for amending provisions of the Statute of the European Investment Bank (no. 5).[47] Each of the two protocols which take over the provisions of the Acts of Accession (Protocols no. 8 and 9) contains a provision enabling the Council, by unanimity and after consulting the European Parliament, to repeal provisions in the Protocol which are no longer applicable.[48]

Five of these provisions allow for the amendment of primary law provisions using QMV in the Council. These are the only five cases in which the Constitution can be amended by QMV and not by unanimous agreement of Council members or of the Governments of the Member States:

- the nature of the composition of the Committee of the Regions and of the Economic and Social Committee may be reviewed by the Council using QMV (Article I-32(5), 2nd subparagraph, Cst);

---

[46] This possibility already exists under the present EC Treaty in Art. 104(14).
[47] See Art. III-393, 4th subpara., Cst. This possibility already exists under the present EC Treaty in Art. 266, 3rd subpara.
[48] See Art. 5 of Protocol no. 8 and Art. 10 of Protocol no. 9.

- two provisions enable the Council and the European Parliament to amend in codecision parts of the Protocol on the Statute of the ECB and on the Statute of the Court (Articles III-187(3) and III-381 Cst);
- two provisions enable the Council to repeal, by QMV, specific rules allowing compensation measures for certain areas affected by the former division of Germany (Articles III-167(2)(c) and III-243 Cst).

Voluntary withdrawal from the EU

Finally, in an enlarged EU, which has committed itself to further enlargements, and could end up with 33 Member States or more,[49] the new provision on voluntary withdrawal from the EU may also be construed as a sort of 'facilitating' mechanism, in the sense that it would be the ultimate way to deal with a serious problem with a Member State.

Article I-60 Cst states that 'any Member State may decide to withdraw from the Union in accordance with its own constitutional requirements'. Then follows a 'divorce' procedure under which, after notification by the Member State concerned, the Union concludes an agreement with that State, setting out the arrangements for its withdrawal. The agreement is to be concluded by the Council, acting by QMV, and the Constitution ceases to apply to the State concerned from the date of entry into force of the agreement or, failing that, two years after the request for withdrawal,

---

[49] According to the Presidency Conclusions following the European Council on 16 and 17 December 2004 (doc. 16238/04):

- the accession negotiations with Bulgaria and Romania were concluded on 14 December 2004, the Accession Treaty with those two States will be signed in April 2005 (it was signed on 25 April) and it will enter into force, subject to ratification, on 1 January 2007 (or on 1 January 2008 at the latest);
- as regards Turkey, if all conditions are met, the accession negotiations would start on 3 October 2005. As regards Croatia, according to the Conclusions of the Council adopted on 16 March 2005, 'the bilateral intergovernmental conference will be convened by common agreement as soon as the Council has established that Croatia is cooperating fully with the ICTY' (see doc. 7138/2/02 REV 2, available on the internet site of the Council). Accession negotiations were launched with Turkey and Croatia on 3 October 2005.

Paras. 40 to 43 of the Presidency Conclusions following the Thessaloniki European Council reaffirmed 'the European perspective of the Western Balkan countries, which will become an integral part of the EU, once they meet the established criteria' (doc. 11368/03).

unless that deadline is prolonged by common accord of the European Council and the State concerned.[50]

Whether such a provision constitutes an advance or a setback may be assessed differently. However, one may note that such a right normally exists in confederations of States but never in federal States. Therefore, this provision on withdrawal could be seen as clarifying a basic issue, i.e. that the Union is actually a voluntary association between States which remain sovereign as to the question of whether or not they remain in that association.

---

[50] For an analysis of withdrawal rights, see R. J. Fried, 'Providing a Constitutional Framework for Withdrawal from the EU: Article 59 of the Draft European Constitution' (2004) vol. 53 *International and Comparative Law Quarterly* 407–428. See also by the same author 'Secession from the European Union; Checking out of the Proverbial "Cockroach Motel"' (2004) 27 no. 2 *Fordham Law Journal* 590–641.

V

Changes in substance

The Constitution does not extend the Union's remit to substantive new areas of competences. Most importantly, and this is where the use of the name 'Constitution' might create some confusion, the Constitution is and remains a treaty and its 'masters' are still the Member States.[1] They have kept for themselves the power to amend the Treaties or, as constitutional lawyers would say, the *Kompetenz Kompetenz*, the power for distributing competences.[2] Like the present Treaties, the Constitution does not allow itself to be amended by a majority of Member States. It requires approval and ratification by each of them.

The Constitution begins with a short and entirely new Preamble which was drafted in the Convention.[3] It states, in particular, that 'the peoples of Europe are determined to transcend their former divisions and, united ever more closely, to forge a common destiny'. Thus, the wording 'united ever more closely' replaces the traditional formula of 'an ever closer union'.

During the Convention and the IGC, some delegations argued that the Preamble should refer directly to God or to Europe's Christian heritage. Others opposed this,[4] and the Preamble limits itself to mentioning 'the cultural, religious and humanist inheritance of Europe'.

---

[1] The expression 'Masters of the Treaties' was used by the German Constitutional Court in its case about the Maastricht Treaty (see judgment of 12 October 1993, Case *Brunner et al. v. The European Union Treaty*, BVerfGE 89, 155).

[2] For an interesting analysis of this issue, see O. Pfersmann, 'The New Revision of the Old Constitution' in J. H. Weiler and C. L. Eisgruber (eds.) *The EU Constitution in a Contextual Perspective. Altneuland* (Jean Monnet Working Paper 5/04), http://www.jeanmonnetprogram.org/papers/04/040501-10.pdf.

[3] The IGC decided to delete the quotation from Thucydides in Ancient Greek which preceded the Preamble drafted in the Convention.

[4] Notably France, Belgium and the Nordic States. It is recalled that the first sentence of Art. 1 of the French Constitution reads 'La France est une République indivisible, laïque, démocratique et sociale' (France is an indivisible, secular, democratic and social Republic).

Contrary to the Treaties of Maastricht and Amsterdam, the Constitution confers only a few new competences of substance on the EU. To a large extent, the substantive content of the present EC Treaty remains the same. The few new competences conferred on the EU in the Constitution are far from being revolutionary. Actually, they mostly codify in specific provisions what has already been done pursuant to the existing Treaties, under general legal bases such as the internal market legal basis (Article 95 EC Treaty) and the so-called 'flexibility clause' (Article 308 EC Treaty, ex-235 (before the Amsterdam Treaty renumbered it)), or under sectoral legal bases.[5]

The most noticeable new legal basis is the one which allows the EU institutions to create Union-wide intellectual property rights which provide uniform protection for intellectual property rights throughout the EU, and to set up centralised Union-wide authorisation, coordination and supervision mechanisms.[6] The other new legal bases concern European space policy,[7] energy policy,[8] tourism,[9] sport,[10] civil protection[11] and humanitarian aid.[12] However, the EC is already now in a position to adopt provisions in these areas. Its competences will therefore not really be widened, but rather made easier to use, due to the fact that these new legal bases provide for QMV (save for language arrangements concerning European intellectual property rights and for measures primarily of a fiscal nature in energy policy, where unanimity will still apply).

---

[5] See Annex 4, list of new legal bases.

[6] Art. III-176 Cst. At present, such EC-wide rights or authorisations have been adopted under the flexibility clause (Art. 308 EC Treaty) or under the internal market provision (Art. 95 EC Treaty).

[7] Art. III-254 Cst. At present, such acts are adopted under R&D provisions (Art. 166 EC Treaty).

[8] Art. III-256 Cst. At present, such acts are adopted under environmental protection provisions (Art. 175 EC Treaty), the internal market provision (Art. 95 EC Treaty), the transeuropean networks provision (Arts. 155 and 156 EC Treaty) or the flexibility clause (Art. 308 EC Treaty).

[9] Art. III-281 Cst. At present, such acts are adopted under the flexibility clause (Art. 308 EC Treaty).

[10] Art. III-282 Cst. At present, such acts are adopted under youth policy provisions (Art. 149 EC Treaty).

[11] Art. III-284 Cst. At present, such acts are adopted under the flexibility provision (Art. 308 EC Treaty).

[12] Art. III-321 Cst. At present, such acts are adopted under development cooperation (Art. 179 EC Treaty).

Apart from these new legal bases, the Constitution mostly strengthens some existing competences, mainly CFSP, defence, JHA, provisions specific to the euro zone, public health and social policy.

One striking characteristic of the Constitution is that it is deeply rooted in human rights. As mentioned by an American author, 'much of the Constitution is given over to the issue of fundamental human rights. It might be said that human rights are the very heart and soul of the document.'[13] The Constitution puts to the forefront the values on which the EU is based (see box 5.1 with the provision on the Union's values). It also takes the highly symbolic steps both of incorporating the Charter for Fundamental Rights, and of providing for an obligation for the EU to accede to the European Convention on Human Rights.

Box 5.1   The Union's values (Article I-2 Cst)

The Union is founded on the values of respect for human dignity, freedom, democracy, equality, the rule of law and respect for human rights, including the rights of persons belonging to minorities. These values are common to the Member States in a society in which pluralism, non-discrimination, tolerance, justice, solidarity and equality between women and men prevail.

This provision on the Union's values is not only declaratory. It is referred to both as a condition which a European State will have to respect in order for that State to be allowed to apply for membership: 'the Union shall be open to all European States which respect its values . . .' (Article I-1 (2) Cst) and, if seriously breached, as a reason for suspending certain of a Member State's rights resulting from Union membership: 'the European Council . . . may adopt a European decision determining the existence of a serious and persistent breach by a Member State of the values mentioned in Article I-2 . . .' (Article I-59(2) Cst).[14] The Union's values are therefore part and parcel of the very essence of the EU.

---

[13] J. Rifkind, *The European Dream* (Tarcher Penguin, 2004), p. 212.

[14] The list of values in Art. I-2 Cst whose breach may result in suspension is longer than the present list in Art. 6(1) EU Treaty (referred to in Art. 7(2) EU Treaty on the suspension of rights): 'The Union is founded on the principles of liberty, democracy, respect for human rights and fundamental freedoms, and the rule of law, principles which are common to the Member States.'

Section 1: Better protection for human rights and fundamental freedoms

The most important change, both symbolic and in substance, brought about by the Constitution as compared with the present Treaties is without any doubt the incorporation of the EU Charter of Fundamental Rights as a full Part of the Constitution. The legal status of the Charter will thus change from one of political declaration, although of a very high value, to the status of 'primary law' or Treaty-level law.

Linked to this was the decision to provide for the accession of the EU to the 1950 European Convention for the Protection of Human Rights and Fundamental Freedoms (ECHR) (Article I-9(2) Cst).

These two important moves were agreed upon in the Convention and the IGC did not question them.

The IGC however had to settle one additional issue which was very important, at least for some Member States (notably Hungary) and which the Convention had not been able to solve. These Member States insisted that a reference should be made to 'the rights of minorities'. However, this request, formulated in such a way, was unacceptable for other Member States. Finally, the compromise was to refer to 'the rights of persons belonging to minorities', therefore excluding collective rights (Article I-2 Cst).

Incorporation of the Charter of Fundamental Rights of the EU

The Constitution incorporates, as its Part II, the whole Charter of Fundamental Rights adopted in Nice in December 2000, together with the Charter's Preamble. This will not increase the competences of the EU, but it will underline the importance for the EU itself and its institutions of respecting fundamental rights and of being a 'Union based on the rule of law' or, in French, 'Union de droit' as the Court has called the Community in its case-law.[15]

---

[15] See Case 294/83, *Les Verts v. Parliament*. For an analysis of the Charter of Fundamental Rights, see F. Benoît-Rohmer, 'La Charte des droits fondamentaux de l'Union européenne' (2001) II fasc. 160 *Juris-Classeur* and (2001) 19 *Le Dalloz* 1483–1492 and 'Valeurs et droits fondamentaux dans la Constitution' (2005) 2 *Revue trimestrielle de droit européen* 261–283.

In accordance with the mandate which the European Council had given in June 1999 to the Convention which drafted it, the Charter contains three categories of rights:

- fundamental rights and freedoms as well as basic procedural rights guaranteed by the ECHR and derived from the constitutional traditions common to the Member States, as general principles of Community law;
- fundamental rights that pertain only to the Union's citizens;
- economic and social rights as contained in the 1961 European Social Charter,[16] and the 1989 Community Charter of the Fundamental Social Rights of Workers.[17]

The Charter therefore reproduces, and in some cases modernises, the rights contained in the ECHR. Part of this modernisation took the form of adding basic provisions which take into account developments in international and Community law, in the case-law and in the constitutional traditions common to the Member States:

- human dignity (Article II-61 Cst), which is of course not new and constitutes the real basis of fundamental rights;
- the right to the integrity of the person (Article II-63 Cst), which takes over rules set out in the 1997 Convention on Human Rights and Biomedicine;[18]
- the protection of personal data (Article II-68 Cst), which derives *inter alia* from the EC Directive on data protection;[19]
- the freedom of the arts and sciences (Article II-73 Cst);

---

[16] The 1961 Charter was adopted in the framework of the Council of Europe and had been ratified by all EU Member States at the time. It may be found at http://conventions.coe.int/treaty/en/treaties/html/035.htm.

[17] The 1989 Charter had been adopted by 11 of the Heads of State or Government of the EU Member States and had been incorporated first as the so-called 'Social Protocol' in the Maastricht Treaty, without the participation of the UK which at the time had opted out from it. When the UK agreed to join it, the Amsterdam IGC made it a fully-fledged Chapter on Social Provisions (Arts. 136 to 145 of the EC Treaty). The text of the 1989 Charter may be found at http://www.psi.org.uk/publications/archivepdfs/Trade%20unions/TUAPP1.pdf.

[18] This Convention may be found at http://conventions.coe.int/treaty/en/treaties/html/164.htm.

[19] Directive 95/46/EC of the European Parliament and of the Council on the protection of individuals with regard to the processing of personal data and on the free movement of such data (OJ No. L281, 23 November 1995, p. 31).

- the right to asylum (Article II-78 Cst), which is guaranteed by the 1951 Geneva Convention on refugees;
- protection in the event of removal, expulsion or extradition (Article II-79 Cst), which derives from the case-law of the Human Rights Court regarding Article 3 of the ECHR;[20]
- the rights of the child (Article II-84 Cst), which derives from the 1989 New York Convention on the Rights of the Child.[21]

The Charter also supplements these classic human rights provisions with a number of provisions on economic and social rights. The Charter has the particularity of containing not only rights, but also 'principles'. The difference between the two is that the rights constitute personal rights which may be directly invoked as such by individuals in the courts while the principles set out an objective to be respected by the legislature towards which, in view of their implementation through legislation, the principles can then be invoked. This is why Article II-112(5) Cst states that these principles 'shall be judicially cognisable only in the interpretation of such acts and in the ruling on their legality'. This distinction gave rise to difficulties between Member States whose constitutional traditions in this respect differ. Some Member States, like the UK, were of the opinion that listing principles alongside real personal rights would mislead the individuals into believing that principles gave them true rights while some other Member States, like France, Spain or Portugal, were used to such a distinction and did not want to give up the idea of including principles.

There is no precise list of what are the rights and what are the principles. Normally the way in which a given provision is drafted enables one to distinguish between a right or a principle, but it is not always easy. Typical drafting for a right would be for instance 'everyone has the right . . .', while typical drafting for a principle would be for instance 'the Union recognises and respects the right of . . .'. Some provisions even contain one paragraph conferring rights and another setting out principles.

Examples of social rights are equality between women and men (Article II-83 Cst), the prohibition of child labour (Article II-92 Cst),

---

[20] See *Ahmed v. Austria*, judgment of 17 December 1996, and *Soering v. United Kingdom*, judgment of 7 July 1989. See internet site of the European Court of Human Rights at http://cmiskp.echr.coe.int.

[21] This Convention may be found at http://www.unhchr.ch/html/menu3/b/k2crc.htm.

the right to engage in work (Article II-75), the right to protection from dismissal for reasons connected with maternity and the right to paid maternity leave and to parental leave (Article II-93 Cst), the right to protection in the event of unjustified dismissal (Article II-90 Cst), the right to fair and just working conditions (Article II-91 Cst), workers' right to information and consultation within undertakings (Article II-87 Cst), the right of collective bargaining and action (Article II-88 Cst) and the right of access to placement services (Article II-89 Cst).

Examples of principles are the right of access to social security and social assistance (Article II-94 Cst) and to health care (Article II-95 Cst), the rights of the elderly (Article II-85 Cst), the right of persons with disabilities to integration in the life of the community (Article II-86 Cst), access to services of general economic interest (Article II-96 Cst), a high level of environmental protection (Article II-97 Cst) and a high level of consumer protection (Article II-98 Cst).

Two issues raised during some of the national ratification debates, notably in France, were whether Article II-62 Cst on the right to life and Article II-70 Cst on the freedom of thought, conscience and religion would contradict or impede national rules, respectively, on the right to abortion and on the principle of '*laïcité*' or secularism.

Article II-62(1) Cst on the right to life reads '1. Everyone has the right to life.' This paragraph is based on the first sentence of Article 2(1) of the ECHR which reads: 'Everyone's right to life shall be protected by law.' Although the Human Rights Court has not so far had an opportunity to interpret this provision, the Human Rights Commission did so partly in 1980 by noting that neither the notion of 'everyone' nor the notion of 'life' was defined in the Convention and that, in the particular case, which was a therapeutic abortion, Article 2(1) of the ECHR did not impede national legislature from authorising such abortion.[22] Thus, neither the Human Rights Court nor the Human Rights Commission has settled the issue of whether the 'unborn' benefit from Article 2(1) ECHR and one may doubt that they will ever do so.

The fact is that a great majority of the States parties to the ECHR, and to the EU, have had abortion laws in force for several years already, with varying conditions and limits, while some States, such as Ireland,[23]

---

[22] Decision of 13 May 1980, Case *X v. UK*, no. 8416/79, DR 19, p. 244.

[23] For instance, Art. 40, Section 3, third subsection, of the Irish Constitution reads: 'The State acknowledges the right to life of the unborn and, with due regard to the equal right to life of the mother, guarantees in its laws to respect, and, as far as practicable, by its laws to defend and vindicate that right.'

Malta, Poland or Portugal, currently forbid abortion (sometimes with the sole exception of a risk to the mother's life). Anyway, it should be made absolutely clear that, like all the other provisions of the EU Charter, Article II-62(1) Cst is solely addressed to the EU institutions, and is addressed to the Member States 'only when they are implementing Union law' and 'does not . . . establish any new power or task for the Union' (Article II-111 Cst). Abortion is exclusively a matter for national law; the EU has no competence whatsoever in this matter, neither under the present Treaties, nor under the Constitution.[24]

Article II-70 Cst on the freedom of thought, conscience and religion reads 'Everyone has the right to freedom of thought, conscience and religion. This right includes freedom to change religion or belief and freedom, either alone or in community with others and in public or in private, to manifest religion or belief, in worship, teaching, practice and observance.' This Article is identical to Article 9(1) of the ECHR. It is particularly the freedom to manifest one's religion in public which, during the French ratification debate, the 'No' camp claimed would contradict the French legislation of February 2004 which prohibits regulates, pursuant to the principle of secularism, the wearing of signs or dress manifesting a religious affiliation in State primary and secondary schools. However, the French Constitutional Council, in its November 2004 decision on the compatibility of the draft EU Constitution with the French Constitution,[25] stated that, given the case-law of the Human Rights Court, and most recently the judgment of June 2004 in a case of a Turkish student who was barred from wearing an Islamic headscarf in a Turkish University,[26] the EU Constitution was compatible with the French Constitution, which states that France shall be a secular Republic

---

[24] The only angle from which the issue of abortion has been examined by the EU Court of Justice was in a case linked to the free movement of services where the Court said that 'medical termination of pregnancy, performed in accordance with the law of the State in which it is carried out, constitutes a service within the meaning of Article 60 [now 50] of the Treaty'. This means that women may freely travel to another Member State to seek such a service. On the issue of whether or not that service was morally acceptable or not, the Court replied that 'whatever the merits of those arguments on the moral plane . . . it is not for the Court to substitute its assessment for that of the legislature in those Member States where the activities in question are practised legally'. See judgment of 4 October 1991, Case C-159/90, *SPUC v. Grogan*, [1991] ECR p. I-04685, paras. 20 and 21.

[25] See decision mentioned above in footnote 46 of chapter III.

[26] See judgment of 29 June 2004 of the Human Rights Court, Case 44774/98, *Sahin v Turkey*. In this case the Court stated that: 'Article 9 does not protect every act motivated or inspired by a religion or belief and does not in all cases guarantee the right to behave in the public sphere in a way which is dictated by a belief' (para. 66); 'in a democratic

('une République laïque'). Again, like the issue of abortion, the issue of secularism and freedom to manifest one's religion in public is exclusively a matter for national law; the EU has no competence whatsoever in this matter, neither under the present Treaties, nor under the Constitution.

A short history of fundamental rights in the EU

The genesis of the protection of fundamental rights in the EU goes back to the sixties. The original version of the EC Treaties did not make any reference to fundamental rights. It was the 1992 Maastricht Treaty which inserted the present Article 6(2) of the EU Treaty providing that 'The Union shall respect fundamental rights, as guaranteed by the European Convention for the Protection of Human Rights and Fundamental Freedoms . . . and as they result from the constitutional traditions common to the Member States, as general principles of Community law.' Before that, the EU Court of Justice had already, in 1969,[27] stated that fundamental human rights are 'enshrined in the general principles of Community law and protected by the Court'. Thereafter, the Court continued building up this protection so that 'respect for human rights is . . . a condition of the lawfulness of Community acts'.[28]

Such a guarantee was a prerequisite to the acceptance by Member States of the principle that EU law has primacy over national law, which the Court of Justice had enunciated in 1964. Without a guarantee that fundamental rights were properly protected at EU level, the conferral by Member States of competences on the EU could have entailed a lowering of the level of protection of human rights. This link with primacy was

---

society the State was entitled to place restrictions on the wearing of the Islamic headscarf if it was incompatible with the pursued aim of protecting the rights and freedoms of others, public order and public safety' (para. 98); 'the principle of secularism in Turkey is undoubtedly one of the fundamental principles of the State, which are in harmony with the rule of law and respect for human rights' (para. 99); and 'a margin of appreciation is particularly appropriate when it comes to the regulation by the Contracting States of the wearing of religious symbols in teaching institutions, since rules on the subject vary from one country to another depending on national traditions . . . and there is no uniform European conception of the requirements of "the protection of the rights of others" and of "public order"'(para. 102).

[27] Judgment of 12 November 1969, Case 29/69, *Stauder*, [1969] ECR p. 425, para. 7.

[28] See Opinion 2/94, *Accession of the EC to the ECHR*, paras. 33 and 34. For a summary of the protection of fundamental rights in the EU, see also paras. 73 to 81 of the judgment of 30 June 2005 of the Human Rights Court, Case 45036/98, *Bosphorus Hava Yollari Turizm v. Ireland*.

made by the German Constitutional Court in its case-law which became known as '*Solange*' (which means 'as long as' in German). In a judgment of 1974 (known as Case '*Solange I*'),[29] the German Court stated that it would review whether EU legislation respects fundamental rights 'as long as' the EU did not have a directly elected parliament, with legislative powers, and a catalogue of fundamental rights. Later on, the German Constitutional Court somewhat relaxed its case-law, in 1986 ('*Solange II*')[30] and in 2000,[31] by stating that as long as the EU's case-law guarantees an effective protection of fundamental rights, actions in the German Court against an EU legal act will be dismissed, unless the applicant shows that the development of EU law and EU case-law falls below a proper level of protection of fundamental rights. The Italian Constitutional Court followed a similar line.[32]

In a judgment of 30 June 2005, the Human Rights Court of Strasbourg followed a similar reasoning in a case where a Member State was sued for having allegedly violated property rights because of applying an EC Regulation. The Court stated that, on condition that the EU 'is considered to protect fundamental rights, as regards both the substantive guarantees offered and the mechanisms controlling their observance, in a manner which can be considered at least equivalent to that for which the [ECHR] provides', the Court will consider that there is a 'presumption . . . that a State has not departed from the requirements of the [ECHR] when it does no more than implement legal obligations flowing from its membership of the [EU]'. It added however that 'any such presumption can be rebutted if, in the circumstances of a particular case, it is considered that the protection of [ECHR] rights was manifestly deficient. In such cases, the interest of international co-operation would be outweighed by the [ECHR] role as a "constitutional instrument of European public order" in the field of human rights.'[33]

---

[29] Case '*Solange I*', BVerfGE 37, 271 of 29 May 1974, which may be found translated into English at http://www.ucl.ac.uk.

[30] Case '*Solange II*', BVerfGE 73, 339 of 22 October 1986; see the above-mentioned site http://www.ucl.ac.uk.

[31] Case '*Bananenmarktordnung*', BVerfGE 102, 147 of 7 June 2000; see the above-mentioned site http://www.ucl.ac.uk.

[32] Case *Frontini* no. 183/73 of 27 December 1973, I, 1974, 314, and Case *Fragd* no. 232/89 of 21 April 1989, I, 1990, 1855.

[33] See paras. 155 and 156 of the above-mentioned *Bosphorus* judgment (footnote 28).

At the initiative of Germany, during its Presidency in the first half of 1999, the European Council meeting in Cologne in June 1999 decided to draw up a Charter of Fundamental Rights for the EU.[34]

The European Council decided to entrust the task of preparing the draft Charter to a body composed of representatives of the national and European parliaments as well as of representatives of the Governments of the Member States and of the Commission. This procedure was chosen in order to enable more publicity and a broader-based participation in the drafting of the text. This body, which called itself a 'Convention', was chaired by Roman Herzog, former President of Germany and former President of the German Constitutional Court.

The Charter of Fundamental Rights of the European Union proposed by that Convention was solemnly proclaimed by the European Parliament, the Council and the Commission in Nice on 7 December 2000.[35] In order to make it easier for the readers to know which sources were used in the drafting of the Charter and what interpretation should be given to its provisions, a set of 'Explanations relating to the Charter of Fundamental Rights' was prepared under the authority of the Praesidium of the Convention which drafted the Charter.[36]

However, the Charter was not incorporated into the Treaties and, therefore, was not given legally binding force. The question of the Charter's legal status was to be considered later and became the second of the four questions in the 2000 Nice Declaration (see above, box 2.2).

The way the Charter of Fundamental Rights is incorporated into the Constitution

Both in the 2000 Nice Declaration and in the 2001 Laeken Declaration, it was agreed that the question of the status of the Charter should be examined, among other matters, by the IGC.

The Convention proposed to incorporate the text of the Charter as such into the Constitution.[37] However, this incorporation gave rise to

---

[34] See 'European Council Decision on the drawing up of a Charter of Fundamental Rights of the European Union' in Annex IV to the Presidency Conclusions of 3 and 4 June 1999, available on the internet site of the Council.

[35] See OJ No. C364, 18 December 2000, p. 1.

[36] See doc. CHARTE 4473/00 which may be found on the internet site of the Convention which drafted the Charter: http://www.europarl.eu.int/charter.

[37] For an analysis of the issues at stake and suggestions made at the time of the Convention, see my contribution of 23 July 2002 to the Working Group II 'Incorporation of the Charter/ Accession to the ECHR' set up by the Convention, in Working Document 13 (WG II-WD 13), page 15, of 5 September 2002 (available on the internet site of the Convention).

acute difficulties. Some Member States (in particular the UK) feared that it could be construed as conferring additional competences on the EU to legislate on the issues covered by the Charter. They also feared that the Charter could somehow make its way into their own internal legal order, to the extent that a purely internal action, having nothing to do with the implementation of EU law, would nevertheless fall within the scope of the Charter.

In order to address these concerns, the Convention agreed that certain amendments should be made to the original Charter as agreed in Nice. The aim was to clarify that the Charter will not extend the field of application of Union law beyond the competences conferred on the Union, and that the Constitution will oblige Member States to respect the Charter only when they are implementing Union law. Article II-111 Cst states that the Charter provisions 'are addressed to the institutions, bodies, offices and agencies of the Union' and not to the Member States, except '. . . when they are implementing Union law'. It adds that the Charter 'does not extend the field of application of Union law beyond the powers of the Union or establish any power or task for the Union, or modify powers and tasks defined in the other Parts of the Constitution'. This corresponds to the present case-law of the EU Court of Justice according to which the Court reviews the respect of fundamental rights by the Member States only when they implement EC law.[38]

However, such legal clarifications might escape the attention of ordinary citizens, who may think that the EU will have a proper 'Bill of Rights', all of whose provisions will be obligatory in full and protect them in all situations. How then to explain that these rights will not apply directly and fully to them in order to protect them from any policy action by any public authorities, but will only be an obligation on the EU institutions and not on the national public authorities, except when they implement EU law? The symbol is powerful, but it could possibly over-simplify the real situation.

Other amendments also stress that fundamental rights recognised in the Charter which resulted from the constitutional traditions common to Member States should be interpreted in harmony with those traditions and that full account should be taken of national laws and practices as specified in the Charter. Another amendment specifies the

---

[38] See for instance judgment of 24 March 1994, Case C-2/92, *Bostock*, [1994] ECR p. I-976, para. 16 and judgment of 18 March 2000, Case C-107/97, *Rombi and Arkopharma*, [2000] ECR p. I-3392, para. 65.

circumstances in which those provisions of the Charter which contain principles rather than rights may be invoked in the courts.

The IGC essentially followed this approach. At the insistence of the UK, it made one more amendment to Article II-112 Cst (which corresponds to the present Article 52 of the Charter). A new paragraph 7 was added, which provides that 'the explanations drawn up as a way of providing guidance in the interpretation of the Charter . . . shall be given due regard by the courts of the Union and of the Member States'. A reference to these explanations, which had originally been drawn up under the authority of the Praesidium of the Charter Convention and had been updated under the responsibility of the Praesidium of the Constitution Convention, was added in the Charter's preamble. These explanations were reproduced in a Declaration no. 12 to the Final Act of the IGC, indicating that the Conference had taken note of them.

Accession of the EU to the European Convention on Human Rights

Finally closing a long saga which started 30 years ago and culminated with the Opinion of the Court of Justice in 1996,[39] which stated that the EC did not have the necessary powers to accede to the ECHR, the Constitution provides that 'the Union shall accede to the [ECHR]. Such accession shall not affect the Union's competences as defined in the Constitution' (Article I-9(2) Cst).

The EU's accession to the ECHR will further reinforce the protection of human rights and fundamental freedoms within the Union, by increasing the uniformity of such protection through a fuller integration of the two systems, while preserving the specific features of both.

The saga started with the 1974 '*Solange*' case-law of the German Constitutional Court (see above under 'A short history of fundamental rights in the EU', p. 140). This worried the Commission which proposed in 1979 that the European Community accede to the ECHR. That proposal did not meet with the approval of the Council. The Commission renewed it in 1990. The European Parliament, for its part, adopted several resolutions in favour of the Community's accession.

Against this background, the Council decided to ask the Court of Justice for an opinion as to whether accession by the Community to the ECHR would be compatible with the EC Treaty. The Court held in 1996

---

[39] See Opinion 2/94, *Accession of the EC to the ECHR*, paras. 27 and 35.

that such an accession would entail a substantial change in the Community system for the protection of human rights in so far as it would entail the Community entering into a distinct international institutional system as well as the integration of all the provisions of the Convention into the Community legal order. Such a modification would be of constitutional significance and could therefore be brought about only by way of Treaty amendment.

In the 2001 Laeken Declaration, the Convention was invited to consider the issue. This was linked with the idea of making the EU Charter of Fundamental Rights legally binding. As this modification of the legal status of the Charter would have increased the risks of discrepancies between the case-law of the two Courts (the EU Court of Justice in Luxembourg and the Human Rights Court in Strasbourg), it was suggested that a specific legal basis should be inserted into the Constitution enabling the Union 'to seek accession' to the ECHR. The Convention suggested that the Council would act unanimously when deciding to seek such accession. This voting rule was changed during the IGC to provide for QMV instead. The text of the legal basis itself was changed to state directly that the Union 'shall accede' to the ECHR.

The IGC also agreed on the text of a new Protocol (Protocol no. 32). This Protocol provides for certain conditions to be respected when proceeding to this accession:

• the specific characteristics of the Union and Union law must be preserved, particularly in relation to the arrangements for the Union's possible participation in the judicial bodies of the ECHR, and in relation to the mechanisms concerning proceedings by non-Member States and individual applications;
• the competences of the Union and the powers of its institutions must not be affected;
• it must be ensured that the accession does not affect the situation of Member States in relation to the ECHR (Protocols, derogations and reservations);
• actions between the Union and its Member States would have to be excluded from the scope of the agreement on accession, in order to take account of the monopoly conferred on the EU Court of Justice in such matters by Article III-375(2) Cst.

Moreover, a Declaration no. 2 was annexed to the Final Act of the IGC, in which the Conference stated that the Union's accession to the ECHR should be arranged in such a way as to preserve the specific features of Union law. The IGC considered, in this connection, that the regular dialogue between the EU Court of Justice and the European Court of Human Rights could be reinforced when the Union acceded to the ECHR.

In any case, since the 25 EU Member States are all Contracting Parties to the ECHR, each of them will have to ratify the amendments that will have to be made to the ECHR in order to allow for the EU to become party to it.

Section 2: Strengthening existing EU competences

Some existing competences will be strengthened by the addition of new possibilities for EU action, or by introducing more efficient structures and decision-making procedures.

The most noticeable improvements and reinforcements concern the areas of foreign policy, defence and justice and home affairs.

Foreign policy (CFSP): new tools for a real foreign policy

The Constitution will provide legal and institutional tools which, if used with the necessary political will, could greatly improve the functioning of the EU Common Foreign and Security Policy, enhance the political visibility and effectiveness of the EU on the world stage, and improve the general consistency of its external action.

A short history of CFSP in the EU

The original Rome Treaty of 1957 focused on economic aspects, i.e. the creation of a common market. Several rather ambitious attempts to add a political and defence dimension failed, these being the European Defence Community, and the associated European Political Community, which failed in 1954, and the so-called 'Fouchet plan', about political cooperation and defence policy, which failed in 1962.

From October 1970 and the 'Davignon report', the Member States endeavoured to consult one another on major international policy problems, in a purely intergovernmental fashion, outside the existing Community institutions, through what was then called 'European political cooperation'. In 1986, the Single European Act (Article 30) formalised this cooperation, according to which 'the High Contracting Parties' endeavoured jointly 'to formulate and implement a European foreign policy'. At that time, the 'common positions' were only to constitute 'a point of reference' for the policies of the Member States. This cooperation had its own structures, under the umbrella of special meetings of the Foreign Ministers of the Member States. It was organised and served by the Presidency, with the help of a small Secretariat, based in Brussels and composed of a few diplomats seconded from the Member States. The Commission was 'fully associated with the proceedings of Political Cooperation'.

It was in 1993, with the entry into force of the Maastricht Treaty,[40] that the European Union as such, and more particularly the Council, was given in Title V of the EU Treaty the power to define a 'Common Foreign and Security Policy' (CFSP) and to adopt, by unanimity, legal acts called common positions and joint actions, which committed the Member States (the so-called 'second pillar'). The CFSP was still led by the Council Presidency, and the Commission was still to be 'fully associated with the work'. However, the structures serving the previous Political Cooperation were integrated into the Council structures (working parties and General Secretariat). In 1999, the Amsterdam Treaty made a further qualitative step, with the creation of the office of High Representative for the CFSP, who was to 'assist the Council [in CFSP matters] . . . in particular through contributing to the formulation, preparation and implementation of policy decisions'. Mr Javier Solana, former Foreign Minister of Spain and former Secretary-General of NATO, was appointed High Representative in 1999 for a period of five years. He was reappointed for another five years in 2004.[41]

In the European Security Strategy which he submitted to the European Council in December 2003,[42] the High Representative indicated that 'the challenge now is to bring together the different instruments and capabilities: European assistance programmes and the European Development Fund, military and civilian capabilities from Member States and other instruments', and that 'Diplomatic efforts, development, trade and environmental policies, should follow the same agenda' (page 15).

The innovations brought about by the Constitution

Both in the Convention and in the IGC, the ambition was to take a real qualitative step forward. The aim was to make the Union more 'present

---

[40] See Arts. J to J.11 of the Treaty on European Union signed on 7 February 1992.
[41] Council Decision of 29 June 2004, OJ No. L236, 7 July 2004, p. 15.
[42] The European Security Strategy (doc. 15849/03) was adopted by the European Council of 12 and 13 December 2003 (see para. 84 of the Presidency Conclusions, doc. 5381/04).

in the world', as the European Council had requested in the 2001 Laeken Declaration, to improve substantially the functioning of the CFSP, as well as the consistency between the different areas of EU external policy (CFSP, trade, development, humanitarian aid and other sectoral external policies in environment, transport, etc.).

Rather than amending the substance of the provisions, such as the scope and content of CFSP, attention focused on how to improve decision-making and working structures.

The idea was developed of merging the roles presently performed by the High Representative and the Commissioner for External Affairs into a new office: the 'Union Minister for Foreign Affairs'. The Minister would also take over the tasks of initiative, chairmanship, representation and implementation currently taken care of by the six-monthly rotating Presidency of the Council. CFSP would essentially remain in the hands of the institutions where the Governments of the Member States are directly represented, namely the European Council and the Council.

The merger into a single Title of all provisions on external action The Constitution merges into a single Title on the 'Union's External Action' (Title V of Part III) all provisions on external action: Common Foreign and Security Policy (which includes the common security and defence policy), trade policy, development cooperation and humanitarian aid.

This has allowed placing the EU's whole external action under a single framework of principles and objectives which are applicable to all these 'policies', on top of their own specific objectives (Article III-292 Cst). It has also allowed making these provisions subject to a single procedure for negotiating and concluding international agreements (Article III-325 Cst; see comments above under 'One legal personality' in chapter III).

The creation of the office of Union Minister for Foreign Affairs The Constitution will create a new office of Union Minister for Foreign Affairs.[43] This new office will be 'triple-hatted' in the sense that it will merge the present tasks of:

- the High Representative for CFSP, who, at present, is in charge of assisting the Council, in particular through 'contributing to the formulation, preparation and implementation of policy decisions'

---

[43] In a declaration of 29 June 2004 in which they indicated that they had decided, in agreement with the President designate of the Commission, Mr Barroso, that Mr Javier Solana would be appointed Union Minister for Foreign Affairs on the day of entry into

and through 'conducting political dialogue with third parties' (Article 26 EU Treaty). The High Representative also has authority over the EU Military Staff[44] and coordinates the work of the EU special representatives.[45] In practice, the High Representative does much more than that and, with the backing of the Council, appears more and more, in a number of important matters, as the voice of the EU;

- the Commissioner for External Affairs, who contributes to the Commission's non-exclusive right of initiative in CFSP (Article 22(1) EU Treaty), as well as the possibility for the Commission to assist the Council Presidency in conducting negotiations for the conclusion of international agreements in the field of CFSP (Article 24 EU Treaty); and

- the six-monthly rotating Presidency of the Foreign Affairs Council, which, at present, 'represent[s] the Union in matters coming within the [CFSP]', is 'responsible for the implementation of decisions', 'express[es] the position of the Union in international organisations and international conferences' (Article 18 EU Treaty), negotiates international agreements on behalf of the Council in CFSP matters (Article 24(1) EU Treaty) and consults the European Parliament on CFSP matters (Article 21 EU Treaty).

The Union Minister for Foreign Affairs will be appointed by the European Council, with the agreement of the President of the Commission (Article I-28(1) Cst). The Commission President, the Minister and the other members of the Commission will be subject, as a body, to a vote of consent by the European Parliament (Article I-27(2), 2nd subparagraph, Cst).

---

force of the Constitution, the Heads of State or Government of the EU Member States underlined 'the commitment of Member States to work in support of the [Secretary-General/High Representative] during the transition to the establishment of the function of Union Minister for Foreign Affairs.' They invited 'the President of the Commission and the [Secretary-General/High Representative] to organise the working relations between them in a way that will ensure a smooth and efficient transition and to take the necessary measures to that end'.

[44] See para. 5, 2nd indent, of the Annex to the Council Decision of 22 January 2001 on the establishment of the Military Staff of the European Union (OJ No. L27, 30 January 2001, p. 7).

[45] See Art. 23(3) of the Council's Rules of Procedure. By October 2005, there was a total of ten EU Special Representatives: M. Otte to the Middle East Peace Process, F. Vendrell to Afghanistan, H. Talvitie to South Caucasus, J. Kubiš to Central Asia, A. J. de Szeged to

The Union Minister for Foreign Affairs will be in charge of:

- ensuring the consistency of the Union's external action, which comprises the whole field of external action, not only CFSP, and coordinating all aspects of the Union's external action (Article I-28 (4));
- conducting the Union's CFSP (including ESDP), which he will 'carry out as mandated by the Council' (Article I-28(2) Cst);
- making proposals in the field of CFSP (Articles I-28(2), III-296(1), III-299(1) and III-325(3) Cst), in some cases jointly with the Commission (e.g. Articles III-293(2), III-322 (1) and III-329(2) Cst);
- presiding over the Foreign Affairs Council (Articles I-28(3) and III-296(1) Cst) and taking part in the work of the European Council (Article I-21(2) Cst);
- as Vice-President of the Commission, being 'responsible within the Commission for responsibilities incumbent on it in external relations ... In exercising these responsibilities within the Commission, and only for these responsibilities, the Union [Minister] shall be bound by Commission procedures to the extent that this is consistent with [his role in CFSP under Article I-28(2) and (3) Cst]' (Article I-28(4) Cst);
- representing the Union for matters relating to CFSP, which includes conducting political dialogue with third parties, expressing the Union's position in international organisations and international conferences and presenting the Union's position in the UN Security Council when the Union has defined a position (Articles III-296(2) and III-305(2), 3rd subparagraph, Cst);
- negotiating international agreements in CFSP matters on behalf of the Union, if so mandated by the Council (Article III-325(3) Cst);
- putting into effect the CFSP and ensuring the implementation of CFSP decisions adopted by the European Council and the Council (Articles I-40(4) and III-296(1) Cst), including organising the coordination of the Member States' action in international organisations and at international conferences (Article III-305(1) Cst);

Moldova, P. Ashdown to Bosnia and Herzegovina, E. Fouéré to FYROM, A. Ajello to the African Great Lakes Region, P. Haavisto to Sudan and S. Lehne to the Kosovo future status process. There are also two EU Personal Representatives of the High Representative (A. Giannella on non-proliferation of weapons of mass destruction and M. Matthiessen on human rights in the area of CFSP). The High Representative also appointed G. de Vries as EU Counter-terrorism Coordinator. For more details, see the home page of High Representative Solana on the internet site of the Council.

- consulting and informing the European Parliament 'on the main aspects and basic choices of the [CFSP and ESDP]' and ensuring that the Parliament's views 'are duly taken into consideration' (Articles I-40(8), I-41(8) and III-304 Cst);
- exercising authority over the EU special representatives appointed by the Council (Article III-302 Cst); and
- being in charge of the 'European External Action Service' which will assist him (Article III-296(3) Cst), including the 130 Union delegations in third countries and at international organisations (Article III-328(2) Cst).

The creation of the office of full-time President of the European Council   The creation of the new office of full-time President of the European Council who will also be in charge 'at his or her level and in that capacity, [of ensuring] the external representation of the Union on issues concerning [CFSP], without prejudice to the powers of the [Minister]' (Article I-22(2), 2nd subparagraph, Cst), will also have an impact on the functioning of CFSP. At the very least, it will entail establishing good cooperation between the two new offices.

A timid opening towards more QMV in CFSP matters   As is the case now, the great bulk of CFSP decisions will still be adopted by unanimity.

QMV will be used only in those few cases which are listed in Article III-300(2) Cst:

- adoption of a decision on the basis of a decision of the European Council on 'the Union's strategic interests and objectives', as referred to in Article III-293(1) Cst (a decision which will have been adopted by unanimity);
- adoption of a decision on the basis of a proposal which the Minister has presented 'following a specific request to him or her from the European Council' (which will have been made by consensus in accordance with Article I-21(4) Cst);
- adoption of implementing decisions;
- appointment of special representatives of the EU in accordance with Article III-302 Cst.

This corresponds to the proposal from the Convention which the IGC decided to accept. It mostly takes over the present situation under Article 23(2) of the EU Treaty, the only addition being the second bullet point above, i.e. in the case of a proposal by the Minister following a specific request from the European Council.

During the IGC, the Italian Presidency had attempted to propose that the Council should act by QMV each time it acted on a proposal from the Minister,[46] but this was never considered to be a realistic proposal and was quietly abandoned some weeks later.

The real novelty in this field is rather the specific 'passerelle' in Article III-300(3) Cst which will enable the European Council, by unanimity and without the need to go through national ratifications in the Member States, to switch more cases to QMV than those listed above. However, this 'passerelle' will not apply to 'decisions having military or defence implications' (Article III-300(4) Cst).

The creation of an External Action Service   Pursuant to the EC Treaty, the Council is presently assisted by a General Secretariat, under the responsibility of a Secretary-General, High Representative for the CFSP, who is assisted by a Deputy Secretary-General. Within this General Secretariat, there are different Directorates General (DG), including one in charge of External Relations (CFSP, ESDP, enlargement, trade and development), as well as the Policy Unit,[47] the Situation Centre[48] and the EU Military Staff.[49]

The Commission has, among its 23 DGs, six DGs dealing directly with external relations matters (DG External Relations, DG Trade, DG

---

[46] See Annex 18 of doc. CIG 52/03 ADD 1 of 25 November 2003 which was presented in Naples.

[47] The 'Policy Planning and Early Warning Unit' was created in 1998 as a consequence of the Amsterdam Treaty, which had created the office of 'High Representative for CFSP', and in accordance with Declaration no. 6 to the Final Act of the Amsterdam IGC. In this Declaration, the Conference had agreed to establish in the General Secretariat of the Council a unit whose task would be, *inter alia*, to monitor and analyse developments in areas relevant to the CFSP, to provide assessments of the Union's CFSP and identify areas on which it could focus, and to provide assessments and early warning of events or situations which might have significant repercussions on CFSP, including potential crises.

[48] The Joint Situation Centre or 'SitCen' was created by the Secretary-General of the Council, High Representative for CFSP. Initially within the Policy Unit, it was later on turned into a separate unit where intelligence is exchanged between relevant services from the Member States. It produces daily assessments for the use of the Political and Security Committee and the High Representative. Its attributions have been expanded to cover JHA matters as well.

[49] The EU Military Staff (EUMS) was established in 2001 (OJ No. L27, 30 January 2001, p. 7) and now employs about 200 persons, of which about 150 military officers are seconded by Member States. It provides military expertise to the Council and its bodies and to the High Representative. It also provides early warning capabilities, plans, assesses

Development, DG Enlargement, DG Humanitarian Aid Office (ECHO) and DG EuropeAid Cooperation Office).

During the Convention, the idea emerged of a Service dealing with all matters in the area of external relations of the Union, encompassing both CFSP (including ESDP), which is presently under the responsibility of services of the General Secretariat of the Council, and other sectors, such as external trade or development cooperation, which are presently under the responsibility of services of the Commission. The creation of an EU Diplomatic Academy and of an EU Diplomatic Service was contemplated. Some ideas about transforming EU delegations into 'Embassies' were also discussed. The final text of the Constitution is less far-reaching than that.

The Constitution contains a new legal basis which will allow the Council to establish an External Action Service. This Service will assist the Union Minister for Foreign Affairs. It will work 'in cooperation with the diplomatic services of the Member States and shall comprise officials from relevant departments of the General Secretariat of the Council and of the Commission as well as staff seconded from national diplomatic services of the Member States' (Article III-296(3) Cst). One may note that this provision is placed in the Chapter on CFSP, within the Title on the EU's external action, although its role would most likely not be limited to purely CFSP matters (see the assessment below).

The organisation and functioning of the External Action Service will be laid down by a decision of the Council, acting by unanimity on a proposal from the Minister, after consulting the European Parliament and obtaining the consent of the Commission. This Service will include a central administration as well as the 130 or so Commission and Council delegations abroad,[50] which will become 'Union delegations', placed under the authority of the Union Minister for Foreign Affairs (Article III-328(2) Cst).

According to a Declaration no. 24 to the Final Act of the IGC: 'as soon as the Treaty establishing a Constitution for Europe is signed, the Secretary-General of the Council, High Representative for the common foreign and security policy, the Commission and the Member States should

---

and makes recommendations on the concept of crisis management and the general military strategy, supports the Military Committee regarding situation assessment and military aspects of strategic planning for EU-led operations, etc.

[50] Of which the Council has only two delegations, one at the UN in Geneva and one at the UN in New York.

begin preparatory work on the European External Action Service'. The Secretary-General of the Council, High Representative for CFSP and the President of the Commission submitted in March 2005 an 'Issues Paper on the European External Action Service' as a preparatory step towards another report for the European Council in June 2005, as requested by the European Council in December 2004. They then submitted to the European Council in June 2005 a 'Joint Progress Report' on the European External Action Service.[51]

The Commission's general role in ensuring the Union's external representation, except for CFSP The Constitution provides for a general rule according to which the Commission 'with the exception of [CFSP], and other cases provided for in the Constitution . . . shall ensure the Union's external representation' (Article I-26(1) Cst). This corresponds more or less to the present practice under which the Commission represents the EC when there is an EC competence and when there is no obstacle to its doing so in the forum where the negotiation takes place.[52]

Assessment of the new provisions

With regard to the future representation of the EU, the picture looks promising. However, it remains to be seen whether the Union Minister for Foreign Affairs will be in a position to fully implement his role of representing the Union, and how this role will be reconciled with those entrusted by the Constitution, both to the President of the European Council and to the Commission.[53]

---

[51] See doc. 9956/05 of 9 June 2005, accessible on the internet site of the Council.

[52] There may be cases where, due to the fact that the EC (or the Commission on behalf of the EC) has no seat or no right to speak in an international organisation, the six-monthly council Presidency will express the position of the EC instead. There are also cases where, because a negotiation concerns both EC competences and national competences (so-called 'mixed agreements') and if the Member States do not want to mandate the Commission to negotiate on matters belonging to their national competences, there will be two 'negotiators': the Commission with regard to EC competences and the Presidency with regard to the national competences.

[53] For an assessment of the provisions of the Constitution on the Union Minister for Foreign Affairs, see B. Crowe, *Foreign Minister of Europe* (Foreign Policy Centre, February 2005), http://fpc.org.uk/fsblob/395.pdf.

With respect to his role regarding the coordination of other aspects of the Union's external action (i.e. other than CFSP), the Minister, who has not been granted legal authority over his fellow Commissioners, will have take into account the actions undertaken by the other members of the Commission, over whom the President of the Commission does have legal authority. He will also have to take into account the different configurations of the Council. On the one hand, the Foreign Affairs Council, under his presidency, will develop the Union's external action on the basis of strategic guidelines laid down by the European Council and will ensure that the Union's action is consistent. On the other hand, it will be for the General Affairs Council to ensure consistency in the work of the different Council configurations (Article I-24(2) Cst), and that configuration will continue to be chaired by the six-monthly rotating Presidency. Other Council configurations, also chaired by the rotating Presidency, will continue, as at present, to play a role in the Union's external action in their respective sectors (such as environment, justice and home affairs, transport, etc.).

As for the European External Action Service, it will be neither an EU institution within the meaning of the Constitution, nor an agency, nor an office attached to the Commission: it will be a 'Service'. This raises a number of issues that need to be addressed during the preparatory work which has already begun following the signature of the Constitution: should this autonomous Service be an integrated and comprehensive structure, or a light coordinating tool? Should it incorporate limited or large parts of the present services within the Commission (certainly the DG on External Relations and probably not DG Trade, but what about the geographical desks in the Enlargement DG or the Development DG?), as well as those within the General Secretariat of the Council dealing with external relations (certainly most of the DG on External Relations and the Policy Unit, but what about the Situation Centre and the EU Military Staff)? Would it also include expertise in certain other areas linked to external relations? How many diplomats would be seconded to the Service by the Member States? Would the Service be called upon to have a role in consular protection, in the issuing of visas, etc.? Would it have the necessary budgetary flexibility in order to enable the Union Minister to act swiftly?

In any case, foreign policy is so close to the heart of the sovereignty of each of the Member States that, despite these new means of action, nothing will be done in this field without a shared political will by all of them. The necessary unanimity will be difficult to obtain in a group of 25 or 27, but one has to recognise that at present there is no realistic alternative in this field.

Defence (ESDP): further steps towards a more efficient policy

The Constitution also greatly improves the provisions on defence, a sector which over the last five years has taken giant steps compared to its progress during the previous 50 years of European integration. These improvements should give the Council and the Member States a wider choice of flexible and efficient solutions in order to conduct the whole range of civil or military operations and therefore improve the specific value-added of the EU in the field of crisis management.

A short history of defence in the EU

ESDP is often presented as one of the recent success stories of the EU, the other one being the single currency, although ESDP still has quite a long way to go to reach a comparable level of integration to the euro. But like the euro, ESDP is the result of a long maturing process.[54]

A first attempt on defence policy had been the Treaty establishing the European Defence Community, signed in May 1952, one year after the Treaty establishing the Coal and Steel Community (ECSC), but it was rejected by the French Parliament in August 1954. This Treaty was very ambitious. It was to establish a supranational Community with common armed forces, its own budget, and institutions comparable to the ones of the newly created ECSC. Another attempt which failed was the so-called 'Fouchet plan' in 1962. In parallel, the less ambitious Western European Union had been established in 1948, and was enlarged to include Germany and Italy in 1954.

Article 30(6) of the Single European Act in 1986 was the first Treaty between the EU's Member States ever to mention the words 'European security'. The word 'defence', however, was not mentioned, because European security was seen only from its 'political and economic

---

[54] See R. A. Wessel, 'The State of Affairs in EU Security and Defence Policy: The Breakthrough in the Treaty of Nice' (2003) Vol. 8, No. 2 *Journal of Conflict and Security Law* 265–288; G. Andréani, C. Bertram and C. Grant, *Europe's Military Revolution*, (London, Centre for European Reform, March 2001), http://www.cer.org.uk/pdf/ p22w_military_revolution.pdf; P. de Schoutheete, *La cohérence par la défense: une autre lecture de la PESD* (Paris, EU Institute for Security Studies, *Cahiers de Chaillot no. 71*, 2004), http://www.iss-eu.org/chaillot71.pdf and *EU Security and Defence Policy: The First Five Years (1999–2004)*, edited by N. Gnesotto, Preface by J. Solana, EU Institute for Security Studies, Paris, 2004, http://www.iss-eu.org/books/5esdpen.pdf.

aspects' on which the 'High Contracting Parties' were to coordinate their positions. This was the lowest common denominator at that time.

It was in the Maastricht Treaty in 1992 that the words 'common defence policy, which might in time lead to a common defence' appeared for the first time, as part of the chapter on the common foreign and security policy. However, this stated ambition remained largely ineffective. The Bosnian war broke out during that period (1992–95) and was widely perceived as a failure for the EU.

The Amsterdam Treaty, signed in October 1997, added a provision to the EU Treaty listing the so-called 'Petersberg tasks'[55] which the EU could undertake. These are 'humanitarian and rescue tasks, peace-keeping tasks and tasks of combat forces in crisis management, including peace-making' (Article 17(2) EU Treaty). But the EU's weakness was about to appear again in Kosovo where the Serbian army started its operations in August 1998. Public opinion as well as governments became frustrated at seeing exposed the EU's incapacity to manage crises effectively, even on its own doorstep.

In December 1998, the UK and France, the two EU countries with the most significant 'power-projection' capabilities in military terms, held a summit in Saint Malo in which they adopted an important Declaration.[56] This was to be the real start for the European Security and Defence Policy: 'The European Union needs to be in a position to play its full role on the international stage . . . This includes the responsibility of the European Council to decide on the progressive framing of a common defence policy in the framework of CFSP . . . To this end, the Union must have the capacity for autonomous action, backed up by credible military forces, the means to decide to use them, and a readiness to do so, in order to respond to international crises . . . In order for the European Union to take decisions and approve military action where the Alliance as a whole is not engaged, the Union must be given appropriate structures and a capacity for analysis of situations, sources of intelligence, and a capability for relevant strategic planning, without

---

[55] Named after the place near Bonn where the Western European Union (WEU) first defined these tasks in 1992.

[56] For a list of important documents on ESDP, see *From St Malo to Nice: European Defence: core documents* (Paris, EU Institute for Security Studies, *Chaillot Paper no. 47*, 2001), www.iss-eu.org/chaillot/chai47e.pdf, which contains the St Malo Joint Declaration. See also *Cahier de Chaillot* no. 75, vol. V (Feb. 2005), which contains basic documents of 2004.

unnecessary duplication, taking account of the existing assets of the WEU and the evolution of its relations with the EU.'

From then on, things developed very fast. In June 1999, the European Council in Cologne decided to establish new bodies within the Council: the Political and Security Committee (PSC) consisting of national representatives based in their respective Permanent Representations in Brussels (which would replace the 'Political Committee' in Article 25 of the EU Treaty), the EU Military Committee (EUMC), made up of national chiefs of defence staff or their deputies and an EU Military Staff (EUMS) attached to the General Secretariat of the Council (which now numbers about 200 persons, of which there are about 150 military officers seconded by the Member States). It also decided that the EU would take over from the WEU the Institute for Security Studies, based in Paris, and the Satellite Centre, based in Torrejón, Spain.[57]

In December 1999, the European Council in Helsinki decided to boost Europe's military capabilities by setting a 'headline goal' according to which by 2003 the Member States would be able to deploy, in the field and within 60 days, up to 60,000 self-sustaining troops for a year (which, with rotations, implies a total pool of at least 200,000 available troops and three mobile corps headquarters). In December 2002, the EU and NATO finally hammered out the so-called 'Berlin plus' Agreement which includes arrangements allowing the Union to have recourse to NATO's assets and capabilities for an EU-led operation.

In parallel, and in order to complement the military side with a civilian side, which constitutes the added-value of the EU in crisis management, the European Council had also decided to set up a Committee for Civilian Aspects of Crisis Management[58] and to define civilian headline goals for crisis management, such as the deployment of policemen (5000 persons), administrators to restore civilian administration, judicial officials (200) and civil protection intervention teams (2000 persons) (see list of ESDP operations in box 5.2).[59]

---

[57] See the two Council Joint Actions of 20 July 2001 (OJ No. L200; 25 July 2001, pp. 1 and 5).

[58] Council Decision no. 2000/354/CFSP of 22 May 2000 (OJ No. L127, 27 May 2000, p. 1).

[59] See Presidency Conclusions of the European Council in Helsinki (Annex IV to the Conclusions, December 1999), Feira (Annex 1 to the Conclusions, June 2000) and in Göteborg (June 2001, Annex III doc. 9526/1/01 REV 1).

Box 5.2   ESDP operations and missions of the EU (2003–2005)[1]

Since 2003, the EU has undertaken ten operations of a military character or of a civilian character:

Military operations

- 'Concordia' was the first EU-led military operation. It made use of common NATO assets and capabilities which it took over on 31 March 2003. This operation was based on UNSC Resolution no. 1371 and an explicit request of the government of the former Yugoslav Republic of Macedonia. It was aimed at contributing further to a stable secure environment in fYROM and allowing the implementation of the August 2001 Ohrid Framework Agreement. The operation lasted from March to December 2003;
- 'Artemis' was the first autonomous EU-led military operation. This operation was conducted in accordance with UNSC Resolution no. 1484. It was aimed, *inter alia*, at contributing to the stabilisation of the security conditions and the improvement of the humanitarian situation in Bunia (Democratic Republic of Congo). The operation lasted from June to August 2003;
- 'Althea' is the EU-led military operation which took over on 2 December 2004 from the NATO SFOR-operation in Bosnia-Herzegovina. It makes use of common NATO assets and capabilities. The aim is to deploy a force (7,000 troops) with a Chapter VII UN Charter mission under UNSC Resolution no. 1551 to ensure continued compliance with the Dayton/Paris Agreement and to contribute to a safe and secure environment in BiH.

Civilian operations

- 'EUPM' is the first EU-led Police mission. It takes place in Bosnia-Herzegovina, where it started on 1 January 2003, following on from the UN's International Police Task Force. It is composed of some 500 police officers from about 30 countries. Pursuant to UNSC Resolution no. 1396, it is aimed at establishing sustainable policing arrangements under BiH ownership in accordance with best European and international practice;

- 'Eupol Proxima' is an EU-led Police mission in the former Yugoslav Republic of Macedonia which was launched on 15 December 2003. Police experts (i.e. around 200 personnel from EU Member States and other countries) are monitoring, mentoring and advising that country's police thus helping to fight organised crime as well as promoting European policing standards;
- 'Eujust Themis' is the first EU Rule of Law operation. It is taking place in Georgia and was launched on 16 July 2004. Senior and highly qualified experts support, mentor and advise Ministers, senior officials and appropriate bodies at the level of the central government;
- 'Eupol Kinshasa' is an EU-led Police mission in the Democratic Republic of Congo launched in January 2005. It aims at assisting in the setting up of an Integrated Police Unit in order to contribute to ensuring the protection of the state institutions and reinforcing the internal security apparatus;
- 'Eujust Lex' is an EU Rule of Law mission in Iraq which the Council agreed on 21 February 2005 and which was launched in July 2005. It aims at improving the Iraqi criminal justice system by providing training for officials in senior management and criminal investigations, primarily from the police, judiciary and penitentiary services, and improving skills and procedures in criminal investigations whilst ensuring full respect for the rule of law and human rights;
- 'Eusec-RD Congo' is an EU advisory and assistance mission for security reform in the Democratic Republic of Congo launched on 8 June 2005;
- 'Aceh Monitoring Mission', launched on 15 September 2005 by the EU and five ASEAN countries, monitors the commitments undertaken by the Government of Indonesia and the Free Aceh Movement (GAM) and will in particular monitor the decommissioning of weapons, re-location of non-organic military forces, reintegration of active GAM members, rulings on disputed amnesty cases, etc.

Note: [1] Further details may be found on the internet site of the Council (http://ue.eu. int) under 'ESDP operations'. The EU will also launch two missions in the Palestinian territories, a police mission (EUPOL COPPS) to help build up the capacity of the Palestinian civil police, and one for border control assistance at the Rafah crossing-point (EU BAM Rafah).

The Nice Treaty, which entered into force in 2003, brought about more innovations, in particular by enhancing the role of the Political and Security Committee in crisis management operations through giving it the right to adopt decisions upon delegation from the Council. Finally, the European Council meeting in December 2003 decided to establish a 'Civil Military Cell' designed, *inter alia*, to enhance the EU's capacity for crisis management planning and to generate the capacity to plan and run autonomous EU operations.[60]

The innovations brought about by the Constitution

The political will to go further in ESDP was clearly present among the drafters of the Constitution. The Convention, while taking over the existing Treaty provisions, proposed several innovations such as the updating of the so-called 'Petersberg tasks', the possibility of entrusting a crisis management task to a group of willing Member States, as well as a 'structured cooperation' between those Member States fulfilling higher criteria in military capabilities, a closer cooperation between willing Member States on mutual defence, the establishment of a Defence Agency, the possibility of having enhanced cooperation in defence and a legal basis to create a start-up fund for financing crisis management tasks. But some of these novelties, such as the 'structured cooperation' between 'the able' and closer cooperation in mutual defence between 'the willing', did not have unanimous support.

Thanks to preparatory talks held between France, Germany and the UK in the autumn of 2003, an informal agreement in the IGC could be reached rather quickly during the Italian Presidency at the IGC meeting in Naples in November 2003, where the provisions on mutual defence and 'structured cooperation' proposed by the Convention were thoroughly redrafted.

Provisions regarding the ESDP are contained mainly in Article I-41 and Articles III-309 to III-313 Cst:

- ESDP will continue to be an integral part of CFSP. The Union may use civilian and military assets on missions outside the Union for peace-keeping, conflict prevention and strengthening international security in accordance with the principles of the United Nations Charter;
- Member States will make civilian and military capabilities available to the Union for the implementation of the ESDP, in order to contribute to the objectives defined by the Council;

---

[60] See Presidency Conclusions of the European Council, 12–13 December 2003, p. 23 and doc. 10580/1/04 REV 1 of 8 September 2005, 'Civil Military Cell – Terms of Reference'.

- the tasks to be performed in this respect will include joint disarmament operations, humanitarian and rescue tasks, military advice and assistance tasks, conflict prevention and peace-keeping tasks, tasks of combat forces in crisis management, including peace-making and post-conflict stabilisation;
- a novelty worth noticing is the use of QMV in certain crucial provisions such as the launching and the membership of a 'permanent structured cooperation' (Article III-312 Cst), the definition of the statute, seat and operational rules of the Defence Agency (Article III-311 Cst) and the establishment of a start-up fund for ESDP operations (Article III-313(3), 3rd subparagraph, Cst).

The clarification of the scope of EU crisis management tasks   The Constitution will clarify the scope of the EU crisis management tasks, by mentioning their two aspects, civilian and military, and bring the list of the so-called 'Petersberg tasks' up to date by explicitly including disarmament operations, military advice and assistance, conflict prevention and post-conflict stabilisation (Articles I-41 and III-309 Cst).

The 'solidarity clauses'   First, the Constitution will introduce, in Article I-41(7), an obligation for all Member States to give aid and assistance by all the means in their power, in accordance with Article 51 of the UN Charter, to a Member State which has been the victim of armed aggression on its territory. In order to reassure those Member States which have adopted a neutrality policy, it is made clear that this 'shall not prejudice the specific character of the security and defence policy of certain Member States'. This provision, which was nicknamed the 'solidarity clause', does not transform the EU into a military alliance. It specifies that 'commitments and cooperation in this area shall be consistent with commitments under the [NATO Treaty] which, for those States which are members of it, remains the foundation of their collective defence and the forum for its implementation'. This solidarity clause is of the utmost symbolic and political importance for the EU. However, it does not amount to a mutual defence clause and does not change anything about the respective position of each Member State vis-à-vis NATO.

Secondly, Articles I-43 and III-329 Cst contain another 'solidarity clause' according to which 'the Union and its Member States shall act jointly in a spirit of solidarity if a Member State is the object of a terrorist attack or the victim of a natural or man-made disaster'. They will assist

such a Member State 'at the request of its political authorities'. The clause
further provides that 'the Union shall mobilise all the instruments at its
disposal, including the military resources made available by the Member
States' for prevention, protection and assistance in case of terrorist
threats or terrorist attacks. For that purpose, the Council will be assisted
by the Political and Security Committee and by the standing committee
referred to in Article III-261 Cst in charge of ensuring that operational
cooperation on internal security is promoted and strengthened within
the Union. The significance of such a provision became all the more
obvious following the terrible terrorist attacks on 11 March 2004 in
Madrid and on 7 July 2005 in London.

**The possibility of entrusting a group of Member States with an ESDP
mission**   The Constitution will introduce the possibility for the Council
to entrust a group of Member States, which are willing and have the
necessary capability, with an ESDP mission having the aim of protecting
EU values and serving its interests (Articles I-41(5) and III-310 Cst).

This is new and will provide the EU with great flexibility in its reaction
to certain crisis situations where a quick response is essential. Because, in
practice, the large Member States have a wider range of capabilities than
the smaller States, this possibility was seen by some small Member States
as a risky trend towards ESDP being taken over by large Member States
and it had therefore been resisted up to now. Anyway, in real life, most EU
missions do not involve all 25 Member States on the ground, but only
those Member States, large or small, which decide to contribute to it
(through providing personnel, transport and all the support necessary to
fulfil the aims of the mission). The possibility opened up by Article I-41
(5) Cst will thus make certain operations easier to manage.

The 'permanent structured cooperation'   The Constitution will create
the possibility of a permanent structured cooperation between willing
Member States 'whose military capabilities fulfil higher criteria' (Articles
41(6) and III-312 Cst and Protocol (no. 23) on permanent structured
cooperation). Under these provisions, 'those Member States whose
military capabilities fulfil higher criteria and which have made more
binding commitments to one another in this area with a view to the
most demanding missions shall establish permanent structured
cooperation within the Union framework' (Article I-41(6) Cst).

Protocol no. 23 provides that this cooperation 'shall be open to any
Member State which undertakes, from the date of entry into force of the

[Constitution], to . . . proceed more intensively to develop its defence capacities . . . and to have the capacity to supply by 2007 at the latest . . . targeted combat units' under specified conditions (Article 1 of the Protocol).[61] To that end, Member States participating in this cooperation will undertake, in particular, to 'take concrete measures to enhance the availability, interoperability, flexibility and deployability of their forces, in particular by identifying common objectives regarding the commitment of forces, including possibly reviewing their national decision-making procedures' (Article 2(c) of the Protocol). The list of the Member States participating in this cooperation will be adopted by the Council, using QMV (Article III-312(2) Cst). This is quite remarkable when compared with the condition for launching an 'enhanced cooperation' in the field of CFSP or ESDP which requires unanimity (Article III-419(2), 2nd subparagraph, Cst).

The 'permanent structured cooperation' is open to any Member State which fulfils the criteria and makes the required commitments. Likewise, any participating Member State may withdraw from the cooperation or be suspended from the cooperation when it no longer fulfils the criteria for participation. Pursuant to Article III-312(3) Cst 'any Member State which, at a later stage, wishes to participate in [the] cooperation shall notify its intention to the Council and to the Union Minister for Foreign Affairs. The Council shall adopt a European decision confirming the participation of the Member State concerned.' Conversely, 'if a participating Member State no longer fulfils the criteria or is no longer able to meet the commitments . . . the Council may adopt a European decision suspending the participation of the Member State concerned' (Article III-312(4) Cst) and 'any participating Member State which wishes to withdraw from [the cooperation] shall notify its intention to the Council . . .' (Article III-312(5) Cst). Again, in both cases (participation at a later stage or suspension of the participation of a Member State), the Council will decide by QMV.

---

[61] The so-called '2010 Headline Goal' agreed in June 2004, and aimed at improving capabilities of the EU Member States so as to be able to respond to the whole spectrum of crisis management operations covered by the EU Treaty, already comprises, as part of the rapid response capability, the so-called 'battlegroups' formed among willing and capable Member States, i.e. groups of at least 1,500 men from one or more Member States with specific capabilities (ability to deploy abroad within ten days, ability to remain in the theatre of operations for a given period, etc.) (see doc. 6309/6/04 Rev 6, available in the Council's Register of Documents on the Council's internet site).

The creation of a Defence Agency   The Constitution will provide for the establishment by the Council, using QMV, of a Defence Agency in the fields of capabilities development, research, acquisition and armaments (Articles I-41(3) and III-311 Cst). Actually, such an Agency has already been established unanimously by the Council on 12 July 2004, on the basis of the present EU Treaty (Article 17), and it has started to operate.[62] The Constitution will therefore enable the Council to amend the statute and operational rules of this Agency using QMV. The mandate of the Agency is to identify operational requirements, promote measures to satisfy those requirements, contribute to identifying and implementing any measure needed to strengthen the industrial and technological base of the defence sector, to participate in defining a European capabilities and armament policy, and to assist the Council in evaluating the improvement of military capabilities.

The possibility of establishing a start-up fund for ESDP operations   The Constitution will facilitate the financing of EU military operations by creating the possibility for the Council to establish, using QMV, a start-up fund, made up of Member States' contributions, designed to finance preparatory activities of such operations (Article III-313(3), 2nd subparagraph, Cst). Again, the use of QMV for such a decision deserves to be noted.

Justice and Home Affairs (JHA): better decision-making, more competences and full judicial control

The Constitution will also greatly improve the provisions on JHA, a sector which is generally considered by EU citizens to be particularly important for the future. In particular, the Constitution will switch almost all JHA matters to QMV and codecision. It will extend the possibility of approximating national rules in the field of judicial cooperation in criminal matters. It will also allow for better police and judicial

---

[62] See Council Joint Action 2004/551/CFSP of 12 July 2004 on the establishment of the European Defence Agency (OJ No. L245, 17 July 2004, p. 17). The Agency employs about 80 persons. In March 2005, its steering board decided that, by the end of the year, 'a voluntary intergovernmental approach to opening up defence procurement to competition within Europe' would be adopted (see report by Mr Solana in his capacity as Head of the Agency, doc. 8967/05 of 17 May 2005, which may be found on the internet site of the Council, under 'Policies', 'Security & Defence' and 'European Defence Agency').

cooperation, notably by making it easier to give new tasks to Europol and Eurojust. It will finally bring the whole JHA sector under the full jurisdiction of the Court of Justice.

A short history of Justice and Home Affairs in the EU

From 1975, there had been some cooperation between Member States, either in the framework of European Political Cooperation or in the margins of the Council, which involved Ministers for Home Affairs on issues such as terrorism and police cooperation, drugs or border controls (the so-called 'Trevi Group' was established informally at the request of the European Council in Rome in December 1975). This also involved Justice Ministers on matters concerning judicial cooperation, although most developments in judicial matters took place within the larger framework of the Council of Europe.

Over time, several Member States realised that establishing complete free movement of persons within the Community, in a way that would be visible for the citizens, would entail the abolition of physical controls on persons at internal borders. This would consequently require a number of so-called 'compensatory measures' such as reinforced controls at external borders, a common visa policy and other measures regarding third country nationals, police and judicial cooperation, information exchange, etc.

In 1986, the Single European Act inserted a new Article 8a in the Treaty (now Article 14 EC Treaty and in the future Article III-130(2) Cst)) which stated that 'the internal market shall comprise an area without internal frontiers, in which the free movement of goods, persons, services and capital is ensured in accordance with the provisions of this Treaty'. A Declaration on this Article confirmed the right of Member States to continue to take measures on 'controlling immigration from third countries, and to combat terrorism, crime, the traffic in drugs and illicit trading in works of art and antiques'. Another Declaration 'on the free movement of persons' stated that 'in order to promote the free movement of persons, the Member States shall cooperate . . . in particular as regards the entry, movement and residence of nationals of third countries. They shall also cooperate in the combating of terrorism, crime, the traffic in drugs and illicit trading in works of art and antiques.'

Behind this was the wish of several Member States to create a 'People's Europe', a Europe which the citizens would see as directly benefiting them. To that end, a committee was created in June 1984 by the European Council in Fontainebleau, whose mandate included the task of making proposals on 'how all police and customs formalities on the movement of persons at borders within the Community could be abolished as quickly as possible'. This began outside the legal framework of the Community. One year later, on 14 June 1985, Belgium, France, Germany, Luxembourg and the Netherlands signed in Schengen, a village in Luxembourg, the 'Schengen Agreement' on the gradual abolition of checks at their common borders. On 19 June 1990, they signed the 'Schengen Implementing Convention' on 'compensatory measures'. They were joined later on by Italy (November 1990), Portugal and Spain (June 1991), Greece (November 1992), Austria (April 1995) and the Nordic countries, Denmark, Finland and Sweden (December 1996). The 'Schengen area' entered into force in March 1995 between the five original States plus Portugal and Spain. It entered into force in October 1997 for Italy, in December 1997 for Austria and in January 2000 for Greece.

In the meantime, as from 1 November 1993, the Treaty of Maastricht had introduced provisions on cooperation in the fields of Justice and Home Affairs in Title VI of the EU Treaty (the so-called 'third pillar'). Ten Articles set out the procedures for dealing with nine areas 'of common interest': asylum policy, rules on crossing by persons of the external borders of the Member States and the exercise of controls there, immigration policy and policy regarding nationals of third countries, combating drug addiction, combating fraud on an international scale, judicial cooperation in civil matters, judicial cooperation in criminal matters, customs cooperation and police cooperation.

As from 1 May 1999, the Treaty of Amsterdam incorporated the Schengen Agreement into the EU legal framework, through a protocol. The JHA provisions were completely rewritten. Measures with respect to external border controls on persons (including visa policy), asylum, immigration and safeguarding the rights of nationals of third countries, as well as measures in the field of judicial cooperation in civil matters, were 'communitarised' (new Title IV in part three of the EC Treaty), whereas the remaining provisions in Title VI of the EU Treaty were limited to police and judicial cooperation in criminal matters.

As from March 2001, the 'Schengen area' covered all Member States, except for Ireland and the UK. Two third countries (Iceland and Norway) were associated with the area, in accordance with Article 6 of the Protocol integrating the Schengen *acquis* into the framework of the European Union. This is because they already had an agreement on free movement of persons with the three Nordic EU countries: Denmark,

Finland and Sweden. Only Ireland and the UK, which 'opted out' at Amsterdam, continued to apply controls on persons at their borders with the other Member States. Denmark also opted out from participating in the adoption of Community measures, but it still applies them when they constitute a development of the Schengen *acquis*, although only as 'an obligation under international law' (Article 5 of the Protocol on the position of Denmark). Following enlargement on 1 May 2004, the process towards fully applying the Schengen rules to the new Member States has started, some of them expecting to be part of the 'Schengen area' in 2007. Moreover, on 26 October 2004, the EU signed an agreement associating Switzerland with the Schengen area, which the Swiss people accepted by a majority of 54.6% in a referendum on 5 June 2005 (see box 5.3 on variable geometry in JHA). The Swiss people also agreed by a majority of 56% in a referendum on 25 September 2005 to extend to the ten new EU Member States the scope of the EU-Switzerland agreement on free movement of persons.

Box 5.3   Variable geometry in JHA

The variety in the nature and geographical scope of the JHA rules is a particular feature of this area which results from the need to accommodate the concerns of certain Member States, whilst not preventing others from going forward. This feature will continue to exist when the Constitution enters into force. This 'variable geometry' results, on the one hand, from Protocols setting out the special positions of certain Member States and, on the other hand, from agreements with third countries; it makes the adoption of acts in this field very difficult and complicated:

- Denmark does not participate in the adoption of Community measures. However, it applies them as a matter of public international law, only where they constitute a development of the Schengen *acquis*. This requires identifying in each case whether the measure in question constitutes a 'development of the Schengen *acquis*', which is not always obvious;
- the UK and Ireland only participate to a limited extent in the Schengen *acquis* and its development. They have opted out from measures in the fields of immigration, asylum and civil law cooperation, with the right to decide on a case by case basis whether they wish to participate in the adoption of a measure;[1]

- the ten new Member States which acceded to the EU in May 2004 are also, for the time being, only partially bound by the provisions of the Schengen *acquis*. Its provisions relating to the lifting of checks on persons at common borders with other Member States will only become applicable once a specific Council Decision is taken to that effect;

- agreements have been negotiated with three third States (Iceland, Norway and Switzerland), allowing for their association with the application, implementation and development of the Schengen *acquis*. For Iceland and Norway, this association entered into force in March 2001. For Switzerland, the association agreement was signed in October 2004 and will be applicable after its entry into force and the adoption of a specific Council Decision on the putting into effect of the Schengen *acquis* for Switzerland.

Note: [1] For an example of this complexity, see the action for annulment which the UK has brought against the Council Regulation establishing the European Agency for the Management of Operational Cooperation at the External Borders of the EU (case C-77/05) because the Council decided that this Regulation constitutes a development of the provisions of the Schengen *acquis* in which the UK does not take part, a decision which the UK contests.

The innovations brought about by the Constitution

From the start, the Convention was nearly unanimous in its wish to strengthen the so-called 'third pillar' and to 'communitarise' it. The IGC decided to follow this path and regarded the JHA chapter as one of the most important for the future of the Union. The innovations in the Constitution with regard to JHA are the following:

QMV and codecision for asylum, immigration and external border controls   The Constitution will switch all the provisions on asylum and immigration policies and on external border controls to QMV and codecision and will make them subject to the principle of solidarity and the fair sharing of responsibility (Articles III-257(2) and III-265 to III-268 Cst).

QMV and codecision for most provisions on criminal matters   The Constitution will widen the possibility for adopting measures on the approximation of laws or minimum rules in the field of judicial cooperation in criminal matters by using QMV and codecision (Articles III-270 and III-271 Cst). However, a new procedural device, called 'brake-accelerator' by the negotiators during the IGC, was inserted in the text in order to make the switch to QMV more acceptable to those Member States most sensitive about it (see box 5.4).

The Constitution will also widen the possibility of adding to the tasks of Eurojust, by QMV and codecision (Article III-273 Cst). Likewise, it will widen the scope of police cooperation as well as the possibility of enlarging the tasks of Europol, again by QMV and codecision (Articles III-275 and III-276 Cst), thus doing away with the requirement that all Member States ratify amendments to the Europol Convention in order to give new tasks to Europol.

Box 5.4   The 'brake-accelerator' system in the area of judicial cooperation in criminal matters

In order to make the switch to QMV more acceptable in the sensitive area of judicial cooperation in criminal matters, the IGC invented a new procedure, quickly nicknamed by the negotiators the 'brake-accelerator', with two elements:

the first one is a so-called 'emergency brake' system which allows a Member State which considers that a draft legislative act 'would affect fundamental aspects of its criminal justice system', to bring the matter to the European Council, in which case the decision-making procedure will be suspended for a duration of four months. After discussion, the European Council must either refer the draft back to the Council, which will terminate the suspension of the procedure, or request the Commission or the group of Member States from which the draft originated to submit a new draft, in which case the act originally proposed will be deemed not to have been adopted (see Articles III-270(3) and III-271(3) Cst);

the second element is a so-called 'accelerator' designed to avoid a stalemate. If, by the end of the four months' period, the European Council has taken no action or if, within twelve months from the submission of a new draft, the legislative act has not been adopted, and at least one-third of the Member States wish to establish an enhanced cooperation on the basis of the draft act in question, they will notify the European Parliament, the Council and the Commission accordingly and the enhanced cooperation will automatically apply between them, thus by-passing some of the preliminary steps which are normally required under the enhanced cooperation procedure and hence 'accelerating' the procedure (see Articles III-270(4) and III-271(4) Cst).

A European Public Prosecutor's Office to protect the EU's financial interests   The Constitution will add a new legal basis empowering the Council to create a European Public Prosecutor's Office. After difficult discussions, the IGC agreed to limit the Prosecutor's tasks to the combating of offences against the EU's financial interests (Article III-274 Cst). It also agreed to subject the creation of the Public Prosecutor to a decision of the Council acting in unanimity (rather than QMV) and with the consent of the European Parliament.

However, the Constitution will allow the European Council to adopt, by unanimity and with the consent of the European Parliament, a decision extending the powers of the Public Prosecutor to include serious crime having a cross-border dimension.

Specific procedures for improving the functioning and democratic control of JHA   The Constitution will introduce some specific institutional elements to improve the functioning of JHA, such as a role for the European Council in defining strategic guidelines (Article III-259(Cst) and the creation of a standing committee within the Council for the promotion of operational cooperation on internal security within the Union (Article III-261 Cst).

It will also improve democratic control in this sector by giving a specific role to national Parliaments in assessing observance of the subsidiarity principle in the areas of judicial cooperation in criminal matters and police cooperation (Article III-259 Cst), in evaluating the implementation of the Union's policies (Article III-260 Cst) and, together with the European Parliament, in controlling the activities of both Europol and Eurojust (Articles III-276(2), 3rd subparagraph, and III-273 (1), 3rd subparagraph, Cst).

Full judicial review   The Constitution will subject the whole JHA area to the full jurisdiction of the Court of Justice, save for the exception provided for in Article III-377 Cst with regard to the validity or proportionality of operations carried out by law-enforcement services of a Member State or the maintenance of law and order and the safeguarding of internal security.

In addition to ensuring a better protection of individuals' rights in JHA matters, this will also improve the enforcement of Member States' implementation of EU legislation in JHA matters, as the Commission will be empowered, as hitherto in Community matters, to bring infringement procedures against Member States which do not implement EU law correctly, or on time.

Keeping unanimity in a few very sensitive cases   The requirement of unanimity in the Council will be retained in a number of specific cases which were considered as being particularly sensitive: measures concerning family law with cross-border implications (Article III-269 (3) Cst), the establishment of certain minimum rules in criminal procedure (Article III-270(2)(d) Cst), the definition of further areas of crime to be made the subject of harmonisation measures (Article III-271 (1), 3rd subparagraph, Cst), measures on operational police cooperation (Article III-275(3) Cst) and the establishment of a European Public Prosecutor's Office (Article III-274 Cst).

Keeping the right of initiative of Member States   The right of initiative of Member States in the areas of judicial cooperation in criminal matters and police cooperation will be retained, but an initiative will have to be made by at least a quarter of the Member States acting jointly (Article III-264 Cst). Article III-396 Cst, on the codecision procedure, addresses this particular rule (paragraph 15), but leaves a number of details to be resolved in practice.

Assessment of the new provisions

The improvements made by the JHA provisions in the Constitution lie mainly in the new institutional arrangements, especially the full jurisdiction of the Court of Justice, and the introduction of more QMV and more codecision with the European Parliament for the adoption of legal acts. However, even if the pillar structure has been abandoned, the serious complications resulting from the 'variable geometry' and from the need to identify what constitutes a 'development of the Schengen *acquis*' will remain.

The introduction of QMV might provide the opportunity to renegotiate and readopt, using the form of one of the new legal instruments which do not require national ratifications, provisions that were introduced or integrated into the Union before the entry into force of the Constitution: the Europol Convention, the Schengen Convention and instruments on judicial cooperation in criminal matters or on the approximation of offences and sanctions. This is what happened to a number of conventions in the field of judicial cooperation in civil matters following the entry into force of the Amsterdam Treaty which 'communitarised', among other things, the Treaty provisions on judicial cooperation in civil matters.[63]

Special clauses which preserve the responsibilities of Member States with regard to the maintenance of law and order and the safeguarding of internal security have been retained (Articles III-262 and III-377 Cst). It is therefore an open question to what extent the Union as such, and more particularly the future standing committee of the Council with responsibility to promote and strengthen 'operational cooperation on internal security' (Article III-261 Cst), will be able to play a real steering role in the organisation of coordinated operational actions by the services of the Member States responsible for law and order and internal security, including border security. Recent discussions in the Council as to the positioning of the Task Force of Chiefs of Police may suggest that the role of the standing committee could become primarily oriented towards the production of common strategic threat analyses.

A most important added value of EU action in the field of JHA consists in the development of systems and mechanisms for the exchange of information between the national services of the Member States, in particular through the setting up of common data-bases or by providing mutual access to national information systems. At present, such systems as the SIS (Schengen Information System) and Eurodac (a fingerprints data base on asylum seekers) are already operational. Soon, Europol and the Customs administrations will have their information systems in place. In the future, a European Visa Information System (VIS) will be set up. The operation of such systems will not only require a common platform for their development and management, but also a general legal framework, including the existence of detailed rules on the protection of personal data.

---

[63] The Council adopted a Regulation recopying the 1968 Brussels Convention on jurisdiction and the enforcement of judgments in civil and commercial matters (see Council Regulation no. 44/2001 of 22 December 2000 on jurisdiction and the recognition and enforcement of judgments in civil and commercial matters, OJ No. L12, 16 January 2001, p. 1). It did the same with the 1998 Convention on jurisdiction and the recognition and enforcement of judgments in matrimonial matters (see Council Regulation no. 1374/2000 of 29 May 2000 on jurisdiction and the recognition and enforcement of judgments in matrimonial matters and in matters of parental responsibility for children of both spouses, OJ No. L160, 30 June 2000, p. 19).

Economic and monetary policy and the 'euro zone': improved decision-making

Although, in substance, the existing Treaty provisions on economic and monetary policy will remain broadly unchanged, the Constitution will add provisions designed to strengthen what is sometimes named 'economic governance' in the euro zone, i.e. the ability of the Council to manage the euro zone better, as well as improvements in the external representation of the euro.

A short history of economic and monetary issues in the EU

The original Rome Treaty in 1957 only summarily addressed the issue of coordination of economic and monetary policy. Article 6 provided for a general obligation on Member States to 'coordinate their respective economic policies to the extent necessary to attain the objectives of the Treaty'. Article 145 (now Article 202 EC Treaty) stated that the Council was to 'ensure coordination of the general economic policies of the Member States'. Articles 103 to 109 dealt with conjunctural policy, exchange rate policy by Member States and assistance and safeguard procedures in case of difficulties in the balance of payments. In 1970, the so-called 'Werner Committee', named after its chairman who was the Prime Minister and Finance Minister of Luxembourg, presented a report on the progressive realisation of Economic and Monetary Union (EMU). The Heads of State or Government meeting in Paris in 1972 agreed on this objective.

However, the collapse of the Bretton Woods system of fixed exchange rates in 1973, combined with the first oil crisis, created serious disturbances in the exchange rates between the Member States, which somewhat held up the move towards EMU. This led to the adoption in 1978 of the 'European Monetary System' (EMS), an exchange rate mechanism established outside the Treaty. The 1986 Single European Act did not add much to that, apart from adding the words 'Economic and Monetary Union' in the title of the chapter on cooperation in economic and monetary policy. It was the liberalisation of capital movements triggered by the Single European Act which boosted again the idea of a fully-fledged EMU. The so-called 'Delors Committee', chaired by the Commission's President, sketched out in its 1989 report the main aspects of what would be included in the 1992 Maastricht Treaty. In three phases, the Treaty led to the introduction, on 1 January 1999, of a single currency, the euro, between 11 Member States, i.e. without Denmark and the UK which had a derogation Protocol, and without Greece and Sweden which did not fulfil the convergence criteria. Greece joined two years later, in January 2001, and the euro became a physical reality, in notes and coins, on 1 January 2002.

The innovations brought about by the Constitution

Both in the Convention and in the IGC, particular emphasis was put on improving economic governance within the EU, particularly within the euro zone.

Improved decision-making and representation for the euro zone The possibility will be given to the Council, with only those Council members representing Member States whose currency is the euro (the 'euro-ins') having the right to vote, to strengthen coordination and surveillance of Member States' budget policies and set out economic policy guidelines (Article III-194 Cst).

The 'euro-ins' will have to give their prior acceptance to a new member joining the euro (Article III-198(2), 2nd subparagraph, Cst).

For the first time, the existence of the 'Eurogroup', which consists of the 'euro-ins' finance ministers, will be given formal recognition. The Constitution also provides that it will be chaired for two and a half years by a President elected by his peers (Article III-195 Cst and the related Protocol).[64]

The international representation of the euro will be further strengthened, thanks to a new provision enabling the Council to adopt by QMV (with only the 'euro-ins' voting) 'common positions on matters of particular interest for economic and monetary union within the competent international financial institutions and conferences' and to adopt 'appropriate measures to ensure a unified representation within the international financial institutions and conferences' (Article III-196 Cst).

Finally, in addition to the European Central Bank formally becoming an 'institution' (Article I-30 Cst), the Constitution will enable the European Council to make appointments to the Executive Board of the European Central Bank by QMV instead of common accord (Article

---

[64] At present, the Eurogroup is already chaired, for a mandate of two years as from 1 January 2005, by Mr Jean-Claude Juncker, Prime Minister and Finance Minister of Luxembourg.

III-382 Cst). In addition, amendments to the Statute of the European System of Central Banks and of the European Central Bank will also be subject to adoption by codecision (i.e. QMV, instead of unanimity) when proposed by the Commission (Article III-187(3)(a) Cst), whereas now QMV applies only when such amendments are recommended by the Central Bank (Article 107(5) EC Treaty).

Improved decision-making in the area of economic and monetary policy The Constitution will abolish the so-called 'cooperation procedure' (the predecessor of codecision), which in the current Treaty is now only applicable in the provisions on economic and monetary union.

Despite the wish of the Commission and some Member States, Council decisions in relation to the coordination of national economic policies and excessive government deficits will mainly continue, as at present, to be taken upon a Commission recommendation, rather than upon a Commission proposal (Articles III-179 and III-184 Cst). The only exception is the first sentence of Article III-184(6) on the existence of an excessive deficit in a Member State, where the Council will act on a proposal, instead of a recommendation, from the Commission (as now under Article 104(6) EC Treaty). The significance of this distinction is that Article III-395(1) Cst, pursuant to which the Council may only amend Commission *proposals* by acting unanimously, does not apply to *recommendations*. The Council may therefore amend the latter as part of the process of adopting the act recommended by the Commission and by using the same voting rule as provided for the adoption of the act.

Public health: higher standards and better monitoring of threats

The Constitution will add two new kinds of measures to the list of 'shared competences' in the field of public health: 'measures setting high standards of quality and safety for medicinal products and devices for medical use' and 'measures concerning monitoring, early warning of and combating serious cross-border threats to health' (Article III-278(4)(c) and (d) Cst).

Social policy: a horizontal clause

The Constitution will insert a new 'horizontal' social clause, according to which the EU must take into account, in the definition and implementation of all its policies, the 'requirements linked to the promotion of a high level of employment, the guarantee of adequate social protection, the fight against social exclusion, and a high level of education, training and protection of human health' (Article III-117 Cst). The insertion of this clause was considered very important by some delegations (Belgium and France in particular).

Moreover, measures in the field of social security, based on Article III-136 Cst, which are necessary to bring about freedom of movement for employed and self-employed migrant workers and their dependants, will be switched to QMV and codecision. These concern technical measures such as the aggregation, for the purpose of acquiring and retaining the right to benefit and of calculating the amount of benefit, of the periods spent in different Member States, and the payment of benefits to persons residing in another Member State.[65]

Apart from that, the provisions on social policy will remain identical to the present ones. Article III-210 Cst on social policy is identical to the present Article 137 of the EC Treaty.[66] Therefore:

---

[65] The procedure of the so-called 'emergency brake' will, however, be applicable. According to this procedure, if a Member State considers that a draft legislative act 'would affect fundamental aspects of its social security system, including its scope, cost or financial structure, or would affect the financial balance of that system', it can bring the matter to the European Council. In that case, the codecision procedure is suspended for a duration of four months. After discussion, the European Council must either refer the draft back to the Council, which will terminate the suspension of the procedure, or request the Commission to submit a new proposal, in which case the act originally proposed is deemed not to have been adopted (see Art. III-136(2) Cst).

[66] A rather large amount of EU legislation has already been adopted in the field of social policy. The first directives were adopted in the 1970s, dealing e.g. with the safeguarding of employees' rights in the event of collective redundancies (Directive 75/129, now replaced by Directive 98/59), transfers of undertakings (Directive 77/187) and insolvency of the employer (Directive 80/987).

A second wave of directives was adopted in the 1980s, dealing essentially with safety and health at work. The number of directives in this field increased substantially when the Single European Act introduced QMV and Art. 118a into the Treaty (see Directive 80/1107 on the protection of workers from the risks related to exposure to chemical, physical and biological agents at work, which at the time had been based on Art. 100 EC Treaty, now Art. 94 EC Treaty, which requires unanimity, and Directive 89/391 on measures to encourage improvements in the safety and health of workers at work, which was based on Art. 118a EC Treaty, now Art. 137, and which contained a 'derived legal basis' on the basis of which 18 Directives have been adopted).

A third wave came in the 1990s when the Maastricht Treaty incorporated the 'Social Protocol', which the Amsterdam IGC afterwards made part of the Social Policy Chapter of the EC Treaty. Examples are directives on working time (Directive 93/104, replaced by Directive 2003/88), on the protection of young people at work (Directive 94/33) and on the information and consultation of employees in Community-scale undertakings (Directive 94/45 and Directive 2002/14)

- as now, the European Parliament and the Council will still be empowered to adopt in codecision, the Council using QMV, 'minimum requirements' for certain matters (Article III-210(2)(b) Cst). QMV will thus continue to apply for adopting measures on the protection of workers' health and safety, working conditions, information and consultation of workers, integration of persons excluded from the labour market and equality between men and women with regard to labour market opportunities and treatment at work;
- as now, unanimity will be kept for the adoption of 'minimum requirements' in the most sensitive matters such as social security and social protection (Article III-210(3) Cst).[67] Unanimity will thus continue to apply for adopting measures on social security and social protection for workers, protection of workers where their employment contract is terminated, the representation and collective defence of the interests of workers and employers and conditions of employment of third-country nationals;
- as now, such minimum requirements 'shall not affect the right of Member States to define the fundamental principles of their social security systems and must not significantly affect the financial equilibrium of such systems' and 'shall not prevent any Member State from maintaining or introducing more stringent protective measures compatible with the Constitution' (Article III-210(5)(b) Cst);
- as now, the right of association, the right to strike and the right to impose lockouts will continue to be excluded from EU competence and remain a purely national competence (Article III-210(6) Cst).

The Constitution has also retained the 'passerelle' allowing for a switch to QMV and codecision with regard to the adoption of minimum requirements on the list of matters which are now subject to unanimity (see Article III-210(3), 2nd subparagraph, Cst).

It has also retained the possibility for social partners, management and labour, to conclude agreements at Union level on matters covered by Article III-210 Cst which, at their joint request, may be transformed into

---

[67] It should be noted that point (g) of Art. III-210(1) Cst on conditions of employment for third-country nationals legally resident in the Union could be considered redundant, as it is superseded by point (b) of Art. III-267(2) on 'the definition of the rights of third-country nationals residing legally in a Member State', which can be regulated by QMV and codecision.

a regulatory act of the Council which is binding throughout the EU (Article III-212 Cst, which is the same as Article 139 EC Treaty).[68]

Public services: a new legal basis

The Constitution will add, in the present general provision in the EC Treaty which underlines the important role played by services of general economic interest (Article 16 EC Treaty), an express legal basis that will enable the legislature to adopt, by QMV and codecision, a European law establishing the principles and conditions on the basis of which such services will operate, so as to 'enable them to fulfil their missions' (Article III-122 Cst).

Article 16 of the EC Treaty already contains a general provision on public services but without a legal basis empowering the Council to adopt legal acts. Adding such a possibility was considered very important by some Member States, in particular France, where the concept of '*services publics*' equally accessible to all is widely considered a great achievement of the twentieth century.

---

[68] Four such 'agreements' have already been adopted by social partners and transformed into Council Directives (Directive 96/34 on parental leave, Directive 1999/63 on the working time of seafarers, Directive 1999/70 on fixed-term work and Directive 2000/79 on the working time of mobile workers in civil aviation).

VI

General assessment

This general assessment will be made on two levels:

- does the Constitution fulfil the mandates that its authors were given by the 2000 Nice Declaration and by the 2001 Laeken Declaration? Would its entry into force succeed in making the Union more democratic and more efficient?
- assessment from a legal, economic and social point of view: would it drive the European economy towards a more 'liberal' or rather towards a more 'social' path? as well as from a political and historical point of view: would it transform the European Union into a federal State or would it rather confirm the present nature of the Union and of its relationship with the Member States?

Section 1: Does the Constitution fulfil the Nice and Laeken mandates?

The Nice mandate

The Constitution addresses all four questions raised in the 2000 Nice Declaration.

The delimitation of powers between the EU and the Member States

The delimitation of powers between the EU and the Member States, though not much altered as compared with the present legal situation, is made clearer for the reader, thanks to the codification, in Part I of the Constitution, of the existing situation both as to the three categories of competences (exclusive, shared and supporting) and as to their content (Articles I-12 to I-17 Cst). However, some competences were difficult to categorise and, in any case, they are subject to possible development.

The status of the Charter of Fundamental Rights

The Charter of Fundamental Rights is incorporated as such into Part II of the Constitution and will become legally binding upon the EU institutions and upon the Member States 'only when they are implementing Union law' (Article II-111(1) Cst). Here again, this does not alter the existing legal situation very much. The Court of Justice stated already in 1969 that 'fundamental human rights [are] enshrined in the general principles of Community law and protected by the Court'[1] and that 'respect for human rights is . . . a condition of the lawfulness of Community acts'.[2] Nevertheless, first, the Charter's content is broader than what is applicable now and, secondly, inserting it into the Constitution is a very powerful symbol, which will make it more apparent to the citizens that the new EU is to be a 'Union based on the rule of law' and has to respect their rights. However, the down-side is that the citizens might have some mistaken illusions that the Charter will always be obligatory for their national authorities, even when the latter are not implementing EU law.

The simplification of the Treaties

The objective of simplifying the Treaties 'with a view to making them clearer and better understood without changing them' has been partly achieved.

To a non-specialist in EU matters, reading the first 60 Articles in Part I of the Constitution (i.e. only 30 pages) will give a reasonably clear idea of what the Union is, what it does and how.

In addition, a more interested reader will now find almost everything in a single document, instead of having to go through 17 Treaties and Acts. He or she will no longer have to wonder about two legal personalities, three 'pillars' or 15 different types of legal instruments. That said, even though the Constitution is structured and drafted in a more coherent and readable way than the present Treaties, it is still a very long text (448 Articles, 36 Protocols and two Annexes), and its drafting is sometimes very complicated (see for instance the definition of QMV in Article I-25 Cst).

It is certainly not easy reading for the non-specialists, but this complexity is unavoidable, given the special characteristics of the Union, as a multi-layered legal order, and the wish of Member States to be very precise, and often detailed, on what and how much power they confer on

---

[1] Case 29/69, *Stauder*, para. 7.
[2] Opinion 2/94, *Accession of the EC to the ECHR*, paras. 33 and 34.

the EU and its institutions. This being said, one could have restricted the text of the Constitutional Treaty itself to Parts I, II and IV alone, without repealing the text of the present Treaties as taken over in Part III of the Constitution, while amending the EC Treaty as necessary.

The role of national Parliaments in the EU architecture

The role of national Parliaments in the EU architecture will be significantly improved as compared with the present situation.

Now, they are only indirectly informed, depending on the goodwill of their national government. The Constitution will transform them into direct actors in the EU legislative process:

- by providing for them to be directly informed by EU institutions on draft EU legislation;
- by giving them, for the first time, a direct role in the EU legislative process, through the possibility of issuing reasoned opinions on compliance with the principle of subsidiarity and, through their government, to trigger an action in the Court of Justice for an infringement of subsidiarity;
- by associating them with the European Parliament in the control mechanisms for Europol and Eurojust.

Finding ways to give the national Parliaments a say in the legislative process of the EU had been a long-standing demand. It was seen as a way to compensate for the perceived loss of influence of national legislatures on matters legislated on at EU level, which they have to transpose afterwards into their national legal order without much room for manoeuvre. It is also considered as a way of giving the EU citizens, through their elected national representatives, more say in the EU legislative process. One may wonder, however, if the Constitution could not have gone further down this road.

The Laeken mandate

The requirements in the 2001 Laeken declaration were less precise than those of Nice. However, the Constitution tries to answer the main expectations raised in Laeken, such as the need for the Union 'to become more democratic, more transparent and more efficient'.

A more democratic and transparent Union

The elements in the Constitution designed to make the Union more democratic may be identified as the following:

- the increased role given to the national Parliaments, as referred to above;
- the increased powers of the European Parliament, both with regard to the scope of codecision (about 40 more instances) and in the budgetary procedure, as well as in the procedure for the appointment of the Commission;
- the direct role given to the EU's citizens, both in the legislative process, through the possibility for one million of them to bring a 'citizens' initiative' inviting the Commission to submit a legislative proposal, and through an increased access to justice, by the widening of the jurisdiction of the Court of Justice, in particular to the JHA field and by making the Charter of Fundamental Rights legally binding;
- the new method for calculating QMV in the Council, which makes it more proportionate to the population in the Member States and, thus, to their citizens;
- the increased number of cases where QMV is going to be applied, because it is much more democratic than voting by unanimity (or by simple majority);
- the increased transparency of the EU legislative process, through a total opening to the public of Council meetings when it deliberates and votes on a draft legislative act;
- and, last but not least, the greater readability of the primary law of the Union and the 'codification' and clarification of existing political and legal principles, which will allow EU citizens to understand better the way the EU institutions work and, therefore, how they might influence or control them.

It follows from the above that a great deal is achieved in the Constitution in favour of progress towards more democracy. However, one has to recognise that EU citizens will probably continue not to feel as though they are the masters of the game, in the same way as they feel in the national or regional political arenas. Therefore, in the future, political control over the EU's activities will continue to be exercised through national institutions as well as through the European Parliament. This issue needs to be discussed in an open way, much more than it has been discussed up to now.

This does not mean that the system established and developed over the years in the EU was not democratic and that decisions were taken in an undemocratic way. EU decision-making has a very effective system of checks and balances. An American observer of EU life noted that 'The EU as a vehicle for sharing power between national governments and an international institution has evolved into a complex but effective system of checks and balances. Policy can be made only by painstaking consensus. By the time 70 percent of the 25 member governments, a technocratic European Commission and a directly elected European Parliament agree to a law, it is almost certain to represent a stable compromise.'[3]

A more efficient Union

The elements in the Constitution designed to make the Union more efficient are the following:

- simplification of structures, instruments and procedures are one of the big successes of the Constitution and will probably be conducive to a clearer and smoother functioning of the EU decision-making process;
- full-time and stable Presidents both for the European Council and for the Foreign Affairs Council, and a stable President for the Eurogroup, in lieu of the six-monthly rotating Presidency, which should produce more stability, more consistency and more visibility;
- a reduced number of Commissioners, which will make the Commission work more efficiently; however, this would only apply as from 2014;
- an increased number of cases (about 40 more) where QMV will apply in the Council, which will facilitate the decision-making in these areas, although a large number of matters (about 70), including a number of important ones, will remain subject to unanimity, common accord or consensus (see annexes 3, 4 and 5), which will continue to make the decision-taking in these areas very difficult in a Union of 27 Member States or more;
- the possibility of using a mechanism, 'enhanced cooperation', which will enable one-third of the Member States to go further than the others, and the 'passerelles', which will allow, by unanimity, but

---

[3] See A. Moravcsik, 'Europe's Slow Triumph', *Newsweek*, 21 June 2004, p. 41. See also J. Rifkind, *The European Dream*, p. 230: 'But the important thing to remember is that the regulatory decisions made in Brussels are themselves the result of a polycentric process of negotiation, compromise and consensus, involving many parties at the regional, national, transnational and global levels.' See also C. Rumford, *The European Union: A Political Sociology* (Oxford, Blackwell Publishers, 2002), M. M. Dean, *Governmentality: Power and Rule in Modern Society* (London, Sage, 1999) and T. R. Reid, *The United States of Europe* (London, Penguin Books, 2005).

without having to follow the full ordinary revision procedure of the Constitution, a switch of a given legal basis from unanimity to QMV in the Council and to codecision with the European Parliament.

With regard to the creation of the new offices of full-time President of the European Council and Union Minister for Foreign Affairs, giving too optimistic a picture of the future might not correspond to the reality, which could see rivalries develop between them and the existing political figures of the Union.

First, the President of the European Council will not be the only one to prepare the work of the institution over which he will preside, and to ensure its follow-up. Another personality will do so, i.e. the six-monthly rotating President of the General Affairs Council, as this configuration of the Council 'shall ensure consistency in the work of the different Council configurations' and 'shall prepare and ensure the follow-up to meetings of the European Council, in liaison with the President of the European Council and the Commission' (Article I-24 (2) Cst).

Secondly, the Union Minister for Foreign Affairs will not be the only one to represent the Union in the world. On the one hand, the President of the European Council will do so 'at his level' on issues concerning CFSP (Article I-22(2) Cst) and, on the other hand, the Commission will be in charge of representing the Union externally on issues other than CFSP (Article I-26(1) Cst).

In any case, trying to foresee the effects and consequences in the future of the establishment of these new offices is not obvious.

According to the opinion of one of the most attentive contributors to the Constitution, i.e. the UK's Foreign Secretary, Jack Straw,[4] the effects of this should be the following:

> The Constitution also shifts power back to Member States, and so to citizens, in another way : by reform of the presidency system. This sounds a bit arcane. But imagine any complex organisation where the leadership had to switch every six months, and it was only your turn once every twelve-and-a-half years. What would happen if that effective power would shift, automatically, to those with some permanence. And no imagination is needed : this is the EU today. Rotating the presidency made sense when the EU had six members. With 25, and soon to be more, it is now a recipe for Member States to lose their grip. A key institutional reform creates a

---

[4] J. Straw, *The Economist*, 30 July 2004, p. 30.

full-time post of president of the European Council (i.e., heads of government) to put into effect its decisions on the EU's strategic direction. This was a British proposal.

This political assessment (shifting power back to the Member States) might prove to be correct in the future. However, a different political development cannot be excluded. One can suppose that two major political personalities will be working full-time in Brussels. In such a case, and in order to be successful and trusted by all, these two personalities would most likely loosen their direct links with a given Member State. They might become real central organs of the Union. Being in Brussels and working full-time for the Union, they might not be at all tempted to pass up the opportunity of being active and of affirming themselves. They might, instead, use their abilities and offices in order to work better towards a more efficient, consistent and visible Union. They might be tempted to work in favour of more common action, not less. If the person who will be elected as President of the European Council is a heavy-weight politician, and given that it has already been decided that Javier Solana will be the first Union Minister for Foreign Affairs, this tandem would be a very powerful team, which would certainly be pro-active in making the Union more results-oriented and more present on the international scene.

The adoption of a 'constitutional text'

The name 'Constitution' goes quite a lot further than what the 2001 Laeken Declaration more timidly alluded to, which was 'in the long run . . . the adoption of a constitutional text in the Union'. Therefore, it does respond to this request, unless this expression had only been intended to mean a text which could be amended by a decision of a constituent body or a constituent procedure, such as by some sort of super-qualified majority of Member States, and no longer through the common agreement of them all.

However, the fact is that it is now, and for the foreseeable future, politically ruled out to think about such an amendment procedure. Member States are not ready to give up unanimity on the procedure for amending the very basic provisions establishing the Union and by which they limit their sovereign rights and transfer powers to the institutions of the Union.

Section 2: Legal, economic and social assessments

Legally, the Constitution is far from being a revolution

Legally, the 'Treaty establishing a Constitution for Europe' remains a Treaty agreed between sovereign States. It can only enter into force and be amended by their common agreement. Calling it a 'Constitution' does not change anything about that.[5] The EU would not become 'sovereign', i.e. it will not have *Kompetenz-Kompetenz*, it will not have the right to define the extent of its own powers. This competence will continue to belong to the 'Masters of the Treaties', i.e. the Member States. The relationship between the EU and its Member States will not be changed. The EU will not become a federal State. The 'Constitution' is not a legal revolution.

If and when it is ratified, the Constitution will be much more satisfactory than the collection of 17 texts presently applicable. European citizens will have the benefit of a single text, shorter, more explanatory, setting out a number of founding concepts and principles, codifying as clearly as possible the applicable law as it results from the practice of the institutions and from the case-law of the Court of Justice.

Up to now, the gradual building up over 50 years of what is now the European Union has been done in a manner that has not attracted the citizens' attention enough. Things happened mainly through deals between government representatives, mostly ratified by national Parliaments. This did not raise much passion in the public, save for the occasional eruption of an emotional debate in this or that Member State when a ratification referendum was organised on an amending Treaty or when some sort of scandal made its way into the headlines, such as the mad cow crisis or the resignation of the Santer Commission in 1999.

And yet, under this veil of indifference or ignorance, shrouded in ambiguity,[6] the European Union has progressively but quite quickly

---

[5] See Art. IV-443 Cst on the revision procedure, which is worded in a similar way to the present Art. 48 EU Treaty, i.e. a treaty procedure negotiated between the Member States and ratified by them. See O. Pfersmann, 'The New Revision of the Old Constitution' in J. H. H. Weiler and C. L. Eisgruber (eds.) *The EU Constitution in a Contextual Perspective. Altneuland* (Jean Monnet Working Paper 5/04) [http://www.jeanmonnetprogram.org/papers/04/040501-10.pdf]. See also J.-L. Halperin 'L'Union européenne, un Etat en voie de constitution?' (2004) no. 4 *Recueil Dalloz* 219–221.

[6] On this ambiguity, see Y. Mény, 'Europe, la grande hésitation', *Le Monde*, 12 June 2004. See also my article 'Does the European Union have a Constitution? Does It Need One?' (1999) 6 *European Law Review* 557–585.

developed into a constitutional order of its own, with what the Court of Justice had called already in 1964 a 'new legal order',[7] established by a 'basic constitutional charter, the Treaty'[8] and 'for the benefit of which the States have limited their sovereign rights, in ever wider fields, and the subjects of which comprise not only Member States but also their nationals'. The essential characteristics of this legal order have been in particular 'its primacy over the law of the Member States and the direct effect of a whole series of provisions which are applicable to their nationals and to the Member States themselves'.[9]

This legal reality of today, i.e. the existence of a Constitutional Charter in a material sense, will be made evident by the so-called 'Constitution'. Long-standing EU legal principles will be stated, such as the principle of conferral of powers on the EU by the Member States and the principle of primacy of EU law over national law, principles that specialists have known for a long time. Moreover, they are expressed in such a way that ordinary citizens can read and understand them. Citizens are no longer left to find out by themselves that the primacy principle was stated by the EC Court of Justice in a judgment of 15 July 1964 to be found on page 593 of the Court Reports, and has been a legal reality since then.

The Constitution explains in plain language that, when the Member States confer competences on the EU, they prescribe in detail the precise limits of these powers (hence the length of the text). It also shows that most of these competences are not exclusive, but will remain shared with the Member States.

The Constitution also stresses that the EU is based on the rule of law and that it has to respect human rights, which are clearly listed in the Constitution itself.

Therefore, although legally the Constitution is not a revolution, as it changes neither the nature of the Union, nor the nature of the latter's relations with the Member States, it is shorter, clearer, and contains many real and welcome improvements and clarifications.

---

[7] Judgment of 13 November 1964, Cases 90/63 and 91/63 of *Commission v. Luxembourg and Belgium*, [1964] ECR p. 625 and Case 6/64, *Costa v. ENEL*, p. 593.
[8] See Case 294/83, *Les Verts v. Parliament*, para. 23. See also Opinion 1/91 of 14 December 1991, *EEA Agreement*, [1991] ECR p. 6102, para. 21.
[9] See para. 21 of Opinion 1/91, *EEA Agreement*.

The Constitution will not bring about major changes in the economic and social fields

The political nature or orientation of the EU will not be changed in one way or the other. The Constitution is neither more 'liberal' (in the French sense of the term), nor more 'socialist' than the present Treaties. In the economic and social fields, it actually reproduces more or less the present Treaty provisions, without changing the existing balance between 'market-friendly' and 'worker-friendly' provisions. Of course, the Constitution, like the present EC Treaty, aims at offering its citizens 'an internal market where competition is free and undistorted', which is the expression of a market economy with free competition, and the Constitution repeats this long-standing objective (Article I-3(2) Cst, which corresponds to Article 3(g) EC Treaty). There is nothing new about that, as it expresses the basic purpose of the original Treaty of Rome which was to establish, within the EU, a 'common market' with the so-called 'four freedoms': free movement for persons, services, capital and goods.

During the French national ratification debate, the reference to 'free and undistorted' competition was used by several 'No' campaigners as an alleged proof that the EU was, in their view, 'ultra-liberal' or 'ultra-capitalist'. They seemed to overlook the fact that this wording, 'undistorted competition', had been in the Treaties since 1951 and 1957 (Coal and Steel and EEC) and that it had been included for good reasons at the time, six years after the Second World War, in view, *inter alia*, of the damage that powerful cartels had caused to the economy and to the political situation. Should one understand the arguments of these campaigners as meaning that competition should be allowed to be 'distorted' through, for instance, 'dumping' or price-fixing between dominant companies? How to reconcile this with the arguments from the very same campaigners against alleged 'social dumping' from poorer States or a more classic version of dumping of low-cost goods from overseas countries, as for instance in the textile sector? It was precisely with a view to ensuring a 'climate of fair competition' (see recital no. 5) that the European Parliament and the Council adopted in 1996 the Directive on the posting of workers in the framework of the provision of services, which stipulates that such workers are subject to the labour law of the State where they are posted, so as to avoid what some call 'social dumping'.[10] The

---

[10] See Directive 96/71 of 16 December 1996, OJ No. L18, 21 January 1997, p. 1.

prime beneficiaries of 'undistorted competition' are of course the consumers who are not taken hostage by cartels of companies which would agree e.g. to fix prices or by very dominant companies which would impose unfair prices or trading conditions.

Article 3(c) and (g) of the EC Treaty provides that the activities of the Community include 'an internal market characterised by the abolition, as between Member States, of obstacles to the free movement of goods, persons, services and capital' and 'a system ensuring that competition in the internal market is not distorted'. The Maastricht Treaty, in view of the planned introduction of the single currency and of the single monetary policy, also introduced several provisions on 'the adoption of an economic policy, which is based on the close coordination of Member States' economic policies . . . and conducted in accordance with the principle of an open market economy with free competition' (Article 3a of the EC Treaty as amended by the Maastricht Treaty, renumbered Article 4 in the present EC Treaty).[11] Here again, this wording has been in the Treaty since 1993 and was ratified by all Member States, including France through the 1992 referendum.

The paradox with the arguments developed by the 'No' campaigners is that the Constitution would introduce for the first time, in Article I-3(3) Cst, as part of the Union's objectives, the notion of 'social market economy', which brings in an important nuance as compared with the present notion of 'open market economy'. The system of 'social market economy' was developed in Germany by Ludwig Erhard, the first economics minister in post-war Germany. Being essentially a balance between the market-principle and the social-principle, it could be said that it is quite representative of the so-called 'European Social Model'. On the one hand, it enables the free play of forces on the market, with the State creating the framework for competition to operate and, on the other hand, it provides for a fully-fledged system of social protection.

In any case, the Constitution is a mere framework. It lists EU competences, which may be exercised by the EU institutions to pursue the policy they choose, whether it be more free-market-oriented or more socially protective. The means for action are put at their disposal and it is up to the competent institutions, and to the Member States as they are represented in these institutions, to push for the type of policy they

---

[11] This particular wording, 'the principle of an open market economy with free competition', may thus be found in Arts. 98 and 105 EC Treaty (reproduced in Arts. III-178 and III-185 EC Cst).

prefer. Therefore, the sometimes Manichean debate one sees in some Member States about the economic or social nature of the Constitution (some UK Tories say it is 'socialist' and some French Socialists that it is 'ultra-liberal') is somewhat artificial and sterile.[12]

Section 3: An important symbolic step from a political point of view

Although, legally and in substance, the Constitution is a mere evolution, building on the previous Treaties, rather than a revolution, it does represent a very important symbolic step from a political point of view.

The use of words like 'laws', 'Minister', 'flag' or 'anthem' and, above all, of the word 'Constitution' has a deep and powerful political effect. Using such words was likely to provoke a psychological earthquake, as the ratification debates have shown, particularly in some of the Member States which hold popular referenda. The title 'Constitution' was deliberately proposed by the Convention and it was then accepted, despite some misgivings, by the 25 Governments of the Member States, with full knowledge of the risks involved. It is as if the 25 EU leaders had decided, deliberately, to have recourse to some sort of 'shock therapy', regardless of the political risks.

For many years, the true extent of EU integration has been understated. It was perceived by the specialists, but not by the people. The intelligentsia in the Member States probably know that the EU has

---

[12] See e.g. Z. Laïdi, 'Europe: la gauche doit dire oui', *Libération*, 22 June 2004. During the IGC, none of the Member States ever suggested that the EU should be given full competence in the field of employment and social policy in general, so that these sectors would be fully regulated by EU legislation, with QMV in the Council. The Member States did not wish to confer more competences on the Union in these fields, where they want to keep their own national powers.

On employment, like now, the EU Council will only adopt by QMV guidelines, recommendations or incentive measures to encourage the Member States to exchange best practices, and nobody proposed giving it powers to adopt directly applicable laws in this field (Arts. III-206 and III-207 Cst, compare with Arts. 128 and 129 EC Treaty).

On social policy, the provisions of Art. III-210 will remain identical to the provisions of Art. 137 EC Treaty (see above in chapter V, under 'Social policy'). Minimum requirements (i.e. Member States are always free to go further) may be adopted at EU level, by QMV on certain aspects of social policy and by unanimity for other aspects (the most sensitive ones such as social security and social protection or protection of workers in case of termination of contract). Some Member States would have liked QMV for these areas, but a majority of other States firmly refused it. This political reality would not change following non-ratification of the Constitution.

already become, for a while, much more than a common market, much more than a mere zone of economic cooperation. They probably feel that it is, even now, what I call a 'Partially Federal Union'.[13] Nevertheless, baptising the founding Treaties, even codified and simplified, by the name of 'Constitution', with all the symbols[14] which accompany it, such as EU laws, the EU flag, the EU anthem and the EU Minister for Foreign Affairs, definitely gives rise to misunderstandings.

Anyway, this political choice has been made by the leaders of the 25 Member States, for better or for worse. It is true that the political step taken to baptise the Treaties as a 'Constitution' does not match the content of the modifications actually made to the Treaties. It may however be seen as the culmination of a slow and successful evolution.[15] From a historical perspective, the present EU is the result of numerous Treaties concluded and ratified over 50 years. 'Europe's slow triumph'[16] is the sum of many small and some big successes, mixed up with trials, errors, crises and compromises.

---

[13] See my article 'The European Union: Towards A New Form of Federalism?' (2003).

[14] See T. Ferenczi, 'Constitution: l'Europe des symboles', Le Monde, 16 October 2004. See also R. Dahrendorf, 'N'accordons pas trop d'importance à la Constitution européenne', Les Echos, 27 July 2004.

[15] As an editorial noted in The Financial Times (30–31 October 2004): 'indeed part of the reason why the new Constitution appears novel is that for the first time it expresses existing EU competences and powers in language ordinary citizens can understand. The difficulty is rather that EU integration is still widely seen as an elite project. The challenge though is to turn it into a democratic one.'

[16] See A. Moravcsik, 'Europe's Slow Triumph', Newsweek, 21 June 2004, p. 41.

Conclusion: What will the final form of the Union be?

My personal point of view is that the European Union already is, and will remain in the future, a 'Partially Federal Union'.[1] This means that the EU is not a federal State and that, in the foreseeable future, it will not become one.

If considered against the classic definition of a State: a people, a territory, an organised government, full sovereignty, the right and means of control over all persons and things within its borders, the capacity for making war and peace and for entering into international relations with other States, the EU does not comply with some or all of these criteria.

Moreover, the EU lacks most of the essential means usually associated with the notion of a State. It lacks proper financial resources and power directly to collect taxes. It is not allowed to establish its own resources, which are laid down in a Decision to be ratified by Member States.[2] The EU budget represents only a tiny proportion of the gross domestic product of the Member States (approximately 1%) and the vast bulk of its expenses (around 85%) is managed by the Member States' administrations.[3] The EU lacks administrative and technical capacities. Its administrative expenditure is less than 5% of its total budget and the human resources of its central organs (about 30,000 people) represent about half of the municipal staff of the city of Paris. The EU lacks administrative and coercive means, it has no fiscal, customs, veterinary, public order or judicial administrations in charge of the daily application of EU law. It has no police, no prisons and no army. It relies entirely on the means of the Member States.

---

[1] See my article 'The European Union: Towards A New Form of Federalism?' (2003).

[2] Article I-54(3) Cst does not change this situation.

[3] Court of Auditors – Annual Report concerning the financial year 2001, paragraph 0.12 on page 6 (OJ C295 of 28 November 2002, p. 1). According to J. O. Karlsson, former President of the Court of Auditors: 'Los Estados Miembros administran el 85% del presupuesto', El País, 14 March 1999.

One could argue that the above elements are not decisive, because they do characterise a classic unitary State with strong central authorities, as distinct from a decentralised federal State relying on a system of 'implementing federalism' or 'indirect administration' whereby the responsibility for implementing and applying EU law belongs to the components.[4] But there are three additional arguments as to why the EU is not a State.

First and above all, the EU does not have a single *demos*. There is no such thing as a European People. The EU has 'peoples', several *demoi*. It is not based on a single popular unit that exercises democratic rights and constitutes a shared identity. It is not based on 'a group of people the vast majority of which feels sufficiently attached to each other to be willing to engage in democratic discourse and binding decision-making'.[5] A *demos* is more than a mere aggregation of individuals, it includes a sense of community, a 'we-feeling', however thinly expressed, for democracy to have a meaning.

Secondly, the EU is not 'sovereign' in the sense that it does not have what the Germans call *Kompetenz-Kompetenz*: it has no right to define the extent of its own powers. This competence belongs to the 'Masters of the Treaties', the Member States. The EU therefore does not derive its authority from its citizens but from its Member States.

Thirdly, the EU lacks a full external identity and the powers that go with it. Foreign affairs and defence remain in the hands of Member States. The EU does not have full treaty-making power, it does not have exclusive competence for those core powers which are the symbol of State sovereignty : foreign policy, security and defence. Member States are obliged to cooperate, coordinate and respect the CFSP instruments, but the effectiveness of these provisions all depend on the goodwill of the Member States. If one or several of them decide not to cooperate or coordinate positions in advance, nobody can force them to do so or enforce the Treaty obligations upon them. The Commission cannot bring them to the EU Court of Justice and the latter has no competence

---

[4] See B. Dubey, 'Administration indirecte et fédéralisme d'exécution en Europe' 1-2/03 *Cahiers de droit européen* 87–133, in particular pp. 90 and 132. This approach, which exists for instance in Germany and in Switzerland, is different from the US 'dualist execution' system under which a power conferred on the federal level comprises not only the power to legislate but also the power to directly implement and apply it.

[5] See L.-E. Cederman, 'Nationalism and Bounded Integration: What It Would Take to Construct a European Demos' European University Institute Working Papers, Florence 2000 (RSC no. 2000:34), p. 7.

in this field. As for the EU High Representative for Foreign Affairs, the creation of this new office in 1999 was indeed a step towards giving some tasks of representation to somebody perceived as impartial, independent from Member States but closely linked to the Council, which is the EU institution where they are all represented. However, if there is no common position to express and defend, if there is no EU policy on a given subject, the High Representative cannot publicly express a position on behalf of the EU.

In the end, the strongest argument of all against the idea of the EU being a State or becoming a State, is that the Member States simply do not want that.

This has been demonstrated again in the Constitution, which does not go in the direction of transforming the Member States into federated entities. On the contrary, Article I-5 obliges the Union to 'respect . . . their national identities, inherent in their fundamental structures, political and constitutional, inclusive of regional and local self-government'. It also obliges the Union to 'respect their essential State functions, including ensuring the territorial integrity of the State, maintaining law and order and safeguarding national security'. Article I-60 Cst gives the right to any Member State to decide to withdraw from the Union, a right which is normally denied in federal States.[6] Moreover, the heterogeneity of the EU is widening with its enlargement.

Besides, as a consequence of globalisation, the very notions of statehood and classic 'sovereignty' are being challenged. Kenneth Clarke addressed his compatriots by saying that 'the most important political lesson of recent years is that no country can exercise complete sovereignty over all its own affairs. Rejecting the EU would mean losing practical sovereign power.'[7] Being what some have described, already in 1993, as 'the first truly postmodern political form',[8] the EU constitutes the beginning of an answer to these challenges.

The answer does not consist in attempting artificially to build an improbable 'super nation-state'. Even if the process of integrating Europe

---

[6] See K. Nicolaïdis, 'We, the Peoples of Europe. . .' (2004) 83(6) *Foreign Affairs*: 'One of the Constitution's most spectacular innovations is to grant member States the right to withdraw from the EU. In so doing, it firmly establishes the EU as a federal union, rather than a federal State, which – as American schoolchildren know well from studying the birth of their own nation – is defined by the very denial of that right.'

[7] K. Clarke, 'The Tories Must Stop being Afraid of Europe', *The Independent*, 6 October 2003.

[8] See J. Ruggie, 'Territoriality and Beyond: Problematizing Modernity in International Relations' (1993) 47 *International Organization* 134–175.

is far from 'completed',[9] the purpose of the EU will continue to be, in the future, to find the right balance between, on the one hand, respect for the national identities of its Member States, their cultures, traditions and diversities and, on the other hand, the necessity to develop an efficient, democratic, transparent, central system of decision-making and to ensure the uniform application of the law this system will make. That is what is needed for Europe to be able to respond effectively to the economic, social, environmental and security challenges of the present century, challenges which none of the Member States, whatever its size and importance, is able to deal with on its own.

Therefore, despite the difficulties in ratifying its 'Constitution', the EU will continue, either through this Treaty or through another Treaty based on it, to progress on its path towards further and deeper integration, especially in the areas of internal and external security, where further cooperation or integration are needed, because Member States will need to integrate some of their policies and means in these areas in order to be able to provide more security to their peoples.

But the Union will continue to be characterised by the fact that its sub-entities, the existing Member States, will keep their external identity in the world. Their participation in the decision-making and implementation of Union law will also continue to be much more preponderant than is the case for the sub-entities of any existing federal State in the world.

If ratified or if its essential content were taken up in another treaty, the Constitution would provide the necessary basis for this evolution. Legally, it would not revolutionise either the specific character of the Union or the nature of its relationship with its Member States, and it would not significantly increase the powers conferred on it by the Member States.[10]

Of course, very much would depend on the personalities of the actors who will have to implement it and on the political and economic climate in which it will be implemented and, therefore, on how and to what extent the Member States and the EU institutions would make use of the new provisions.

In any case, if it, or its essential content in another treaty, were to enter into force and if all actors involved were to take sufficiently into account

---

[9] As was declared in the Conclusions of the Presidency of the European Council on 17 and 18 June 2004, doc. 10679/04 ADD 1 (see above in Chapter 1).

[10] R. Dehousse, 'Convention européenne: pourquoi les anti-fédéralistes ont gagné' (2003) 2 L'Europe en formation 25–42.

the needs of the citizens when implementing its provisions, that would lead to a stronger, more efficient, more useful and more popular Union. The process which began in 1951 and in 1957 with the Treaties of Paris and Rome would continue on this new basis, for the benefit of all States and peoples of Europe, within the limits desired and decided by them according to their real needs, and without artificially building an improbable European Federal State.

Given the present political climate and the current economic situation, in particular in the very heart of Europe, immediate or rapid moves are unlikely. One cannot help noticing the lack of enthusiasm in launching national debates on the future of the Constitutional Treaty. Therefore, on the timing, one has to be realistic.

The process to re-launch the European project will take time. This means that the path towards a possible ratification of the Constitution for Europe – or more probably towards the negotiation of another treaty based on its content – will take a few years. To re-open the debate too early would be counter-productive. Before that, it is necessary to rebuild a favourable political climate in Europe. In order to try and reach this aim, it would be wiser for the EU institutions to concentrate on concrete projects and to encourage economic reforms in the Member States.

The objective should be to re-establish the European Union as a useful and effective way to help its Member States in finding solutions to their problems and as beneficial to their peoples. This has been the major success of the European Union in the past. It will also be the case in the future.

The global assessment of 50 years of European integration is already strikingly positive.

On a continent ravaged by centuries of wars, that built and destroyed several empires, that waged religious or colonial wars all over the planet, the Europeans decided, half a century ago, to sit around a table and to talk and, from then on, they have stopped fighting each other but they have never stopped talking to each other. At the start, their leaders could meet in a small drawing-room, by a fire-place; they now need a very large meeting room with 60 interpreters.

As a result, the European continent has been at peace for 60 years. Democracy has been deeply entrenched. The political, economic and social rights and conditions of the European peoples have been greatly improved. The attraction of the EU has contributed, with the help of the USA, to destroy the Iron Curtain and put an end to the division of the continent. The Union has helped to maintain peace outside its borders.

While pushing its Member States to improve their respective governance and to modernise their economies with the result of increasing their standards of living, the EU has helped to make a reality of the principle of equality between men and women, to improve consumer protection, to raise standards of environmental protection, to strengthen respect for human rights.

The reality is that in a world of increasing globalisation, statehood and the very notion of sovereignty are being eroded. No Member State, whatever its size, is able to face alone the challenges of the twenty-first century. None of them has enough leverage to negotiate, on its own, with the USA or with China or in the WTO. The solution has been for the Member States to pool or transfer certain powers to the EU, because they see it as more robust and better equipped to compete and resist in the global sphere.

All this has been done quietly, by constant dialogue, by free will, through negotiations resulting in compromises and agreements for the benefit of all European States, whether large or small, as well as for their citizens.

The authors of the Coal and Steel Treaty in 1951 wrote in its preamble that 'world peace can be safeguarded only by creative efforts commensurate with the dangers that threaten it' and that they were 'resolved to substitute for age-old rivalries the merging of their essential interests'. In view of what the European Union has achieved to date, the recent accident in the ratification process of the Constitution for Europe, though a serious setback, will not dismantle these deeply rooted and noble foundations. The European project will continue its patient building up.

Annex 1

Laeken Declaration on the Future of the European Union

I. Europe at a crossroads

For centuries, peoples and states have taken up arms and waged war to win control of the European continent. The debilitating effects of two bloody wars and the weakening of Europe's position in the world brought a growing realisation that only peace and concerted action could make the dream of a strong, unified Europe come true. In order to banish once and for all the demons of the past, a start was made with a coal and steel community. Other economic activities, such as agriculture, were subsequently added in. A genuine single market was eventually established for goods, persons, services and capital, and a single currency was added in 1999. On 1 January 2002 the euro is to become a day-to-day reality for 300 million European citizens.

The European Union has thus gradually come into being. In the beginning, it was more of an economic and technical collaboration. Twenty years ago, with the first direct elections to the European Parliament, the Community's democratic legitimacy, which until then had lain with the Council alone, was considerably strengthened. Over the last ten years, construction of a political union has begun and cooperation been established on social policy, employment, asylum, immigration, police, justice, foreign policy and a common security and defence policy.

The European Union is a success story. For over half a century now, Europe has been at peace. Along with North America and Japan, the Union forms one of the three most prosperous parts of the world. As a result of mutual solidarity and fair distribution of the benefits of economic development, moreover, the standard of living in the Union's weaker regions has increased enormously and they have made good much of the disadvantage they were at.

Fifty years on, however, the Union stands at a crossroads, a defining moment in its existence. The unification of Europe is near. The Union is about to expand to bring in more than ten new Member States, predominantly Central and Eastern European, thereby finally closing one of the darkest chapters in European history: the Second World War and the ensuing artificial division of Europe. At long last, Europe is on its way to becoming one big family, without bloodshed, a real transformation clearly calling for a different approach from fifty years ago, when six countries first took the lead.

The democratic challenge facing Europe

At the same time, the Union faces twin challenges, one within and the other beyond its borders.

Within the Union, the European institutions must be brought closer to its citizens. Citizens undoubtedly support the Union's broad aims, but they do not always see a connection between those goals and the Union's everyday action. They want the European institutions to be less unwieldy and rigid and, above all, more efficient and open. Many also feel that the Union should involve itself more with their particular concerns, instead of intervening, in every detail, in matters by their nature better left to Member States' and regions' elected representatives. This is even perceived by some as a threat to their identity. More importantly, however, they feel that deals are all too often cut out of their sight and they want better democratic scrutiny.

Europe's new role in a globalised world

Beyond its borders, in turn, the European Union is confronted with a fast-changing, globalised world. Following the fall of the Berlin Wall, it looked briefly as though we would for a long while be living in a stable world order, free from conflict, founded upon human rights. Just a few years later, however, there is no such certainty. The eleventh of September has brought a rude awakening. The opposing forces have not gone away: religious fanaticism, ethnic nationalism, racism and terrorism are on the increase, and regional conflicts, poverty and underdevelopment still provide a constant seedbed for them.

What is Europe's role in this changed world? Does Europe not, now that it is finally unified, have a leading role to play in a new world order, that of a power able both to play a stabilising role worldwide and to point the way ahead for many countries and peoples? Europe as the continent of humane values, the Magna Carta, the Bill of Rights, the French Revolution and the fall of the Berlin Wall; the continent of liberty, solidarity and above all diversity, meaning respect for others' languages, cultures and traditions. The European Union's one boundary is democracy and human rights. The Union is open only to countries which uphold basic values such as free elections, respect for minorities and respect for the rule of law.

Now that the Cold War is over and we are living in a globalised, yet also highly fragmented world, Europe needs to shoulder its responsibilities in the governance of globalisation. The role it has to play is that of a power resolutely doing battle against all violence, all terror and all fanaticism, but which also does not turn a blind eye to the world's heartrending injustices. In short, a power wanting to change the course of world affairs in such a way as to benefit not just the rich countries but also the poorest. A power seeking to set globalisation within a moral framework, in other words to anchor it in solidarity and sustainable development.

The expectations of Europe's citizens

The image of a democratic and globally engaged Europe admirably matches citizens' wishes. There have been frequent public calls for a greater EU role in justice and security, action against cross-border crime, control of migration flows and reception of asylum seekers and refugees from far-flung war zones. Citizens also want results in the fields of employment and combating poverty and social exclusion, as well as in the field of economic and social cohesion. They want a common approach on environmental pollution, climate change and food safety, in short, all transnational issues which they instinctively sense can only be tackled by working together. Just as they also want to see Europe more involved in foreign affairs, security and defence, in other words, greater and better coordinated action to deal with trouble spots in and around Europe and in the rest of the world.

At the same time, citizens also feel that the Union is behaving too bureaucratic-ally in numerous other areas. In coordinating the economic, financial and fiscal environment, the basic issue should continue to be proper operation of the internal market and the single currency, without this jeopardising Member States' individuality. National and regional differences frequently stem from history or tradition. They can be enriching. In other words, what citizens understand by 'good governance' is opening up fresh opportunities, not imposing further red tape. What they expect is more results, better responses to practical issues and not a European superstate or European institutions inveigling their way into every nook and cranny of life.

In short, citizens are calling for a clear, open, effective, democratically con-trolled Community approach, developing a Europe which points the way ahead for the world. An approach that provides concrete results in terms of more jobs, better quality of life, less crime, decent education and better health care. There can be no doubt that this will require Europe to undergo renewal and reform.

II.   Challenges and reforms in a renewed Union

The Union needs to become more democratic, more transparent and more efficient. It also has to resolve three basic challenges: how to bring citizens, and primarily the young, closer to the European design and the European institutions, how to organise politics and the European political area in an enlarged Union and how to develop the Union into a stabilising factor and a model in the new, multipolar world. In order to address them a number of specific questions need to be put.

A better division and definition of competence in the European Union

Citizens often hold expectations of the European Union that are not always fulfilled. And vice versa – they sometimes have the impression that the Union takes on too much in areas where its involvement is not always essential. Thus the important thing is to clarify, simplify and adjust the division of competence between the Union and the Member States in the light of the new challenges facing the Union. This can lead both to restoring tasks to the Member States and to assigning new missions to the Union, or to the extension of existing powers, while constantly bearing in mind the equality of the Member States and their mutual solidarity.

A first series of questions that needs to be put concerns how the division of competence can be made more transparent. Can we thus make a clearer distinction between three types of competence: the exclusive competence of the Union, the competence of the Member States and the shared competence of the Union and the Member States? At what level is competence exercised in the most efficient way? How is the principle of subsidiarity to be applied here? And should we not make it clear that any powers not assigned by the Treaties to the Union fall within the exclusive sphere of competence of the Member States? And what would be the consequences of this?

The next series of questions should aim, within this new framework and while respecting the *acquis communautaire,* to determine whether there needs to be any reorganisation of competence. How can citizens' expectations be taken as a guide here? What missions would this produce for the Union? And, vice versa, what tasks could better be left to the Member States? What amendments should be made to the Treaty on the various policies? How, for example, should a more coherent common foreign policy and defence policy be developed? Should the Petersberg tasks be updated? Do we want to adopt a more integrated approach to police and criminal law cooperation? How can economic-policy coordination be stepped up? How can we intensify cooperation in the field of social inclusion, the environment, health and food safety? But then, should not the day-to-day administration and implementation of the Union's policy be left more emphatically to the Member States and, where their constitutions so provide, to the regions? Should they not be provided with guarantees that their spheres of competence will not be affected?

Lastly, there is the question of how to ensure that a redefined division of competence does not lead to a creeping expansion of the competence of the Union or to encroachment upon the exclusive areas of competence of the Member States and, where there is provision for this, regions. How are we to ensure at the same time that the European dynamic does not come to a halt? In the future as well the Union must continue to be able to react to fresh challenges and developments and must be able to explore new policy areas. Should Articles 95 and 308 of the Treaty be reviewed for this purpose in the light of the '*acquis jurisprudentiel*'?

Simplification of the Union's instruments

Who does what is not the only important question; the nature of the Union's action and what instruments it should use are equally important. Successive amendments to the Treaty have on each occasion resulted in a proliferation of instruments, and directives have gradually evolved towards more and more detailed legislation. The key question is therefore whether the Union's various instruments should not be better defined and whether their number should not be reduced.

In other words, should a distinction be introduced between legislative and executive measures? Should the number of legislative instruments be reduced: directly applicable rules, framework legislation and non-enforceable instruments (opinions, recommendations, open coordination)? Is it or is it not desirable to have more frequent recourse to framework legislation, which affords the Member States more room for manoeuvre in achieving policy objectives? For which areas of competence are open coordination and mutual recognition the most appropriate instruments? Is the principle of proportionality to remain the point of departure?

More democracy, transparency and efficiency in the European Union

The European Union derives its legitimacy from the democratic values it projects, the aims it pursues and the powers and instruments it possesses. However, the European project also derives its legitimacy from democratic, transparent and efficient institutions. The national parliaments also contribute towards the legitimacy of the European project. The declaration on the future of the Union, annexed to the Treaty of Nice, stressed the need to examine their role in European integration. More generally, the question arises as to what initiatives we can take to develop a European public area.

The first question is thus how we can increase the democratic legitimacy and transparency of the present institutions, a question which is valid for the three institutions.

How can the authority and efficiency of the European Commission be enhanced? How should the President of the Commission be appointed: by the European Council, by the European Parliament or should he be directly elected by the citizens? Should the role of the European Parliament be strengthened? Should we extend the right of co-decision or not? Should the way in which we elect the members of the European Parliament be reviewed? Should a European electoral constituency be created, or should constituencies continue to be determined nationally? Can the two systems be combined? Should the role of the Council be strengthened? Should the Council act in the same manner in its legislative and its executive capacities? With a view to greater transparency, should the meetings of the Council, at least in its legislative capacity, be public? Should citizens have more access to Council documents? How, finally, should the balance and reciprocal control between the institutions be ensured?

A second question, which also relates to democratic legitimacy, involves the role of national parliaments. Should they be represented in a new institution, alongside the Council and the European Parliament? Should they have a role in areas of European action in which the European Parliament has no competence? Should they focus on the division of competence between Union and Member States, for example through preliminary checking of compliance with the principle of subsidiarity?

The third question concerns how we can improve the efficiency of decision-making and the workings of the institutions in a Union of some thirty Member States. How could the Union set its objectives and priorities more effectively and ensure better implementation? Is there a need for more decisions by a qualified majority? How is the co-decision procedure between the Council and the European Parliament to be simplified and speeded up? What of the six-monthly rotation of the Presidency of the Union? What is the future role of the European Parliament? What of the future role and structure of the various Council formations? How should the coherence of European foreign policy be enhanced? How is synergy between the High Representative and the competent Commissioner to be reinforced? Should the external representation of the Union in international fora be extended further?

Towards a Constitution for European citizens

The European Union currently has four Treaties. The objectives, powers and policy instruments of the Union are currently spread across those Treaties. If we are to have greater transparency, simplification is essential.

Four sets of questions arise in this connection. The first concerns simplifying the existing Treaties without changing their content. Should the distinction between the Union and the Communities be reviewed? What of the division into three pillars?

Questions then arise as to the possible reorganisation of the Treaties. Should a distinction be made between a basic treaty and the other treaty provisions? Should this distinction involve separating the texts? Could this lead to a distinction between the amendment and ratification procedures for the basic treaty and for the other treaty provisions?

Thought would also have to be given to whether the Charter of Fundamental Rights should be included in the basic treaty and to whether the European Community should accede to the European Convention on Human Rights.

The question ultimately arises as to whether this simplification and reorganisation might not lead in the long run to the adoption of a constitutional text in the Union. What might the basic features of such a constitution be? The values which the Union cherishes, the fundamental rights and obligations of its citizens, the relationship between Member States in the Union?

III. Convening of a Convention on the Future of Europe

In order to pave the way for the next Intergovernmental Conference as broadly and openly as possible, the European Council has decided to convene a Convention composed of the main parties involved in the debate on the future of the Union. In the light of the foregoing, it will be the task of that Convention to consider the key issues arising for the Union's future development and try to identify the various possible responses.

The European Council has appointed Mr V. Giscard d'Estaing as Chairman of the Convention and Mr G. Amato and Mr J. L. Dehaene as Vice-Chairmen.

Composition

In addition to its Chairman and Vice-Chairmen, the Convention will be composed of 15 representatives of the Heads of State or Government of the Member States (one from each Member State), 30 members of national parliaments (two from each Member State), 16 members of the European Parliament and two Commission representatives. The accession candidate countries will be fully involved in the Convention's proceedings. They will be represented in the same way as the current Member States (one government representative and two national parliament members) and will be able to take part in the proceedings without, however, being able to prevent any consensus which may emerge among the Member States.

The members of the Convention may only be replaced by alternate members if they are not present. The alternate members will be designated in the same way as full members.

The Praesidium of the Convention will be composed of the Convention Chairman and Vice-Chairmen and nine members drawn from the Convention (the representatives of all the governments holding the Council Presidency during the Convention, two national parliament representatives, two European Parliament representatives and two Commission representatives).

Three representatives of the Economic and Social Committee with three representatives of the European social partners; from the Committee of the Regions: six representatives (to be appointed by the Committee of the Regions from the regions, cities and regions with legislative powers), and the European Ombudsman will be invited to attend as observers. The Presidents of the Court of Justice and of the Court of Auditors may be invited by the Praesidium to address the Convention.

Length of proceedings

The Convention will hold its inaugural meeting on 1 March 2002, when it will appoint its Praesidium and adopt its rules of procedure. Proceedings will be completed after a year, that is to say in time for the Chairman of the Convention to present its outcome to the European Council.

Working methods

The Chairman will pave the way for the opening of the Convention's proceedings by drawing conclusions from the public debate. The Praesidium will serve to lend impetus and will provide the Convention with an initial working basis.

The Praesidium may consult Commission officials and experts of its choice on any technical aspect which it sees fit to look into. It may set up ad hoc working parties.

The Council will be kept informed of the progress of the Convention's proceedings. The Convention Chairman will give an oral progress report at each European Council meeting, thus enabling Heads of State or Government to give their views at the same time.

The Convention will meet in Brussels. The Convention's discussions and all official documents will be in the public domain. The Convention will work in the Union's eleven working languages.

Final document

The Convention will consider the various issues. It will draw up a final document which may comprise either different options, indicating the degree of support which they received, or recommendations if consensus is achieved.

Together with the outcome of national debates on the future of the Union, the final document will provide a starting point for discussions in the Intergovernmental Conference, which will take the ultimate decisions.

Forum

In order for the debate to be broadly based and involve all citizens, a Forum will be opened for organisations representing civil society (the social partners, the business world, non-governmental organisations, academia, etc.). It will take the form of a structured network of organisations receiving regular information on the

Convention's proceedings. Their contributions will serve as input into the debate. Such organisations may be heard or consulted on specific topics in accordance with arrangements to be established by the Praesidium.

Secretariat

The Praesidium will be assisted by a Convention Secretariat, to be provided by the General Secretariat of the Council, which may incorporate Commission and European Parliament experts.

Annex 2

Existing legal bases switched to ordinary legislative procedure (codecision)

Article in Cst	Subject matter	Procedure in present Treaties
I-37(3)	rules and general principles for controlling the exercise of implementing measures	**unanimity** in Council + EP consultation (Art. 202 EC)
III-139, 2nd subp.	exclusion in a Member State of certain activities from the application of provisions on the freedom of establishment	QMV in Council, without EP participation (Art. 45, 2nd subp. EC)
III-144, 2nd subp.	extension of the benefit of the freedom to provide services to third country nationals established within the EU	QMV in Council, without EP participation (Art. 45, 2nd subp. EC)
III-147	liberalisation of a specific service	QMV in Council + EP consultation (Art. 52(1) EC)
III-157(2)	adoption of other measures on the movement of capital to or from third countries involving direct investments	QMV in Council, without EP participation (Art. 57(2) EC)
III-174	measures necessary to eliminate distortions in the internal market due to differences between national rules or action	QMV in Council, without EP participation (Art. 96 EC)
III-179(6)	multilateral surveillance	cooperation procedure (Art. 99 (5) EC)
III-187(4)	modification of the ESCB and ECB protocol	**unanimity** in Council + EP consultation (Art. 107(5) EC)
III-191	measures necessary for use of the euro	QMV in Council, without EP participation (Art. 123(4) EC)

Annex 2 (*cont.*)

Article in Cst	Subject matter	Procedure in present Treaties
III-223(1), 1st subp., +(2)	Structural Funds (from 2013)	- now: unanimity in Council + EP assent - from 1.1.2007: QMV in Council[1] + EP assent (Art. 161 EC)
III-223(1), 1st subp., +(2)	Cohesion Fund (from 2013)	- now: unanimity in Council + EP assent - from 1.1.2007: QMV in Council[2] + EP assent (Art. 161 EC)
III-230(1)	application of competition rules to production and trade in agricultural products	QMV in Council + EP consultation (Art. 36 EC)
III-231(2)	common organisation of markets and general objectives in agriculture and fisheries policy	QMV in Council + EP consultation (Art. 37(2) EC)
III-265(2)	visas, checks on persons who cross external borders, conditions under which third-country nationals may travel freely within the EU for a short period, integrated management system for external borders, absence of controls on persons when crossing internal borders	since 1.1.2005: codecision for all but legal immigration (Art. 62 EC) (Council Decision no. 2004/927/ EC of 22 Dec. 2004 making use of 'passerelle' in Art. 67(2) 2nd indent, EC)
III-266(2)	uniform status of asylum and uniform subsidiary protection for third-country nationals, common system of temporary protection for displaced persons, criteria and	since 1.1.2005: codecision for all but legal immigration (Art. 63 (1) + (2) EC) (Council Decision no. 2004/927/ EC of 22 Dec. 2004 making use of 'passerelle' in Art. 67(2) 2nd indent, EC)

	mechanisms for determining which Member State is responsible, etc.	
III-267(2)	common immigration policy and combating trafficking in persons, in particular women and children	since 1.1.2005: codecision for all but legal immigration (Art. 63 (3) + (4) EC) (Council Decision no. 2004/927/ EC of 22 Dec. 2004 making use of 'passerelle' in Art. 67(2) 2nd indent, EC)
III-270 (1)+ (2)[3]	judicial cooperation in criminal matters (mutual recognition of judicial decisions, prevention of conflicts of jurisdiction, training, cooperation in criminal proceedings and enforcement, minimum rules for certain aspects of criminal procedure)	**unanimity** in Council + EP consultation (Art. 31 EU)
III-271 (1)+ (possibly) 2[4]	minimum rules on definition of criminal offences and sanctions in a list of areas of serious crime	**unanimity** + EP consultation (Art. 31 EU)
III-273(2), 1st subp.	Eurojust	**unanimity** + EP consultation Art. 31(2) EU)
III-275(2)	police cooperation (certain aspects)	**unanimity** + EP consultation (Art. 30 EU)
III-276(2), 1st subp.	Europol	**unanimity** + EP consultation (Art. 30 EU)
III-315(2)	definition of framework for implementing the common commercial policy	QMV in Council, without EP participation (Art. 133(2) EC)
III-319(2)	economic, financial and technical cooperation measures with third countries	QMV in Council + EP consultation (Art. 181A EC)
III-359	establishment of specialised courts	**unanimity** + EP consultation (Art. 225A EC)
III-364	jurisdiction of the Court in European intellectual property rights	**unanimity** in Council + EP consultation + national ratification (Art. 229A EC)

Annex 2 (*cont.*)

Article in Cst	Subject matter	Procedure in present Treaties
III-381	modification of the Court statute, except Title I and Article 64	**unanimity** in Council + EP consultation (Art. 245 EC)
III-412(1)	financial rules (codecision coupled with unanimity in the Council until 31.12.2006)	– now: unanimity in Council + EP consultation – from 1.1.2007: QMV in Council + EP consultation (Art. 279(1) EC)
III-427	staff regulations for officials + employment conditions for other servants of the EU	QMV in Council + EP consultation (Art. 283 EC)

[1] On condition that, by that date, the multiannual financial framework applicable from 1.1.2007 and the Interinstitutional Agreement relating to it have been adopted.
[2] On condition that, by that date, the multiannual financial framework applicable from 1.1.2007 and the Interinstitutional Agreement relating to it have been adopted.
[3] Coupled with a 'brake-accelerator' procedure (see box 5.4 above).
[4] Coupled with a 'brake-accelerator' procedure (see box 5.4 above).

Annex 3

Existing legal bases switched to qualified majority voting in the Council

Article in Cst	Subject matter	Act and Procedure in Cst	Article in EU/EC
I-24(6)	Presidency of the Council	European Council decision (no Commission proposal)	203 EC
I-37(3)	rules and general principles concerning mechanism for control by Member States of the Commission's exercise of implementing powers	law **codecision**	202 EC
III-127	measures to facilitate diplomatic and consular protection	law of the Council	20 EC
III-136[1]	coordination of social security for migrant workers (employed and self-employed)	law or framework law **codecision**	42 EC
III-141	provisions on the taking-up and pursuit of self-employed activities even if they entail amendments of existing principles laid down by law in Member States	framework law **codecision**	47(2) EC

Annex 3 (*cont.*)

Article in Cst	Subject matter	Act and Procedure in Cst	Article in EU/EC
III-179(4)	violation of BGEP[2] or risk jeopardising the proper functioning of EMU	Council recommendation, on a recommendation from the Commission	99(2) EC
III-184(6)	– decision on whether an excessive deficit exists – measures with a view to bringing that situation to an end	– Council decision, on a proposal from the Commission – Council recommendation, on a recommendation from the Commission	104(6)EC
III-184 (9)+ (10)+ (11)	measures for the deficit reduction	Council decision, on a recommendation from the Commission	104(9), (10) + (12) EC
III-187(3)	modifications of certain provisions of the ESBC and ECB Statute	law **codecision** either on a proposal from the Commission or on a recommendation from the ECB	107(5)EC
III-223(1)	Structural Funds and Cohesion Fund (as from 2013)	law **codecision**	161 EC
III-236(2)	provisions on principles of the transport regulatory system (also those liable to have serious effects on the standard of living and employment in certain areas and on transport facilities)	law **codecision**	71(2) EC

III-263	administrative cooperation in the area of freedom, security and justice	Council regulation EP consultation	66 EC + 34 (1) EU
III-265	border checks	law or framework law **codecision**	67 EC
III-266	asylum	law or framework law **codecision**	67 EC
III-267	immigration	law or framework law **codecision**	67 EC
III-270(2)+ (4)	judicial cooperation in criminal matters	law or framework law[3] **codecision**	31(1)(a) to (d) EU
III-271(2) to (4)	minimum rules on definition of criminal offences and sanctions in a list of areas of serious crime	framework law[4] **codecision**	31(1)(e) EU
III-273	Eurojust	law **codecision**	31(2) EU
III-275(2)	police cooperation	law or framework law **codecision**	30(1)(b) to (d) EU
III-276	Europol	law **codecision**	30(2) EU
III-280(5)	incentive measures in the field of culture	law or framework law **codecision**	151(5) EC
III-300(2)	– CFSP decisions on the basis of a European Council decision based on Art. III-293 (1); – CFSP decision on a proposal from the EU Minister following a request from the European Council; – implementing a CFSP decision – appointment of EU special representatives	Council decision (CFSP) (no Commission proposal)	23(2) EU

Annex 3 (*cont.*)

Article in Cst	Subject matter	Act and Procedure in Cst	Article in EU/EC
III-382(2)	appointment of ECB members	European Council decision, on a recommendation from the Council (no Commission proposal)	112 EC

[1] Coupled with a 'brake-accelerator' procedure (see box 5.4 above).
[2] Abbreviation for the 'Broad Guidelines of the Economic Policies' adopted by the Council.
[3] Coupled with a 'brake-accelerator' procedure (see box 5.4 above).
[4] Coupled with a 'brake-accelerator' procedure (see box 5.4 above).

Annex 4

New legal bases

New legal bases where QMV *in the* Council *will apply*

Article in Cst	Subject matter	Act and procedure in Cst	EP role
I-9	accession to the European Convention for the Protection of Human Rights	Council decision, on a recommendation/ proposal from the EU negotiator (see Art. III-325)	consent
I-32(5)	revision of rules on the nature of the composition of the Committee of the Regions and of the Economic and Social Committee	Council decision	
I-47(4)	establishment of procedures and conditions for citizens' initiatives	law	codecision
I-54(4)	implementing measures of the Union's own resources system	law of the Council	consent
I-60(2)	agreement on the withdrawal of a Member State	Council decision, on a recommendation/ proposal from the EU negotiator (see Art. III-325)	consent

Annex 4 (*cont.*)

Article in Cst	Subject matter	Act and procedure in Cst	EP role
III-122	principles and conditions for the functioning of the services of general economic interest	law	codecision
III-176, 1st subp.	creation of European intellectual property rights and setting up of a centralised Union-wide authorisation system	law	codecision
III-196 (1)+(2)	common positions and unified representation of the euro within the international financial institutions and conferences	Council decision on a Commission proposal	
III-254	European space policy	law or framework law	codecision
III-256(2)	energy policy	law or framework law	codecision
III-272	measures to promote and support Member States' action in crime prevention	law or framework law	codecision
III-281	tourism	law or framework law	codecision
III-282(1) (g)	sport	law or framework law	codecision
III-284	civil protection	law or framework law	codecision
III-285	administrative cooperation	law	codecision
III-311(2)	definition of the Defence Agency's statute, seat and operational rules	Council decision (no Commission proposal)	
III-312(2)	establishment of permanent structured cooperation in the field of the defence	Council decision (no Commission proposal)	
III-312(3)			

	participation of a Member State in a permanent structured cooperation for defence	Council decision (no Commission proposal)	
III-312(4)	suspension of the participation in a Member State to a permanent structured cooperation for defence	Council decision (no Commission proposal)	
III-313(3), 3rd subp.	start-up fund for ESDP: – procedures for setting up and financing the fund – procedure for administering the fund – financial control procedures	Council decision on a proposal from the EU Minister	
III-321(3)	humanitarian aid	law or framework law	codecision
III-321(5)	European Voluntary Humanitarian Aid Corps	law	codecision
III-398(2)	European administration	law	codecision

New legal bases where unanimity *in the* Council *will apply*

Article in Cst	Subject matter	Act and procedure in Cst	EP role
I-55(2)	multiannual financial framework	law of the Council	consent
III-158(4)	decision on compatibility with the Cst of a restrictive national tax measure concerning third countries	Council decision on application by the Member State concerned	

Annex 4 (*cont.*)

Article in Cst	Subject matter	Act and procedure in Cst	EP role
III-176, 2nd subp.	language arrangements for the European intellectual property rights	law of the Council	consultation
III-256(3)	measures in the field of energy policy which are primarily of fiscal nature	law of the Council	consultation
III-269(3), 2nd subp.	switching to codecision for the adoption of measures concerning family law with cross-border implications (sectoral 'passerelle')	Council decision (no Commission proposal)	consultation
III-270(2) (d)	extension of EU competence in criminal procedure	Council decision (no Commission proposal)	consent
III-271(1), 3rd subp.	extension of the areas of crime that meet the criteria specified in the paragraph	Council decision (no Commission proposal)	consent
III-274(1)	establishment of a European Public Prosecutor's Office	law of the Council	consent
III-312(6)	decisions on permanent structured cooper-ation in defence (other than its establishment or a Member State's participation or suspension)	Council decision (no Commission proposal)	
III-313(3), 1st subp.	specific procedures for guaranteeing rapid access to appropria-	Council decision (no Commission proposal)	consultation

	tions in EU budget for urgent financing of CFSP initiatives		
III-329(2)	implementation of the solidarity clause	Council decision on a joint initiative by the Commission and the EU Minister	information
III-386, 1st subp.	composition of the Committee of the Regions	Council decision on a Commission proposal	
III-389	composition of the Economic and Social Committee	Council decision on a Commission proposal	
III-393	modification of the EIB Statute	law of the Council	consultation
III-422		Council decision (no Commission proposal)	consultation

New legal basis where QMV in the European Council will apply

Article in Cst	Subject matter	Act and procedure in Cst	EP role
I-24(4)	list of Council configurations	European Council decision (no Commission proposal)	

New legal bases where unanimity in the European Council will apply

Article in Cst	Subject matter	Act and procedure in Cst	EP role
I-20(2)	composition of the EP	European Council decision (no Commission proposal)	initiative + consent
I-26(6)	modification of the number of Commissioners (from 2014)	European Council decision (no Commission proposal)	

Annex 4 (*cont.*)

Article in Cst	Subject matter	Act and procedure in Cst	EP role
I-40(7)	switching to QMV in the field of CFSP (excluding defence) (sectoral 'passerelle') (+ Art. III-300(3))	European Council decision (no Commission proposal)	
I-55(4)	switching to QMV for the multiannual financial framework	European Council decision (no Commission proposal)	
I-60(3)	extension of the period of two years before the withdrawal of a Member State	European Council decision (no Commission proposal)	
III-274 (4)	extension of the powers of the European Public Prosecutor's Office	European Council decision (no Commission proposal)	consent
IV-440 (7)	modification of the status, with regard to the Union, of one of the Danish, French or Netherlands ultraperipheral or overseas countries or territories	European Council decision, on an initiative from the Member State concerned	
IV-444	switching to QMV or codecision in Part III (general 'passerelle')	European Council decision *nihil obstat* of national Parliaments (no Commission proposal)	consent
IV-445	simplified revision procedure concerning internal Union policies and action (Title III of Part III)	European Council decision on a proposal from a Member State, the EP or the Commission, approval by the Member States in accordance with their constitutional requirements	consultation

New legal bases where consensus *in the* European Council *will apply*

Article in Cst	Subject matter	Act and procedure in Cst	EP role
Art. III-136	coordination of social security for migrant workers (employed and self-employed) – emergency brake (referral back to Council or request to submit new draft)	(act not specified)	
III-258	strategic guidelines for legislative and operational planning within the area of freedom, security and justice	(act not specified)	
III-270(3)	judicial cooperation in criminal matters – emergency brake (referral back to Council or request to submit new draft)	(act not specified)	
III-271(3)	minimum rules on definition of criminal offences and sanctions – emergency brake (referral back to Council or request to submit new draft)	(act not specified)	

Annex 5

Existing legal bases where unanimity, common accord or consensus will continue to apply

Existing legal bases where unanimity *in the* Council *will continue to apply*

Article in Cst	Subject matter	Act and Procedure in Cst	Article in EU/EC
I-18	flexibility clause	– Any legal act – Council act with EP consent	308 EC
I-41(4)	ESDP (ordinary framework)	– Council decisions – on a proposal from the EU Minister or on an initiative from a Member State (no Commission proposal) – (see also Art. III-300 (1))	23(1) EU
III-124(1)	measures to combat discrimination based on sex, racial or ethnic origin, religion or belief, disability, age or sexual orientation	– law or framework law of the Council – EP consent	13(1) EC
III-125(2)	measures concerning passports, identity cards, residence permits and measures concerning social security or social protection	– law or framework law of the Council – EP consultation	18(3) EC

III-126	arrangements for exercising the right to vote and to stand as a candidate in municipal elections and EP elections in the Member State of residence without being a national of that State	– law or framework law of the Council – EP consultation	19 EC
III-157(3)	step backwards in Union law as regards liberalisation of movement of capital to or from third countries	– law or framework law of the Council – EP consultation	57(2) EC
III-168(2), 3rd subp.	compatibility with the internal market of an aid granted by a Member State or through State resources (derogation from Art. III-167 or from regulations based on Art. III-169)	– Council decision – on application by a Member State (no Commission proposal)	88(2), 3rd subp. EC
III-171	harmonisation of legislation concerning turnover taxes, excise duties and other forms of indirect taxes	– law or framework law of the Council – EP consultation	93 EC
III-173	approximation of legislation which directly affects the establishment or functioning of the internal market (in cases other than those covered by Art. III-172)	– law or framework law of the Council – EP consultation	94 EC
III-184(13), 2nd subp.	modification/replacement of the Protocol on the excessive deficit procedure	– law or framework law of the Council – EP and ECB consultation	104(14), 2nd subp. EC

Annex 5 (*cont.*)

Article in Cst	Subject matter	Act and Procedure in Cst	Article in EU/EC
III-185(6)	specific tasks for the ECB concerning policies relating to prudential supervision	– law of the Council – EP and ECB consultation	105.6 EC
III-198(3)	fixing of the rate at which the euro is to be substituted for the currency of the Member State(s) concerned	– Council regulation or decision – with the agreement of the Council member representing the Member State(s) concerned – ECB consultation	123(5) EC
III-210(3), 1st subp.	– social security and social protection of workers; – protection of workers where their employment contract is terminated; – representation and collective defence of the interests of workers and employers, including co-determination; – conditions of employment for third-country nationls legally residing in Union territory	– law or framework law of the Council – EP consultation	137(2), 2nd subp. EC
III-212(2)	implementation of agreements between management and labour in the fields of Art. III-210(3) where unanimity is required	– Council regulation or decision – at the request of the signatory parties – on a Commission proposal – EP information	139(2) EC

III-223(2)	first provisions of Structural Funds and Cohesion Fund to be adopted following those in force on 29.10.2004	– law of the Council – EP consent	161 EC
III-234(2) 1st subp.	environment: – provisions primarily of a fiscal nature; – measures affecting town and country planning, quantitative management of water; or – land use; – measures significantly affecting a Member State's choice between different energy sources and the general structure of its energy supply	– law or framework law of the Council – EP consultation	175(2) 1st subp. EC
III-237	derogation from the obligation of non-discrimination based on nationality in the field of transport	Council decision (no Commission proposal)	72 EC
III-269(3) 1st subp.	measures concerning family law with cross-border implications	– law or framework law of the Council – EP consultation	67 EC
III-275(3)	operational police cooperation	– law or framework law of the Council – EP consultation	30(1) EU
III-277	conditions and limitations under which the competent authorities of the Member States may operate in the territory of another Member State	– law or framework law of the Council – EP consultation	32 EU

Annex 5 (*cont.*)

Article in Cst	Subject matter	Act and Procedure in Cst	Article in EU/EC
III-291	association of the countries and territories of the Union	– law, framework law, regulation or decision of the Council – on a Commission proposal – EP consultation on the laws and framework laws	187 EC
III-300(1)	CFSP (ordinary framework)	– Council decisions – on an initiative from a Member State, on a proposal from the EU Minister or on a proposal from the EU Minister with the Commission's support (no Commission proposal)	23(1) EU
III-313(2)	operating expenditure for CFSP	– Council decisions (no Commission proposal)	28(3) EU
III-315(4)	common commercial policy: exceptions to QMV for agreements on: – trade in services; commercial aspects of intellectual property and foreign direct investment; – trade in cultural and audiovisual services, where these agreements risk prejudicing the Union's cultural and linguistic diversity;	– conclusion by a Council decision – EP consent if agreement covers fields to which codecision applies or in which the Council adopts laws with EP consent – EP consultation in other cases	133(5)+(6) EC

	– trade in social, education and health services, where these agreements risk seriously disturbing the national organisation of such services and prejudicing the responsibility of Member States to deliver them		
III-325(8)	– agreements covering a field for which unanimity is required for the adoption of a Union act; – association agreements; – agreements with neighbours which are candidates for accession (Art. III-319)	– conclusion by a Council decision – EP consent if association agreement or if covering fields to which codecision applies or in which the Council adopts laws with EP consent – EP consultation in other cases	300 EC
III-326(1)	agreements on an exchange-rate system for the euro in relation with third States' currencies	– Council decision – on a recommendation from ECB or on a Commission recommendation + ECB consultation – EP consultation	111(1) EC
III-330(2)	rules or conditions relating to the taxation of MEPs or former MEPs	– law or framework law of the EP; – on its own initiative – Commission opinion – Council consent	190(5) EC
III-354	increasing the number of Advocates-General	– Council decision – on a request from the ECJ	222 EC
III-359(4)	appointment of the members of the specialised courts	– non-specified act of the Council – after consultation of the Art. III-357 panel	225a EC

Annex 5 (*cont.*)

Article in Cst	Subject matter	Act and Procedure in Cst	Article in EU/EC
III-412(1) + (3)	**until 31.12.2006** – financial rules; – rules on checks on the responsibility of financial actors	– law in codecision – consultation of the Court of Auditors	279(1) EC
III-412(2) + (3)	**until 31.12.2006** methods and procedure whereby the budget revenue provided under the EU's own resources is made available to the Commission and measures to be applied to meet cash requirements	– Council regulation – EP and Court of Auditors consultation	279(2) EC
III-421	derogation from normal rule on expenditure resulting from implementation of enhanced cooperation	– Council decision – EP consultation (no Commission proposal)	44 EU
Art. III-433	rules governing the language regime of the Union's institutions	– Council regulation (no Commission proposal)	290 EC
Art. III-436 (2)	changes to the list of arms, munitions and war material	– Council decision – on a Commission proposal	296(2) EC

Existing legal bases switched from QMV to unanimity *in the* Council

III-419(2)	authorisation to proceed with enhanced cooperation in CFSP	– Council decision – at the request of the Member States concerned (at least $\frac{1}{3}$ of EU Member States) – consultation of EU Minister and of Commission – EP information	27c EU
III-420(2)	acceptance of the participation of a Member State in an existing enhanced cooperation in CFSP	– Council decision – on request from the Member State concerned – consultation of EU Minister	27e EU

Existing 'passerelles' where unanimity *in the* Council *will continue to apply*

III-210(3), 2nd subp.	switching to codecision in the three last matters mentioned in Art. III-310 (3), 1st subp. (social policy)	– Council decision – on a Commission proposal – EP consultation	137(2), 2nd subp. EC
III-234(2) 2nd subp.	switching to codecision in matters mentioned in Art. III-234(2), 2nd subp. (certain measures in environment policy)	– Council decision – on a Commission proposal – EP consultation	175(2) 2nd subp. EC

Existing legal bases where unanimity *in the* Council *will continue to apply, followed by approval or adoption by Member States, in accordance with their constitutional requirements*

I-41(2), 1st subp.	establishment of a common EU defence	– Council decision – adoption of the decision by the Member States in accordance with their respective constitutional requirements (no Commission proposal)	17(1) EU

Annex 5 (*cont.*)

I-54(3)	system of own resources	– law of the Council – EP consultation – approval by the Member States in accordance with their constitutional requirements	269 EC
I-58(2)	conclusion of accession negotiations	– non-specified act of the Council – EP consent – Commission consultation – accession agreement to be ratified by each Contracting Party, in accordance with its respective constitutional requirements	49 EU
III-129, 2nd subp.	addition of new rights for European citizens	– law or framework law of the Council – EP consent – approval by the Member States in accordance with their constitutional requirements	22 EC
III-330(1)	measures for the election of EP members by direct universal suffrage	– law or framework law of the Council – on initiative from, and after obtaining consent of, EP – approval by the Member States in accordance with their constitutional requirements	190(4) EC

Existing legal bases where unanimity *in the* European Council *will continue to apply*

I-59(2)	existence of a serious and persistent breach by a Member State of the EU's values	– European Council decision – on the initiative of $\frac{1}{3}$ of the Member States or on a Commission proposal – EP consent	7(2) EU
III-293(1)	strategic interests and objectives related to CFSP and other areas of EU external action	– European Council decisions – on a recommendation from the Council	13(2) EU

Existing legal bases where common accord *of the* Member States *will continue to apply*

I-29(2)	appointment of judges and Advocates-General of the Court of Justice and of the General Court	– common accord of the governments of the Member States – consultation of the Art. III-357 panel (see Art. III-355 + III-356)	223 + 224 EC
III-432	deciding on the seats of the institutions	common accord of the governments of the Member States	289 EC
Art. IV-443	ordinary revision of the Constitution	– common accord of the IGC in the form of an international agreement – ratification by all the Member States in accordance with their constitutional requirements	48 EU

Annex 6

Table of equivalences between the provisions of the Treaty establishing a Constitution for Europe and the provisions of the EU and EC Treaties

Treaty establishing a Constitution for Europe	EU and EC Treaties[1]
Part I	
Title I – Definition and objectives of the Union	
I-1	1 and 49 EU
I-2	6(1) EU
I-3	2 and 6(4) EU, 2 EC
I-4	14(2) and 12(1st subp.) EC
I-5	6(3), 11(2) and 33 EU, 10 EC
I-6 **new** *(Primary of Union law)*	
I-7	24 EU (concl. of international agreements), 281 EC
I-8 **new** *(The symbols of the Union)*	
Title II – Fundamental rights and citizenship of the Union	
I-9	6(2) EU
I-10	17 to 21 EC
Title III – Union competences	
I-11	5 EC
I-12 **new** *(Categories of competences)*	
I-13 **new** *(Areas of exclusive competence)*	
I-14 **new** *(Areas of shared competence)*	
I-15	99(1), 126(2) EC
I-16	11 and 17(1) EU
I-17 **new** *(Areas of supporting action)*	
I-18	308 EC

Annex 6 (*cont.*)

Treaty establishing a Constitution for Europe	EU and EC Treaties
Title VI – The democratic life of the Union	
I-45 **new** *(The principle of democratic equality)*	
I-46	1(2nd subp.) and 6(1) EU, 189(1st subp.) and 191(1st subp.) EC
I-47 **new** *(The principle of participatory democracy)*	
I-48	138(1) EC
I-49	195 EC
I-50	1(2nd subp.) EU, 207(3)(2nd subp.) and 255 EC
I-51	286 EC
I-52 **new** *(Status of churches and non-confessional organisations)*	(Declaration no. 11 to the Final Act of the Amsterdam IGC)
Title VII – The Union's finances	
I-53	268, 270, 271, 274(1st subp.) and 280(1) and (2) EC
I-54	6(4) EU, 269 EC
I-55 **new** *(The multiannual financial framework)*	
I-56	272 EC
Title VIII – The Union and its neighbours	
I-57 **new** *(neighbours)*	
Title IX – Union membership	
I-58	49 EU
I-59	7 EU, 309 EC
I-60 **new** *(Voluntary withdrawal from the Union)*	
Part II **The Charter of Fundamental Rights of the Union**	
Title I – Dignity	
II-61	1 Charter

II-62	2 Charter
II-63	3 Charter
II-64	4 Charter
II-65	5 Charter

Title II – Freedoms

II-66	6 Charter
II-67	7 Charter
II-68	8 Charter
II-69	9 Charter
II-70	10 Charter
II-71	11 Charter
II-72	12 Charter
II-73	13 Charter
II-74	14 Charter
II-75	15 Charter
II-76	16 Charter
II-77	17 Charter
II-78	18 Charter
II-79	19 Charter

Title III – Equality

II-80	20 Charter
II-81	21 Charter
II-82	22 Charter
II-83	23 Charter
II-84	24 Charter
II-85	25 Charter
II-86	26 Charter

Title IV – Solidarity

II-87	27 Charter
II-88	28 Charter
II-89	29 Charter
II-90	30 Charter
II-91	31 Charter
II-92	32 Charter
II-93	33 Charter
II-94	34 Charter
II-95	35 Charter
II-96	36 Charter
II-97	37 Charter
II-98	38 Charter

Annex 6 (*cont.*)

Treaty establishing a Constitution for Europe	EU and EC Treaties
Title V – Citizens' rights	
II-99	39 Charter
II-100	40 Charter
II-101	41 Charter
II-102	42 Charter
II-103	43 Charter
II-104	44 Charter
II-105	45 Charter
II-106	46 Charter
Title VI – Justice	
II-107	47 Charter
II-108	48 Charter
II-109	49 Charter
II-110	50 Charter
Title VII – General provisions governing the interpretation and application of the Charter	
II-111	51 Charter
II-112	52 Charter
II-113	53 Charter
II-114	54 Charter

Part III
The policies and functioning of the Union

Title I – Provisions of general application	
III-115	3 EU
III-116	3(2) EC
III-117 **new** (*social clause*)	(for employment: 127(2) EC)
III-118	13 EC
III-119	6 EC
III-120	153(2) EC
III-121	Protocol on protection and welfare of animals
III-122	16 EC

Title II – Non-discrimination and
  citizenship

III-123	12(2nd subp.) EC
III-124	13 EC
III-125	18(2) and (3) EC
III-126	19 TCE
III-127	20 TCE
III-128	21(3rd subp.) EC
III-129	22 EC

Title III – Internal policies and action
Chapter I – Internal market
Section 1 – Establishment and functioning
  of the internal market

III-130	14 and 15 EC
III-131	297 EC
III-132	298 EC

Section 2 – Free movement of persons
  and services

III-133	39 EC
III-134	40 EC
III-135	41 EC
III-136	42 EC
III-137	43 EC
III-138	44 EC
III-139	45 EC
III-140	46 EC
III-141	47 EC
III-142	48 EC
III-143	294 EC
III-144	49 EC
III-145	50 EC
III-146	51 EC
III-147	52 EC
III-148	53 EC
III-149	54 EC
III-150	55 EC

Section 3 – Free movement of goods

III-151	23 to 27 EC
III-152	135 EC
III-153	28 and 29 EC
III-154	30 EC
III-155	31 EC

Annex 6 (*cont.*)

Treaty establishing a Constitution for Europe	EU and EC Treaties
Section 4 – Capital and payments	
III-156	56 EC
III-157	57 EC
III-158	58 EC
III-159	59 EC
III-160 **new** (*freezing of assets, etc. JHA*)	(60 EC)
Section 5 – Rules on competition	
III-161	81 EC
III-162	82 EC
III-163	83 EC
III-164	84 EC
III-165	85 EC
III-166	86 EC
III-167	87 EC
III-168	88 EC
III-169	89 EC
Section 6 – Fiscal provisions	
III-170	90 to 92 EC
III-171	93 EC
Section 7 – Common provisions	
III-172	95 EC
III-173	94 EC
III-174	96 EC
III-175	97 EC
III-176 **new** (*intellectual property rights*)	
Chapter II – Economic and monetary policy	
III-177	4 EC
Section 1 – Economic policy	
III-178	98 EC
III-179	99 EC
III-180	100 EC
III-181	101 EC
III-182	102 EC
III-183	103 EC
III-184	104 EC
Section 2 – Monetary policy	
III-185	105 EC
III-186	106 EC
III-187	107 EC

III-188	108 EC
III-189	109 EC
III-190	110 EC
III-191	123(4) EC
Section 3 – Institutional provisions	
III-192	114(2) to (4) EC
III-193	115 EC
Section 4 – Provisions specific to Member States whose currency is the euro	
III-194 **new** *(reinforcement of budget and economic coordination)*	
III-195 **new** *(Euro Group)*	
III-196 **new** *(external representation of EMU)*	(111(4) EC)
Section 5 – Transitional provisions	
III-197	122(1), and (3) to (5) EC
III-198	121(1), 122(2) and 123(5) EC
III-199	117(2) and 123(3), EC
III-200	124(1) EC
III-201	119 EC
III-202	120 EC
Chapter III – Policies in other areas	
Section 1 – Employment	
III-203	125 EC
III-204	126 EC
III-205	127 EC
III-206	128 EC
III-207	129 EC
III-208	130 EC
Section 2 – Social policy	
III-209	136 EC
III-210	137 EC
III-211	138 EC
III-212	139 EC
III-213	140 EC
III-214	141 EC
III-215	142 EC
III-216	143 EC
III-217	144 EC
III-218	145 EC
III-219	146 to 148 EC

Annex 6 (*cont.*)

Treaty establishing a Constitution for Europe	EU and EC Treaties
Section 3 – Economic, social and territorial cohesion	
III-220	158 EC
III-221	159 EC
III-222	160 EC
III-223	161 EC
III-224	162 EC
Section 4 – Agriculture and fisheries	
III-225	32(1) (2nd sentence) EC
III-226	32(1) (1st sentence) and (2) to (4) EC
III-227	33 EC
III-228	34 EC
III-229	35 EC
III-230	36 EC
III-231	37 EC
III-232	38 EC
Section 5 – Environment	
III-233	174 EC
III-234	175 and 176 EC
Section 6 – Consumer protection	
III-235	153 EC
Section 7 – Transport	
III-236	70 and 71 EC
III-237	72 EC
III-238	73 EC
III-239	74 EC
III-240	75 EC
III-241	76 EC
III-242	77 EC
III-243	78 EC
III-244	79 EC
III-245	80 EC
Section 8 – Trans-European networks	
III-246	154 EC
III-247	155 and 156 EC

Section 9 – Research and technological
   development and space

III-248	163 EC
III-249	164 EC
III-250	165 EC
III-251	166 EC
III-252	167 to 170 and 172 (2nd subp.) EC
III-253	171 and 172 (1st subp.) EC
III-254 **new** *(space policy)*	
III-255	173 EC

Section 10 – Energy

III-256 **new** *(energy)*

Chapter IV – Area of freedom, security
   and justice

Section 1 – General provisions

III-257	29 EU, 61 EC
III-258 **new** *(role of the European Council)*	
III-259 **new** *(role of the national* *parliaments)*	
III-260 **new** *(evaluation mechanism)*	
III-261	36 EU
III-262	33 EU and 64(1) EC
III-263	66 EC
III-264 **new** *(administrative cooperation)*	

Section 2 – Policies on border checks,
   asylum and immigration

III-265	62 EC
III-266	63(1) and (2) and 64(2) EC
III-267	63(3) and (4) EC
III-268 **new** *(principle of solidarity)*	

Section 3 – Judicial cooperation in civil
   matters

III-269	65 EC

Section 4 – Judicial cooperation in criminal
   matters

III-270	31(1)(a) to (d) EU
III-271	31(1)(e) EU
III-272 **new** *(crime prevention)*	
III-273	31(2) EU
III-274 **new** *(European Public Prosecutor)*	

Annex 6 (*cont.*)

Treaty establishing a Constitution for Europe	EU and EC Treaties
Section 5 – Police cooperation	
III-275	30(1) EU
III-276	30(2) EU
III-277	32 EU
Chapter V – Areas where the Union may take coordinating, complementary or supporting action	
Section 1 – Public health	
III-278	152 EC
Section 2 – Industry	
III-279	157 EC
Section 3 – Culture	
III-280	151 EC
Section 4 – Tourism	
III-281 **new** *(tourism)*	
Section 5 – Education, youth, sport, and vocational training	
III-282	149 EC
III-283	150 EC
Section 6 – Civil protection	
III-284 **new** *(civil protection)*	
Section 7 – Administrative cooperation	
III-285 **new** *(administrative cooperation)*	
Title IV – Association of the overseas countries and territories	
III-286	182 and 188 EC
III-287	183 EC
III-288	184 EC
III-289	185 EC
III-290	186 EC
III-291	187 EC
Title V – The Union's external action	
Chapter I – Provisions having general application	
III-292	3 (2nd subp.) and 11 EU, 133(1), 174(1) and 177 EC
III-293	13(2) EU

Annex 6 (*cont.*)

Treaty establishing a Constitution for Europe	EU and EC Treaties
Section 3 – Humanitarian aid	
III-321 **new** (*humanitarian aid*)	
Chapter V – Restrictive measures	
III-322	301 EC
Chapter VI – International agreements	
III-323	300(7) EC, 24(6) EU
III-324	310 EC
III-325	300 EC, 24 EU
III-326	111(1) to (3) and (5) EC
Chapter VI – The Union's relations with international organisations and third countries and Union delegations	
III-327	302 to 304 EC
III-328 **new** (*Union delegations*)	
Chapter VIII – Implementation of the solidarity clause	
III-329 **new** (*solidarity clause*)	
Title VI – The functioning of the Union	
Chapter I – Provisions governing the institutions	
Section 1 – The institutions	
Subsection 1 – The European Parliament	
III-330	190 EC
III-331	191(2) EC
III-332	192 EC
III-333	193 EC
III-334	194 EC
III-335	195 EC
III-336	196 EC
III-337	197 and 200 EC
III-338	198 EC
III-339	199 EC
III-340	201 EC
Subsection 2 – The European Council	
III-341 **new** (*European Council*)	

Subsection 3 – The Council of Ministers	
III-342	204 EC
III-343	205(1) and (3) and 206 EC
III-344	207 EC
III-345	208 EC
III-346	209 EC
Subsection 4 – The European Commission	
III-347	213(2) EC
III-348	215 EC
III-349	216 EC
III-350	217 EC
III-351	219 EC
III-352	212 and 218(2) EC
Subsection 5 – The Court of Justice of the European Union	
III-353	221 EC
III-354	222 EC
III-355	223 EC
III-356	224 EC
III-357 **new** *(selection committee for judges)*	
III-358	225 EC
III-359	220n (2nd subp.) and 225A EC
III-360	226 EC
III-361	227 EC
III-362	228 EC
III-363	229 EC
III-364	229A EC
III-365	230 EC
III-366	231 EC
III-367	232 EC
III-368	233 EC
III-369	234 EC
III-370	235 EC
III-371	46(e) EU
III-372	236 EC
III-373	237 EC
III-374	238 EC
III-375	239, 240 and 292 EC
III-376	46(f) EU
III-377	35(5) EU, 68(2) EC
III-378	241 EC

Annex 6 (*cont.*)

Treaty establishing a Constitution for Europe	EU and EC Treaties
III-379	242 and 243 EC
III-380	244 EC
III-381	245 EC
Subsection 6 – The European Central Bank	
III-382	112 EC
III-383	113 EC
Subsection 7 – The Court of Auditors	
III-384	248 EC
III-385	247(2) to (7) EC
Section 2 – The Union's advisory bodies	
Subsection 1 – The Committee of the Regions	
III-386	263 EC
III-387	264 EC
III-388	265 EC
Subsection 2 – The Economic and Social Committee	
III-389	258 EC
III-390	259 EC
III-391	260 EC
III-392	262 EC
Section 3 – The European Investment Bank	
III-393	266 EC
III-394	267 EC
Section 4 – Provisions common to Union institutions, bodies, offices and agencies	
III-395	250 EC
III-396	251 EC
III-397	218(1) EC
III-398 **new** (*European administration*)	
III-399	255 EC
III-400	210, 247(8) and 258 (4th subp.) EC
III-401	256 EC
Chapter II – Financial provisions	
Section 1 – The multiannual financial framework	
III-402 **new** (*multiannual financial framework*)	

Section 2 – The Union's annual budget

III-403	272(2) EC
III-404	272(2) to (10) EC
III-405	273 EC
III-406	271 EC

Section 3 – Implementation of the
  budget and discharge

III-407	274 EC
III-408	275 EC
III-409	276 EC

Section 4 – Common provisions

III-410	277 EC
III-411	278 EC
III-412	279 EC
III-413 **new** *(availability of financial means)*	
III-414 **new** *(interinst. consultation)*	

Section 5 – Combating fraud

III-415	280 EC

Chapter III – Enhanced cooperation

III-416	43(b), (e) and (f) EU, 11(3) EC
III-417	43(h) and 44(2) EU
III-418	27D and 43B EU
III-419	27B, 27C and 40A EU, 11 EC
III-420	27E and 40B EU, 11A EC
III-421	44A EU
III-422 **new** *(passerelle)*	
III-423	45 EU

Title VII – Common provisions

III-424	299(2)(2nd subp.) EC
III-425	295 EC
III-426	282 EC
III-427	283 EC
III-428	284 EC
III-429	285 EC
III-430	287 EC
III-431	288 EC
III-432	289 EC
III-433	290 EC
III-434	291 EC
III-435	307 EC
III-436	296 EC

Annex 6 (*cont.*)

Treaty establishing a Constitution for Europe	EU and EC Treaties
Part IV	
General and final provisions	
IV-437 **new** (*Repealing of earlier Treaties*)	
IV-438 **new** (*Succession and legal continuity*)	
IV-439 **new** (*Transitional provisions relating to certain institutions*)	
IV-440	299(1) and (2)(1st subp.) and (3) to (6) EC
IV-441	306 EC
IV-442	311 EC
IV-443	48 EU
IV-444 **new** (*Simplified revision procedure*)	
IV-445 **new** (*Simplified revision procedure concerning internal Union policies and action*)	
IV-446	51 EU, 312 EC
IV-447	52 EU, 313 EC
IV-448	53 EU, 314 EC

[1] The equivalence is only indicative and does not mean that the provisions are identical. Most of them have been either slightly modified in order to be adapted to the specific terminology used in the Constitution or amended more thoroughly, while retaining an identifiable common origin. As regards Part I, which is a sort of summary of what is in the Constitution, the indications of equivalence are of a general nature.

Annex 7

List of 'passerelles' and provisions on a simplified revision procedure

Passerelles

A 'passerelle' (or 'bridge') is a provision in the Constitution which enables passing from one procedure or voting rule to another (from a consultation procedure to codecision procedure, from unanimity to qualified majority voting). There are seven 'passerelles' in the Constitution:

Articles in the Constitution	Subject matter
IV-444	**general 'passerelle'** regarding the legal bases on internal EU competences in Part III
I-40(7) and III-300(3) and (4)	common foreign and security policy (except for defence)
I-55(4)	multiannual financial framework
III-210(3)(2nd subpara.)	social policy[1]
III-234(2)(2nd subpara.)	certain measures in the field of environment (fiscal measures, country planning, etc.)[2]
III-269(3)(2nd subpara.)	aspects of family law with cross-border implications
III-422	reinforced cooperation (except for defence)

[1] This provision already exists in Art. 137(2)(2nd subpara.) EC Treaty.
[2] This provision already exists in Art. 175(2)(2nd subpara.) EC Treaty.

Provisions on a simplified revision procedure

These provisions allow for amending one or several articles of the Constitution or of a Protocol thereto. There are 13 provisions on a simplified revision procedure:

Revision of articles in the Constitution	Subject matter
Article IV-445	**general provision** which allows for amending articles in Part III on internal EU competences in Part III of the Constitution, by a unanimous decision of the European Council, followed by a ratification procedure within Member States, but without the need to convene a Convention and an Intergovernmental Conference
Article I-32(5)(2nd subpara.)	enables the Council, by QMV, to review the nature of the composition of the Committee of the Regions and of the Economic and Social Committee
Article III-129(2nd subpara.)	enables the Council, by unanimity, to add to the rights of the EU citizens[1]
Articles III-167(2)(c) and III-243	enables the Council, by QMV, to repeal a provision on aid granted to the economy of certain areas of Germany affected by the division of Germany
Article III-271(1)(3rd subpara.)	enables the Council, by unanimity, to extend the list of areas of crime which may be subject to minimum EU rules
Article III-274(4)	enables the European Council, by unanimity, to extend the powers of the European Public Prosecutor's Office
Article III-184(13)	enables the replacement of the Protocol on the excessive deficit procedure[2]
Article III-187(3)	allows for amending certain articles of the ECB Protocol[3]
Article III-381	allows for amending certain articles of the Protocol on the Court of Justice[4]
Article III-393	allows for amending certain articles of the EIB Protocol[5]
Article 5 of Protocol no. 8	allows for repealing Elapsed provisions of the Enlargement Protocol
Article 10 of Protocol no. 9	allows for repealing Elapsed provisions of the Enlargement Protocol

[1] This provision already exists in Art. 22(2nd subpara.) EC Treaty.
[2] This provision already exists in Art. 104(14)(2nd subpara.) EC Treaty.
[3] This provision already exists in Art. 107(5) EC Treaty.
[4] This provision already exists in Art. 245(2nd subpara.) EC Treaty.
[5] This provision already exists in Art. 266(3rd subpara.) EC Treaty.

References

Books

Andréani, G., Bertram, C. and Grant, C. *Europe's Military Revolution* (London, Centre for European Reform, March 2001) [http://www.cer.org.uk/pdf/ p22w_military_revolution.pdf]

Blanchet, T. 'Le succès silencieux de dix ans d'Espace économique européen: un modèle pour l'avenir avec d'autres voisins?', *Liber Amicorum in Honour of Sven Norberg* (Brussels, Bruylant éd., to be published in 2006)

Cederman, L.-E. 'Nationalism and Bounded Integration: What It Would Take to Construct a European Demos' (European University Institute Working Papers, Florence 2000, RSC no. 2000:34)

Crowe, B. *Foreign Minister of Europe* (Foreign Policy Centre, February 2005) [http://fpc.org.uk/fsblob/395.pdf]

Dean, M. M. *Governmentality: Power and Rule in Modern Society* (London, Sage, 1999)

de Schoutheete, P. *La cohérence par la défense: une autre lecture de la PESD* (Paris, EU Institute for Security Studies, *Cahiers de Chaillot no. 71*, 2004) [http:// www.iss-eu.org/chaillot71.pdf]

Durand, G. *A European Parliament really Closer to the People* (European Policy Centre, Ideas Factory Europe no. 5, December 2004) [http://www.theepc.be/]

Engström, M. *Rebooting Europe: Digital Deliberation and European Democracy* (The Foreign Policy Centre, Nov. 2002)

European Democracy: A Manifesto (Arbuthnott, T. and Leonard, M. eds, the Foreign Policy Centre, British Council, Nov. 2003) [http://fpc.org.uk/fsblob/219.pdf]

EU Security and Defence: Core Documents 2004, (Paris, EU Institute for Security Studies, *Cahiers de Chaillot no. 75,* 2005) [http://www.iss-eu.org/chaillot/ chai75e.pdf]

EU Security and Defence Policy: The First Five Years (1999–2004), edited by N. Gnesotto, Preface by J. Solana. EU Institute for Security Studies, Paris, 2004 [http://www.iss-eu.org/books/5esdpen.pdf].

From St Malo to Nice: European Defence: core documents (Paris, EU Institute for Security Studies, *Chaillot Paper no. 47,* 2001) [www.iss-eu.org/chaillot/ chai47e.htm]

Galloway, D. *The Treaty of Nice and Beyond: Realities and Illusions of Power in the EU* (Sheffield Academic Press, 2000)

Gormley, L. W. 'The Judicial Architecture of the European Union in the Constitution' in Peter G. Xuereb (ed.), *The Constitution for Europe: An Evaluation* (EDRC, Medial Centre Print, Malta, 2005) pp. 57–72.

Grant, C. *What Happens if Britain Votes No? Ten Ways Out of a European Constitutional Crisis* (Centre for European Reform, March 2005)

Habermas, J. *Between Facts and Norms: Contributions to a Discourse Theory* (Cambridge, Polity Press, 1996)

Herbillon, M. *La Fracture européenne: Après le Référendum du 29 mai, 40 propositions concrètes pour mieux informer les Français sur l'Europe* (Paris, La documentation française, June 2004) [http://lesrapports.ladocumentation francaise.fr/BRP/054000424/0000.pdf]

Klingemann, H. D. 'Mapping Political support in the 1990's' in Pippa Norris (eds.), *Critical Citizens. Global Support for Democratic Governance. Critical citizens* (Oxford University Press, 1999) pp. 11–56

Lamassoure, A. *Histoire secrète de la Convention européenne* (Paris, Albin Michel éd., 2004).

Louis, J.-V. and Ronse, T. *L'ordre juridique de l'Union européenne* (Brussels, Bruylant éd., 2005)

McDonagh, B. *Original Sin in a Brave New World, An Account of the Negotiation of the Treaty of Amsterdam* (Dublin, Institute of European Affairs, 1998)

Marquardt, S. 'The Conclusion of International Agreements under Article 24 of the Treaty on European Union', Chapter 16 in *The European Union and the International Legal Order: Discord or Harmony?* (The Hague, ed. Vincent Kronenberger, T. M. C. Asser Instituut, 2001) 333–349

Marquardt, S. 'La capacité de l'Union européenne de conclure des accords internationaux dans le domaine de la coopération policière et judiciaire en matière pénale', in G. de Kerchove and A. Weyembergh (eds), *Sécurité et justice: enjeu de la politique extérieure de l'Union européenne*, Institut d'Etudes Européennes, Université de Bruxelles, 2003) 179–194

Meny, Y. and Surel, Y. *Par le peuple, pour le peuple: le populisme et les démocraties* (Paris, éd. Fayard, 2000)

Milton, G. and Keller-Noëllet, J. with Bartol-Saurel, A. *The European Constitution: Its Origins, Negotiation and Meaning* (John Harper Publishing, 2005)

Norman, P. *The accidental Constitution: the making of Europe's Constitutional Treaty* (Brussels, EuroComment, 2005)

Pfersmann, O. 'The New Revision of the Old Constitution' in Weiler, J. H. H. and Eisgruber, C. L. (eds.) *The EU constitution in a Contextual Perspective. Altneuland* (Jean Monnet Working Paper 5/04) [http://www.jeanmonnetprogram. org/papers/04/040501-10.pdf]

Pharr, S. and Putnam, R. *Disaffected Democracies* (Princeton University Press, 2000)

Piris, J.-C. 'The European Union: Towards A New Form of Federalism?' (2003) in Basil Markesinis and Jörg Fedtke (eds.), *Patterns of Regionalism and Federalism: Lessons for the UK* (Oxford, Hart Publishing, forthcoming)

Reid, T. R. *The United States of Europe* (London, Penguin Books, 2005)

Reynié, D. and Cautrès, B. *L'opinion européenne* (Paris, IEP, 2001)

Rifkind, J. *The European Dream* (Tarcher Penguin, 2004)

Risse, T. 'Who Are We? A Europeanization of National Identities?' in M. G. Cowles, J. A. Caporaso, and T. Risse (eds.), *Transforming Europe* (Ithaca, Cornell University Press, 2001)

Rumford, C. *The European Union: A Political Sociology* (Oxford, Blackwell Publishers, 2002)

Ryborg, O. V. *Det utaenkelige nej . . .? Historien om 6 måneder, 0 dage og 17 timer, der rystede Europa* (Copenhagen, Schultz ed. 1998)

Schmidt, V. A. *The EU: Democratic Legitimacy in a Regional State* (Centre for European Studies, Working Paper no. 112, 2004) [http://www.ces.fas.harvard.edu/publications/VSchmidt.pdf]

Shaw, J. 'Failure to Ratify the Constitutional Treaty: What Next?' in Ingolf Pernice/Jiří Zemánek (eds.), *A Constitution for Europe: The IGC, the Ratification Process and Beyond* (Nomos Verlag, Baden-Baden, 2005, European Constitutional Law Network-Series, Bd. 5)

Smith, R. 'Constitutionalising the European Union (Bristol, *Working Paper Series of the School for Policy Studies, no.6,* 2003) [http://www.bris.ac.uk/sps/downloads/working_papers/sps06_rs.pdf]

van der Eijk, C. and Frank, M. N. *Choosing Europe* (University of Michigan Press, 1996)

Weiler, J. H. H. *The Constitution of Europe* (Cambridge University Press, 1999)

de Witte, B. 'The Process of Ratification and the Crisis Options: A Legal Perspective' in *The EU Constitution: The Best Way Forward?*, Asser Institute Colloquium on European Law, The Hague, 13–16 October 2004

Articles

Benoît-Rohmer, F. 'La Charte des droits fondamentaux de l'Union européenne' (2001) II fasc. 160 *Juris-Classeur* and (2001) 19 *Le Dalloz* 1483–1492

Benoît-Rohmer, F. 'Valeurs et droits fondamentaux dans la constitution' (2005) 2 *Revue trimestrielle de droit européen* 261–283

Blanchet, T. 'Les instruments juridiques de l'Union européenne et la réduction des bases juridiques: situation actuelle et rationalisation dans la constitution' (2005) 2 *Revue trimestrielle de droit européen* 319–343

Bréchon, P. 'Des valeurs politiques entre pérennité et changement' (2002) 277 *Futuribles* 92–128

Cangelosi, R. 'Il progetto di Trattato Costituzionale, la Presidenza italiana e la Conferenza intergovernativa. Da Roma a Bruxelles: cronaca di un negoziato' (2003) 4 *La Comunità Internazionale* 533–560

Dehousse, R. 'Convention européenne: pourquoi les anti-fédéralistes ont gagné' (2003) 2 *L'Europe en formation* 25–42

Dubey, B. 'Administration indirecte et fédéralisme d'exécution en Europe' 1–2/03 *Cahiers de droit européen* 87–133

Franklin, M. N., van der Eijk, C. and Marsh, M. 'Referendum Outcomes and Trust in Government: Public Support for Europe in the Wake of Maastricht' (1995) 18–3 *West European Politics* 101–117

Fried, R. J. 'Providing a Constitutional Framework for Withdrawal from the EU: Article 59 of the Draft European Constitution' (2004) 53 *International and Comparative Law Quarterly* 407–428

Fried, R. J. 'Secession from the European Union; Checking Out of the Proverbial "Cockroach Motel"' (2004) 27 no. 2 *Fordham Law Journal* 590–641

Grimm, D. 'Does Europe Need a Constitution?' (1995) 1–3 *European Law Journal* 282–303

Halperin, J.-L. 'L'Union européenne, un Etat en voie de constitution?' (2004) no. 4 *Recueil Dalloz* 219–221

Høegh, K. 'The Danish Maastricht Judgment' (1999) 24 *European Law Review*, 80–90

Jacqué, J.-P. 'La simplification et la consolidation des traités' (1997) 33(4) *Revue trimestrielle de droit européen* 195–205

Jarlebring, J. 'Taking Stock of the European Convention: What Added Value does the Convention bring to the Process of Treaty Revision?' (2003) 8 *German Law Journal*, European & International Law

Justus Lipsius (alias for J.-C. Piris) 'The 1996 Intergovernmental Conference' (1995) 20 *European Law Review* 235–267

Leonard, M. *Why Europe will Run the 21st Century* (London, Fourth Estate, Harper Collins Publishers, 2005)

Magnette, P. and Nicolaïdis, K. 'The European Convention: Bargaining in the Shadow of Rhetoric' (2004) vol. 27, no. 3 *West European Politics* 381–404

Piris, J.-C. 'The 1996 Intergovernmental Conference' (1995) 20 *European Law Review* 235–267

Piris, J.-C. 'Does the European Union have a Constitution? Does It Need One?' (1999) 6 *European Law Review* 557–585

Piris, J.-C. 'The Treaty of Nice: an Imperfect Treaty but a Decisive Step Towards Enlargement' (2000) 3 *The Cambridge Yearbook of European Legal Studies* 15–36

Reif, K. and Schmitt, H. 'Nine Second-Order National Elections' (1980) 8 *European Journal of Political Research* 3–44

Rossi, L. S. 'What if the Constitutional Treaty is Not Ratified?' (30 June 2004) *EPC Commentary* [http://www.theepc.net/]

Rossi, L. S. 'En cas de non-ratification . . . Le destin périlleux de ce Traité-Constitution' (2004) 4 *Revue trimestrielle de droit européen* 621–637

Ruggie, J. 'Territoriality and Beyond: Problematizing Modernity in International Relations' (1993) 47 *International Organization* 134–175

Schoettl, J.-E. 'La ratification du "Traité établissant une Constitution pour l'Europe" appelle-t-elle une révision de la Constitution française?' (2004) vol. 393, no. 238 *Les Petites Affiches* 3–25

'Scientists for a democratic Europe' reproduced in [http://www.ruhr-uni-bochum. de/mathphys/politik/eu/open-letter.htm]

Torrent, R. 'Whom is the European Central Bank the Central Bank of? Reaction to Zilioli and Selmayr' (1999) vol. XXXVI *Common Market Law Review* 1229–1241

Wessel, R. A. 'The State of Affairs in EU Security and Defence Policy: The Breakthrough in the Treaty of Nice' (2003) Vol. 8, No. 2 *Journal of Conflict and Security Law* 265–288

Zilioli, C. and Selmayr, M. 'The External Relations of the Euro Area: Legal Aspects' (1999) vol. XXXVI *Common Market Law Review* 273–349

Zilioli, C. and Selmayr, M. 'The European Central Bank: an Independent Specialized Organization of Community Law' (2000) vol. XXXVII *Common Market Law Review* 591–644

Newspapers

Agence Europe, 21 July 2005

Clarke, K. 'The Tories Must Stop Being Afraid of Europe', *The Independent*, 6 October 2003

Dahrendorf, R. 'N'accordons pas trop d'importance à la Constitution europé-enne', *Les Echos*, 27 July 2004

Ferenczi, T. 'Constitution: l'Europe des symboles', *Le Monde*, 16 October 2004

July, S. *Libération*, 30 May 2005

Karlsson, J. O. *El Pais*, 14 March 1999

Laïdi, Z. 'Europe: la gauche doit dire oui', *Libération*, 22 June 2004

Le Monde, 30 June 2005

Le Nouvel observateur, no. 2117, 2 to 8 June 2005

Le Point, no. 1707, 2 June 2005

L'Express, no. 2813, 30 May to 5 June 2005

Mény, Y. 'Europe, la grande hésitation', *Le Monde*, 12 June 2004

Moravcsik, A. 'Europe's Slow Triumph', *Newsweek*, 21 June 2004, p. 41

Siedentop, L. 'Giving the EU Frontiers, in Minds as well as in Space remains a Priority', *The Wall Street Journal*, 17 June 2005

Straw, J. *The Economist*, 10 July 2004, p. 30
Straw, J. *The Economist*, 30 July 2004, p. 30
Editorial of *The Financial Times*, 30–31 October 2004
The International Herald Tribune, 17 June 2005
Wolf, M. *The Financial Times*, 3 June 2005

References to useful internet sites

General internet site of the EU and EC (europa):	http://europa.eu.int
Internet site of the European Parliament:	http://www.europarl.eu.int
Internet site of the Council of the European Union:	http://ue.eu.int
Internet site of the Council's Registry of documents:	http://register.consilium.eu.int
Internet site of the Convention for the future of Europe:	http://european-convention.eu.int
Internet site of the Convention on the EU Charter of Fundamental Rights:	http://www.europarl.eu.int/charter
Internet site of the University of Pittsburg 'Archive of European Integration':	http://aei.pitt.edu
Internet site of the European Court of Human Rights:	http://cmiskp.echr.coe.int

INDEX